Taiwan Cinema

M000211088

The book examines recent developments in Taiwan cinema, with particular focus on a leading contemporary Taiwan filmmaker, Wei Te-sheng, who is responsible for such Asian blockbusters as *Cape No.7*, *Warriors of the Rainbow: Seediq Bale* and *Kano*. The book discusses key issues, including why (until about 2008) Taiwan cinema underwent a decline, and how cinema is portraying current social changes in Taiwan such as changing youth culture, and how it represents indigenous people in the historical narrative of Taiwan. The book also explores the reasons why current Taiwan cinema is receiving a much less enthusiastic response globally compared to its reception in previous decades.

Kuei-fen Chiu is Professor of Taiwan Literature and Transnational Cultural Studies at National Chung Hsing University, Taiwan.

Ming-yeh T. Rawnsley is Research Associate in the Centre of Taiwan Studies at the School of Oriental and African Studies, University of London, UK.

Gary D. Rawnsley is Professor of Public Diplomacy in the Department of International Politics at Aberystwyth University, UK.

Media, Culture and Social Change in Asia Series

Series Editor: Stephanie Hemelryk Donald, University of Liverpool

Editorial Board:
Gregory N. Evon, University of New South Wales
Devleena Ghosh, University of Technology, Sydney
Peter Horsfield, RMIT University, Melbourne
Michael Keane, Curtin University
Tania Lewis, RMIT University, Melbourne
Vera Mackie, University of Wollongong
Kama Maclean, University of New South Wales
Laikwan Pang, Chinese University of Hong Kong
Gary Rawnsley, Aberystwyth University
Ming-yeh Rawnsley, School of Oriental and African Studies, University of London
Jo Tacchi, Lancaster University
Adrian Vickers, University of Sydney
Jing Wang, MIT
Ying Zhu, City University of New York

The aim of this series is to publish original, high-quality work by both new and established scholars in the West and the East, on all aspects of media, culture and social change in Asia.

Taiwan Cinema

International Reception and Social Change

Edited by
Kuei-fen Chiu, Ming-yeh T. Rawnsley and
Gary D. Rawnsley

Routledge
Taylor & Francis Group

LONDON AND NEW YORK

First published 2017 by Routledge

2 Park Square, Milton Park, Abingdon, Oxfordshire OX14 4RN

52 Vanderbilt Avenue, New York, NY 10017

Routledge is an imprint of the Taylor & Francis Group, an informa business

First issued in paperback 2019

Copyright © 2017 selection and editorial matter, Kuei-fen Chiu, Ming-yeh T. Rawnsley and Gary D. Rawnsley; individual chapters, the contributors

The right of Kuei-fen Chiu, Ming-yeh T. Rawnsley and Gary D. Rawnsley to be identified as the authors of the editorial material, and of the authors for their individual chapters, has been asserted in accordance with sections 77 and 78 of the Copyright, Designs and Patents Act 1988.

All rights reserved. No part of this book may be reprinted or reproduced or utilised in any form or by any electronic, mechanical, or other means, now known or hereafter invented, including photocopying and recording, or in any information storage or retrieval system, without permission in writing from the publishers.

Notice:
Product or corporate names may be trademarks or registered trademarks, and are used only for identification and explanation without intent to infringe.

British Library Cataloguing in Publication Data
A catalogue record for this book is available from the British Library

Library of Congress Cataloging in Publication Data
Names: Chiu, Kuei-fen, editor. | Rawnsley, Ming-yeh T., editor. | Rawnsley, Gary D., editor.
Title: Taiwan cinema : international reception and social change / edited by Kuei-fen Chiu, Ming-yeh T. Rawnsley and Gary D. Rawnsley.
Description: Milton Park, Abingdon, Oxon ; New York : Routledge, 2017. | Series: Media, culture and social change in Asia ; 51 | Includes bibliographical references and index. | Includes filimography.
Identifiers: LCCN 2016058075| ISBN 9781138668164 (hardback) | ISBN 9781315170244 (ebook)
Subjects: LCSH: Motion pictures–Taiwan–History and criticism. | Motion pictures–Social aspects–Taiwan.
Classification: LCC PN1993.5.T28 T3455 2017 | DDC 791.430951249–dc23
LC record available at https://lccn.loc.gov/2016058075

ISBN: 978-1-138-66816-4 (hbk)
ISBN: 978-0-367-87706-4 (pbk)

Typeset in Times New Roman
by Taylor & Francis Books

Contents

Illustrations

Figures

Table

Contributors

Berry, Chris is Professor of Film Studies at King's College London. In the 1980s, he worked for China Film Import and Export Corporation in Beijing, and his academic research is grounded in work on Chinese-language cinema. Books include: *Cinema and the National: China on Screen*; *Postsocialist Cinema in Post-Mao China: The Cultural Revolution after the Cultural Revolution*; *Chinese Cinema* (4 vols); *Public Space, Media Space*; *The New Chinese Documentary Film Movement: For the Public Record*; *Electronic Elsewheres: Media, Technology, and Social Space*; *Cultural Studies and Cultural Industries in Northeast Asia: What a Difference a Region Makes*; *TV China*; *Chinese Films in Focus II*; and *Island on the Edge: Taiwan New Cinema and After*.

Chan, Felicia is Lecturer in Screen Studies at the University of Manchester and founding member of the Chinese Film Forum UK (CFFUK). Her research explores the construction of national, cultural and cosmopolitan imaginaries in cinema, as well as the influence of institutional and industrial practices on the production, distribution and reception of film. She is author of *Cosmopolitan Cinema: Cross-cultural Encounters in East Asian Film* (2017) and co-editor (with Andy Willis) of *Chinese Cinemas: International Perspectives* (2016).

Chiu, Kuei-fen holds a PhD from the University of Washington, Seattle, and is Distinguished Professor of Taiwan Literature and Transnational Cultural Studies at National Chung Hsing University in Taiwan. She has written extensively on postcolonial literary historiography, contemporary Taiwan documentaries, and indigenous literature in Taiwan. In addition to several books in Chinese and *New Chinese-language Documentaries* (co-authored with Yingjin Zhang), she has published in leading journals such as *New Literary History*, *The Journal of Asian Studies*, *The China Quarterly*, *Continuum: Journal of Media and Cultural Studies*, and contributed to edited volumes from international publishers like Routledge.

Hu, Brian, PhD, is the Artistic Director of Pacific Arts Movement and the San Diego Asian Film Festival, for which he is the head of programming. In addition to programming an annual Taiwan Film Showcase at the festival, he has curated retrospectives on Tsai Ming-liang, Vietnamese American film and video, and queer Korean cinema. His writings on Chinese-languages cinemas and Asian American media have appeared in scholarly collections and journals such as *Screen, Velvet Light Trap,* and the *Journal of Chinese Cinemas.* His dissertation on cosmopolitanism in Hong Kong and Taiwan was completed in Cinema and Media Studies at UCLA. He currently teaches at the University of San Diego.

Lee, Yu-lin is Professor and Director of the Graduate Institute of Taiwan Literature and Transnational Cultural Studies, and the Director of the Research Centre for Humanities and Social Sciences at National Chung Hsing University, Taiwan. His recent publications include *Liminality of Translation: Subjectivity, Ethics, and Aesthetics* (2009), and *The Fabulation of a New Earth* (2015). He has co-edited *Cyborg and Posthumanism* (2013), *Deleuze and Asia* (2014), and *The Empires on Taiwan* (2016). He is also a Chinese translator of *Deleuze on Literature* and *Deleuze on Music, Painting, and the Arts.* He is now working on a book project on digital archivisation and historical memories.

Liao, Ping-hui is currently ChuanLyu Endowed Chair Professor in Taiwan Studies at UC San Diego. He has co-edited with Shu-mei Shih *Comparatizing Taiwan* (Routledge, 2015), and with David Der-wei Wang *Taiwan under the Japanese Colonial Rule* (2006), in addition to authoring a dozen books in Chinese and hundreds of essays in English. Among his forthcoming essays are 'Sinophone Literature', 'Travels in Modern China', 'Chen Yingzhen', and 'Modes of Modern Taiwan Literature', to be published by Blackwell, Harvard, Oxford, and Routledge in the new history or handbook series of modern Chinese literature.

Ma, Ran is Associate Professor, Global-30 "Japan-in-Asia" Cultural Studies Program, Graduate School of Humanities, Nagoya University, Japan. Her doctoral project examines Chinese independent cinema on the global film festival network, while her postdoctoral research (2010–13) extends to explore participatory art projects in Asian cities. Dr Ma's current research interests include Asian independent cinemas and film festival studies, for which topics she has published several journal articles and book chapters, including recent contributions to *Chinese Film Festivals: Sites of Translation* (2017), and upcoming anthologies such as *Japanese Cinema Book* (British Film Institute).

Mello, Cecília is Lecturer in Film Studies at the Department of Film, Radio and Television, School of Communications and Arts, University of São Paulo. She was FAPESP Postdoctoral Fellow at the University of São Paulo (2008–11), has an MA in Film and Television Production, University of Bristol (1998) and a PhD in Film Studies, Birkbeck College, University of London (2006). Her research focuses on world cinema, with an emphasis on British and Chinese cinemas, and on issues of audiovisual realism, cinema and urban spaces and intermediality. She has published several essays and co-edited with Lúcia Nagib the book *Realism and the Audiovisual Media* (Palgrave Macmillan, 2009).

Pollacchi, Elena teaches Chinese cinema and culture at Ca' Foscari University of Venice and has been Visiting Associate Professor at Stockholm University since 2015. She completed her PhD at the University of Cambridge, discussing the changes in the Chinese film industry in the years 1989–2004. She has worked extensively on the development of the Chinese film market and its transnational connections. She also serves as a programme consultant for the selection of Chinese-language and Korean films for the Venice International Film Festival. Her current research focuses on Chinese documentary films, film festivals in Asia and the circulation of Chinese-language films at European film festivals. Her most recent publications include a set of articles on documentary filmmaker Wang Bing, and book chapters in *Chinese Film Festivals: Sites of Translations* (eds Chris Berry & Luke Robinson, Palgrave Macmillan, 2017) and *Screening Soft Power in China* (eds Paola Voci & Victor Hui, Routledge, 2017).

Rawnsley, Gary D. is Professor of Public Diplomacy in the Department of International Politics, Aberystwyth University. Working at the intersection of international politics and international communications, he has published widely on propaganda, public and cultural diplomacy, soft power, and election campaigning (with particular reference to East Asia). He is also interested in political cinema and was co-editor (with Ming-yeh T. Rawnsley) of *Global Chinese Cinema: The Culture and Politics of Hero* (2010). He is also co-editor of the *Routledge Handbook of Chinese Media* (2015, with Ming-yeh T. Rawnsley), and the *Routledge Handbook of Soft Power* (2016, with Naren Chitty et al.).

Rawnsley, Ming-yeh T. is Research Associate, Centre of Taiwan Studies, School of Oriental and African Studies (SOAS). She is also Secretary-General, European Association of Taiwan Studies (EATS, 2012–present). She worked as a researcher at the University of Nottingham (1999–2005) and became Head of Chinese Studies at the University of Nottingham Ningbo China (2005–07). Before she joined SOAS, Dr Rawnsley researched and taught East Asian film industries at the University of Leeds (2007–13). She has published widely in both English and Chinese on Chinese-language cinema and culture. She is also a prolific writer and researcher on the media and democratisation in Taiwan. She is a founding member of *The International Journal of Taiwan Studies*, jointly supported by EATS and Academia Sinica in Taiwan.

Rosenstone, Robert A., Professor Emeritus of History at the California Institute of Technology, is the leading international scholar in the field devoted to studying the relationship between history and the visual media. He has written two books on the topic, *Visions of the Past: The Challenge of Film* *to Our Idea of History* (1995), and *History on Film/Film on History* (2006, 2nd edition 2012), and has edited an influential collections of essays, *Revisioning History: Film and the Construction of a New Past* (1995). His most recent addition to the field (co-edited with Constantin Parvulescu) is *A Blackwell Companion to Historical Film* (2013). His books and essays have been translated into 12 languages. He has lectured at more than 50 universities on six continents.

Sterk, Darryl is a Chinese–English literary translator, best known for his translation of Wu Ming-yi's *The Man with the Compound Eyes* (*Fuyanren*). He is Associate Professor of Translation in the Graduate Program in Translation and Interpretation, National Taiwan University. He studies indigenous representations by indigenous and non-indigenous directors and writers in Taiwan. He also studies translation. Two current projects are the role of grammatical analysis in Chinese–English literary translation, and Dakis Pawan's translation of Wei Te-sheng's script for the film *Seediq Bale* (*Warriors of the Rainbow*) into the Tgdaya dialect of Seediq.

Vitali, Valentina is Professor of Film Studies at the University of East London. She is the author of *Capital and Popular Cinema: The Dollars are Coming!* (2016), *Hindi Action Cinema: Industries, Narratives, Bodies* (2008), and the co-editor (with Paul Willemen) of *Theorising National Cinema* (2006). Her work has appeared in a number of journals, including *Boundary2, Inter-Asia Cultural Studies, Cinema Journal*, and *Journal of Asian Studies*; and in the anthologies *Chinese Cinemas: International Perspectives, Beyond the Boundaries of Bollywood, Genre in Asian Film and Television, Narratives of Indian Cinema, Hong Kong Connections: Transnational Imagination in Action Cinema*, and *Shirin Neshat: The Secret of the Veil.*

Wang, Chialan Sharon is Assistant Professor in the Foreign Language Centre at Feng Chia University in Taiwan. She received her doctoral degree in Comparative Literature at the University of Southern California. Her doctoral dissertation, entitled 'Nostalgia for the Future to Come: National Consciousness in Post-87 Taiwanese Literature and Cinema', focuses on the tropes of nationhood in Taiwanese literary and cinematic works since the 1980s within, particularly, the problems of gender, ethnicity and post-coloniality. Her current research interests include postcolonial studies, Chinese-language literature and film, and trauma theory.

Willis, Andy is Reader in Film Studies at the University of Salford, a co-founder of the Chinese Film Forum UK (CFFUK) and a Senior Visiting Curator for Film at HOME, Manchester. In these roles he has worked extensively with independent cinemas in the UK, programming seasons and events related to Asian cinemas. He is the co-editor (with Wing Fai Leung) of *East Asian Film Stars* (2014) and (with Felicia Chan) of *Chinese Cinemas: International Perspectives* (2016).

Editorial note

This book follows the Chinese convention for Chinese names, that is, family names precede personal names (for example, Wei Te-sheng, Tsai Ming-liang). However there are two exceptions. First, the names of the contemporary Chinese authors of both English-language and Chinese-language sources follow the English convention of the personal name preceding the family name (for example, Hong-chi Shiau, Chin-ching Lee). Second, if a Chinese individual has adopted a particular English name that is well known in the field, the book will use the English formation (for example, Ang Lee, Edward Yang, Midi Z).

The Chinese pinyin system is adopted for the Romanisation of Chinese names (e.g. Mao Zedong, Feng Xiaogang) unless the individual has already obtained a particular English spelling of the name that is well known in the field (for example, Chiang Kai-shek, Hou Hsiao-hsien, Sylvia Chang). The Chinese pronunciation of important Chinese phrases, film titles and terms that are directly relevant to the discussion of the book are given in pinyin in Mandarin after the English translation. For example, *Gallants* (*Da lei tai*), *Orphan of Asia* (*Yaxiya de guer*). We apologise for not providing Romanisation for the pronunciation of these terms in other languages simply for practicality. The editors provide a selected Chinese glossary at the end of the book which gives conventional English spelling, pinyin in Mandarin, Complex Chinese characters (used in Taiwan) and Simplified Chinese characters (used in the People's Republic of China), to minimise confusion.

When a film is referred to for the first time in a chapter, we give the film's English title, the director's name and the distribution year. If it is a Chinese or a Taiwanese film, we also offer the original title in pinyin in Mandarin. The exceptions are three features films: *Cape No.7* (*Haijiao qihao*, dir. Wei Te-sheng, 2008), *Warriers of the Rainbow: Seediq Bale* (*Sai de ke ba lai*, dir. Wei Te-sheng, 2011), and *Kano* (*Kano*, dir. Umin Boya, 2014). As these three films are repeatedly discussed throughout the book, we sometimes simply refer to them as *Cape No.7*, *Seediq Bale*, and *Kano*. We also offer a Chinese filmography at the end of the book for easy identification.

Regarding referencing, this book adopts the Harvard system. We give the author's surname, followed by the publication year, in the in-text citation. When publications contain the same surnames and publication years, we also give the author's first-name initial in citation so that the readers are able to identify the correct item in the bibliography at the end of the book.

Acknowledgements

The editors have been assisted by many people and institutions, and wish to record our appreciation for their help. We are particularly grateful to the Chiang Ching-kuo Foundation for granting a publication subsidy that enabled us to acquire appropriate film stills. We appreciate the effort of individual contributors to source and secure permission from image copyright holders. We must thank Ms Huang Quiong-hui of National Chung Hsing University for contacting Central Motion Picture and ARS Film Production on our behalf; Director Wei Te-sheng for agreeing to take time out of his busy schedule for an interview; the School of Oriental and African Studies (SOAS), University of London, for their administrative support; and Dr Wikanda Promkhuntong of Aberystwyth University for her editorial assistance in consolidating the entire manuscript before its submission to the publisher.

This project was initiated by Professor Kuei-fen Chiu of Chung Hsing University at the end of 2014. In January 2015, she organised a workshop in Taiwan where many film scholars enjoyed a valuable and productive exchange of views about the necessity of having fresh perspectives on the younger generation of Taiwanese filmmakers. This is a vision shared by the wider academic community: at the 12th annual conference of the European Association of Taiwan Studies (EATS) in Krakow, Poland, in April 2015, several papers examined Wei Te-sheng and his films from many different disciplinary approaches. Although this volume cannot include all the excellent researchers writing on Taiwan cinema, we have learned a great deal from all of them and so register our appreciation of their work in these pages.

The editors naturally acknowledge the work and friendship of all the contributors. We admire not only their scholarship but also their work ethic. The editors often asked for revisions and additional materials within specific, sometimes tight deadlines. The dedication and cooperation we received from our contributors has made our involvement in this project a pleasure and a privilege.

We also say a huge thank you to Professor Stephanie Donald for commissioning the book as part of her influential and long-standing series, 'Media, Culture and Social Change in Asia'. We believe that the reputation and existing networks established by this series will place our publication in a favourable position to reach the wider readership it deserves. Last but not least, our debt of gratitude must be reserved for our publisher at Routledge,

Mr Peter Sowden. Peter's faith in our project gave us the confidence to focus on the intellectual integrity of the book and the quality of individual chapters without being overly concerned with production costs. As always, he was also a valuable source of advice when we had queries about publishing practices. It is often observed that publishing in the UK is a gentlemen's industry. Publishers like Peter are a testimony to that statement.

Meanwhile, we should express our gratitude to the countless individuals who have dedicated their careers to Taiwan's film industry. Their work deserves to be known by a wider global audience, and we hope that this volume of essays goes some way to helping achieve that.

1 From Taiwan New Cinema to post-New Cinema

An introduction

Kuei-fen Chiu, Ming-yeh T. Rawnsley and Gary D. Rawnsley

A new beginning with new questions

Taiwan New Cinema (*Taiwan xin dianying*, or TNC) is a cinematic move-ment that emerged in the 1980s just as democracy was introduced to the island. Its impact cannot be overstated: TNC not only expanded cultural frontiers, but also made possible multiple and alternative onscreen representa-tions of Taiwanese identities and historiographies. Since Hou Hsiao-hsien – one of the most respected TNC filmmakers – received the Golden Lion award at the Venice Film Festival in 1989 for his masterpiece, *A City of Sadness* (*Beiqing chengshi*), Taiwan New Cinema has carved a niche status in the global markets of arthouse cinema and 'stands tall in the history of world cinema' (Lim 2013: 161). Today, the work of cinematic auteurs associated with the first and second waves of Taiwan New Cinema[1] continues to attract accolade at prestigious film festivals. Recent examples include the Best Director Award for Hou Hsiao-hsien's *The Assassin* (*Nie yin niang*) at the 2015 Cannes Film Festival and the Grand Jury Prize for Tsai Ming-liang's *Stray Dogs* (*Jiao you*) at the 70th Venice International Film Festival in 2013 (see Mello, Vitali, and Pollacchi in this volume). On the other hand, Taiwan's film industry experienced serious setbacks when the domestic commercial film market became completely dominated by Hollywood in the 1990s (Curtin 2007: 86). The long-term decline continued into the twenty-first century until the appearance of Wei Te-sheng's debut feature film, *Cape No.7* (*Haijiao qihao*, 2008), which became the most profitable locally made movie in Taiwan's history (see Ma, Hu, Chan & Willis, Wang, and Berry in this volume).

It is worth noting that prior to *Cape No.7*, there were several local pro-ductions that caught the popular imagination, including the horror film *Double Vision* (*Shuang tong*, dir. Chen Guo-fu, 2002), road movie *Island Etude* (*Lian xi qu*, dir. Chen Huai-en, 2006), and youth romance *Secret* (*Buneng shuo de mimi*, dir. Jay Chou, 2007). However, the popularity of these films did not stimulate a revival, and the struggle for screenings in movie theatres continued (Rawnsley 2016a: 384–385). In contrast, the box office performance of *Cape No.7* gathered momentum in 2008 and encouraged positive signs of improvement. An estimated 30–50 feature films (including documentaries) are now produced in Taiwan each year, while the number of registered film production companies also increased from 556 in 2005 to 914 in October 2010 (Gao 2011: 5).

Arguably, '*Cape No.7* has done for Taiwan cinema within its domestic market what *Crouching Tiger, Hidden Dragon* [*Wo hu cang long*, dir. Ang Lee, 2000] did for transnational Chinese cinemas on a global scale: both smashed box office records and injected a new confidence in their products in their respective markets and audiences' (Lim 2013: 157, quoted in Chan & Willis in this volume). While this domestic success has yet to raise the profile of Taiwanese commercial cinema outside Asia, it has inspired many Taiwan-based filmmakers to move away from 'the auteur-centered, film-festival-participating domestic-audience-alienating TNC period of the 1980s and 1990s' to a 'more popular mode of filmmaking that aims to appeal to a wider audience' (Lim 2013: 158, quoted in Chan & Willis in this volume).

For researchers of Taiwan cinema and cinephilia, this new period of movie-making and consumption raises several questions: Did *Cape No.7* usher in a new dawn of filmmaking on the island? What are the characteristics of the so-called 'post-New Cinema', and who are its representatives? What is the relationship between the younger generations of Taiwanese filmmakers and the renowned TNC masters? Can we claim that post-New Cinema embodies the legacies of Taiwan New Cinema, or does it demonstrate their complete rupture? Moreover, how do these new Taiwan-based filmmakers maintain their presence on the international film festival circuit, and are their films reaching global audiences? The contributors to this volume bring to these and other questions their unique perspectives on Taiwan cinema and the international film environment, and consider how cinema has impacted on society. They also provide insight into Taiwan's position in the ever-evolving global cinema landscape.

Why Wei Te-sheng?

Song-yong Sing (2010: 148–149) suggests that the foremost characteristics of 'post-New Cinema' are a penchant for a 'post-sadness'[2] approach to traumatic historical subjects, and an emphasis on a more ambivalent interpretation of events through well-designed audiovisual strategies. Sing considers Wei's *Cape No.7* one of the most important examples of the post-New Cinema. In addition, Min-xu Zhan (2010) calls attention to Wei's emphasis on the multi-ethnic and transnational configuration of grassroots Taiwan. If Sing's essay helps to situate Wei in the history of contemporary Taiwan Cinema, Zhan's analysis of the multi-ethnic composition and his awareness of a 'Taiwan-Japan-China complex' provide a historicised contextualisation for interpreting Wei's films. Thus this collection of essays uses Wei Te-sheng as a gateway to analyse and understand both the idea and development of Taiwan's national cinema within a social and political context that has experienced profound change.

At the time of editing this volume (September 2016), Wei is known for his two directorial films, *Cape No. 7* (2008) and *Warriors of the Rainbow: Seediq Bale* (*Sai de ke ba lai*, 2011), as well as a film he produced, *Kano* (dir. Umin Boya, 2014). All three experienced box office successes in Taiwan. Wei attracted back to cinema houses large numbers of local film-goers, while turning attention to otherwise forgotten episodes in Taiwan's history.

Song Hwee Lim (2013: 161) defined Taiwan New Cinema as 'another kind of cinema, delivering qualitative pleasure derived from a deep and penetrating investment aesthetically, emotionally, intellectually, and politically'. We may find evidence that audiences in Taiwan who watched *Cape No. 7*, *Seediq Bale*, and *Kano* also experienced these emotional responses to the films, though probably in very different ways. Such 'qualitative pleasure' is discussed in Part I of this collection through the lens of cinephilia and by addressing discourses of international film festivals. The contributors in Part II unpack the multiple layers of emotional and intellectual investment of Taiwanese audiences in Wei's works through film analysis, studies of genres and styles of history films, and historiographical approaches to Taiwan cinema. While each contributor offers an exciting new perspective from their own backgrounds and interests, collectively their work announces a common theme: an international/global versus national/local paradigm can trigger quite varied expectations of and responses to movies.

As Guo-juin Hong (2011), Sheng-mei Ma (2015), and many contributors of this volume (e.g. Berry, Chiu, Liao, Mello, and Vitali) remark, although Wei's films are embraced by local audiences, they fail to inspire the same enthusiasm and interest when screened outside Taiwan and Asia. Cecília Mello (Chapter 2) discovers that the dominant criteria adopted by post-war French cinephilia in film festivals serves Tsai Ming-liang well but fails Wei Te-sheng. Valentina Vitali (Chapter 3) concurs that the logic of international arthouse discourses that helped to elevate Hou Hsiao-hsien from a national to a global auteur status cannot easily apply to Wei. Moreover, Elena Pollacchi (Chapter 4) and Ran Ma (Chapter 5) remind us that there are a variety of stakeholders and constantly changing cultural and political factors to be taken into account in the organisation of international film festivals.

Song Hwee Lim (2013: 157) describes the present state of post-New Cinema as a 'bifurcation between Taiwan cinema's international profile and its domestic self-image'. Clearly Taiwan is not alone. In their study on Singapore cinema, Berry and Farquhar (2006: 213–222; also see Berry in this volume) noted that 'crossover films that attempt to make it out from international festivals into the global exhibition marketplace' have become increasingly rare and thus the local markets are left with *either* 'low-budget films aimed at international festivals and with no domestic market' *or* 'popular films whose heavy reliance on local culture and issues to attract domestic audiences impedes export'. In other words, if post-Taiwan New Cinema – or Singapore and other Asian cinema – is to break away from a seemingly zero-sum arthouse-versus-commercial binary it will, on the one hand, require the international festival professionals to reflect more critically on existing aesthetic ideologies and practices in global film festivals and markets. On the other hand, local practitioners also need to understand how international networks and mechanisms function so they may move towards a more innovative, nuanced and mutually beneficial working relationship with festival organisers.

Some of our contributors have pondered on whether or not it is possible to reconcile the need to create an international presence (especially through film festivals) with the appetite of local movie-goers for popular locally produced and locally relevant output. For example, Mello (Chapter 2) suggests that the new generations of international film enthusiasts are likely to obtain an increasingly more plural understanding of Taiwan cinema within a new cinephilic landscape that has both shaped and been reshaped by digital and online technologies. Chan and Willis (Chapter 7) champion strategic cultural intervention in film programming to bridge the gap left by conventional international distribution and exhibition channels. Similarly, Brian Hu (Chapter 6) proposes a new approach to curating film events that may bring together multiple imaginings of Taiwan to an overseas audience which will animate existing discussions in a more thought-provoking manner.

Wei Te-sheng rejects the arthouse film mode of aesthetics that has advanced Taiwan New Cinema and its auteurs to the global stage. Instead he chooses to work within a commercial framework and adopts Hollywood formats and melodramatic performances. One may argue that Wei prefers to entertain local viewers rather than privileging international cinephilia, and this above everything sets him apart from TNC auteurs and their followers. However, close examination of Wei's movies and filmmaking practices reveals undeniable similarities with his TNC predecessors.

Like many TNC filmmakers (for example, Hou Hsiao-hsien, Wan Jen, and Wang Tong), Wei Te-sheng demonstrates a deep interest in suppressed Taiwanese collective historical memories. *Cape No.7*, *Seediq Bale* and *Kano* are all based on real historical events. As the chapters in this volume testify, these films generate critical debates about the past, present and future of Taiwan and its film industry. They are variably understood as a 'reinvention of national narrative' (Wang, Chapter 8), cinematic dramatisations of the island's 'orphan' complex (Berry, Chapter 9), stories about competing modernities powered by 'transregional, transcultural, post-colonial and intergenerational dynamics' (Liao, Chapter 10), interventional historiographies with conflicting indigenous perspectives (Chiu, Chapter 12), 'the invention of a people to come' (Lee, Chapter 13), or 'an allegory of Taiwan's contemporary political situation' (Sterk, Chapter 14). In short, Wei's films provoke a rich reflection on modern Taiwan – just as the first wave of Taiwan New Cinema did in the 1980s – and generate a wide spectrum of political readings. In the words of Robert A. Rosenstone (Chapter 11), for Taiwanese people these fictionalised cinematic renderings of their history invite a new way of 'understanding [their] relationship to the past, another way of pursuing that conversation about where [they] came from, where [they] are going and who [they] are'.

The Japanese colonial legacy, absent from discussion in the martial law period, appears prominently in both Taiwan New Cinema and in Wei's films. Kuei-fen Chiu (2007) has observed that most pre-TNC films tend to cast Japanese characters in a very negative light, while many TNC outputs offer less negative and non-judgemental portrayals. As Chiu (2007: 29) argued, under authoritarian rule 'the Taiwanese enacted a negation of their association with the Japanese culture so as to have their Chinese identity validated'. However, democratisation in the 1980s empowered filmmakers to try to 'reclaim the island's Japanese colonial heritages' in order to distinguish their unique Taiwanese identity from the increasingly powerful Han Chinese identity (Chiu 2007: 30).

Wei's post-millennium films push beyond the TNC and construct an ambivalent rapport between the Taiwanese characters and their Japanese colonisers. At the heart of *Cape No.7* is a romance story between a Taiwanese girl student and her Japanese teacher during the colonial period. *Kano* focuses on the bond between a Taiwanese baseball team and their Japanese coach in the 1930s. Even *Seediq Bale*, which depicts an indigenous uprising against the Japanese in 1930, disrupts the otherwise antagonistic confrontation between the Taiwanese and Japanese when the commander, Kamada Yahiko, acknowledges similarities between the rebellious Seediq warriors and the influence of the Japanese samurai code, *bushido*. Commenting on E.M. Forster's rhetoric of the colonial relationship in *A Passage to India*, R. Radhakrishnan observes a 'fleeting moment of coming together': 'In the time of colonialism', he said, 'recognition can go this far and no further' (Radhakrishnan 2009: 466).

It is not surprising that Wei's portraits of Taiwan's colonial relationship with Japan are controversial. If we find Chiu's analysis convincing, we may agree that 'the resurrection of suppressed colonial memories' and the recasting of Japanese figures in a positive light demonstrate Wei's 'active participation in the revision of Taiwanese historiography' (Chiu 2007: 30). However, the interventions by Ping-hui Liao and Chris Berry in this volume provide very different perspectives. Berry interprets this rapport in terms of a 'Japan complex' which reveals Taiwan's 'colonial dependence mentality' and longing for recognition by their Japanese colonisers. Liao, on the other hand, emphasises the depiction of the two main Japanese characters in *Kano* to show how the 'sympathetic affinity with local cultural dynamics' on the part of the colonisers reveals 'conflicting, competing, and collaborative forces in the making of a specific moment' in Taiwan's 'colonial and even postcolonial histories'.

Another noteworthy feature of Wei's films is the weight of indigenous culture and history. Both *Seediq Bale* and *Kano* cast indigenous people as the main characters. From the outset Wei was determined to involve Taiwan's indigenous communities in the making of *Seediq Bale*, and made sure they were taught how to speak their lines in the almost extinct Seediq languages (mainly Tgdaya and Toda). At all stages of production, Wei consulted with experts in the Seediq culture. Moreover, the whole story is told mainly from the perspective of the Seediq warriors, and the focus of the story is their leader, Mona Rudo. Wei was the producer of *Kano*, which is directed by Umin Boya, the indigenous actor cast in *Seediq Bale* as Mona Rudo's rival from another tribe. Four out of the nine baseball players in *Kano* are from various indigenous communities. Therefore, these two films make an extremely positive contribution to the representation of Taiwan's indigenous people, in terms of story and production, as well as their part in Taiwan's history. Finally, the multicultural band in *Cape No.7* featured guitarist Lao-ma. Although not a central character, his inclusion is an important demonstration of the declining divisions in Taiwan society. The attention to indigenous culture and history in Wei's films is rarely found in Taiwan New Cinema.

Taiwan New Cinema, post-New Cinema, and Wei Te-sheng

In her work on cultural democratisation and Taiwan cinema, Ming-yeh T. Rawnsley (2016a: 378–383) has explained that the cultural legacies of Taiwan New Cinema have manifested across several dimensions, including: the flexible use of languages; accommodating multiple viewpoints and interpretations of different Taiwanese histories; nuanced approaches to modernity and youth; and a commitment to foster a more vibrant domestic film culture and film education. Rawnsley (2016a: 385) argued that Wei Te-sheng's *Cape No.7* 'acted as the catalyst for the culmination of all the structural changes [in democratic Taiwan] … and finally led to a tentative revival of Taiwan cinema today'.

However, the contributors to this volume draw attention to how the image of Taiwan cinema during the post-New Cinema period has experienced profound change, mainly in the way they build a rapport with their audiences. Many younger filmmakers relate more to their peers and identify with local audiences rather than global auteurs or with cinephilia of international film festivals, as suggested by their preference for the popular commercial mode of filmmaking rather than arthouse aesthetics. The rejuvenation of the Taiwanese movie industry through commercial means is an important motive for this turn, but as our studies of Wei Te-sheng suggest, some filmmakers are also inspired by the ambition to popularise Taiwanese history. In addition, Wei gives more prominence to indigenous culture and history than his TNC predecessors. The result of this critical engagement with multiple Taiwanese identities and the Japanese colonial legacy turns Wei's films into multilingual platforms where a diversity of cultural dynamics intersect.

Without doubt, Wei Te-sheng is one of the most interesting and innovative post-New Cinema film directors working in Taiwan today. His films offer specific and localised interpretations of Taiwan's history and identity, but they also voice universal concerns such as love, heroism, family, friendship, life and death. The diversity of audience reception and interpretation of post-New

Cinema represented by Wei – in cinemas and in the more formal space of film festivals – lies at the heart of this volume which not only brings together the local and the global, but also chronicles the development of Taiwan's film industry. This narrative is set against the background of another, equally exciting story of social and political liberalisation and democratisation that has impacted on how people in Taiwan see themselves and their history. These forces, external to the movie industry, have shaped and in some instances have been shaped by the power of cinema.

Notes

1 The first wave of Taiwan New Cinema (TNC) refers to a movement in the early 1980s in which the younger generation of filmmakers made a conscious decision to film the island's society and history as they understood it, not as the official rhetoric preferred. Their films challenged government censorship and were thus very different from the locally produced commercial movies. Hou Hsiao-hsien and Edward Yang are two of the most revered first wave of TNC auteurs. The second wave of TNC refers to the international film festival-oriented arthouse filmmaking in Taiwan in the 1990s, represented by Tsai Ming-liang and Ang Lee (Rawnsley 2016a: 386).

2 Hou Hsiao-hsien's *A City of Sadness* can be considered a watershed movie in the history of Taiwan cinema for at least two reasons: first, it was the first Taiwanese film to receive the highest recognition at a major international film festival; and second, the February 28th Incident of 1947 (i.e. 2/28), a traumatic event that haunted Taiwan's political and social life for 40 years during the martial law era, was openly depicted on the big screen for the first time. Since then, *A City of Sadness* has become a critical social text and has inspired multidimensional discourses about Taiwan's past and future (Rawnsley 2011). Many local filmmakers were influenced by Hou and subsequently produced a series of works on similar topics. Therefore, 'sadness' (*beiqing*) became a shorthand catch-all term to describe a particular characteristic of Taiwan cinema in the late twentieth century. 'Post-sadness' here refers to the younger generations of filmmakers' search for new paths in interpreting history which are different from *A City of Sadness*.

Part I
International reception and Taiwan cinema

2 Taiwan cinema across the globe

A Brazilian perspective

Cecília Mello

The aim of this chapter is to examine the reception of Taiwan cinema in Brazil between the 1980s and the 2010s, leading to a broader reflection on the process of distribution and exhibition of Taiwanese films abroad. This discussion is moved by an initial observation concerning, on the one hand, the prestige of cinematic auteurs from Taiwan such as Hou Hsiao-hsien, Edward Yang and Tsai Ming-liang and, on the other hand, the relative invisibility of Wei Te-sheng's work to Brazilian audiences, be they arthouse/festival-oriented or more commercially inclined. By trying to understand the main reasons for this disparity, which finds that Wei's films, despite being highly popular in Taiwan, fail to resonate with a Brazilian audience, I hope to shed some light on how Taiwan cinema connects with the world. This also allows for an investigation into the commercial, political and artistic forces that inevitably affect the international reception of a national cinema.

This chapter will develop in such a manner that freely intertwines collected data and observations drawn from my own relationship with Taiwan cinema, which started in the mid-1990s in the city of São Paulo. The personal perspective undoubtedly runs the risk of instilling an anecdotal tone, but the chapter should not be taken as such; rather, it aims at a general approach to the international reception of Taiwan cinema and includes the first-person accounts as representative of both a stratum of Brazilian cinema audiences and of an academic perspective of Taiwan cinema studies from across the globe. It starts by describing how Taiwan cinema became an object of interest to me, both personally and academically, followed by an overall account of the reception of Taiwan cinema in Brazil. This leads to a reflection on the migratory forces at work in Brazilian society and, more specifically, its embrace of the cinema of Japan, which could explain a certain preference for Taiwanese auteurs whose work was influenced by Japanese cinematic traditions. It then addresses the virtual anonymity of Wei Te-sheng in the country and how this might relate to changes in the cinematic landscape of Taiwan at the beginning of the twenty-first century. Finally, this chapter suggests that the current commercial trend in Taiwan cinema has provoked a significant shift in the perception of national identity as related to cinema, and that in the new century, when cinephilia no longer means what it once did, there might still be a place for Taiwanese films among Brazilian cinema audiences.

Taiwan screen memories

In her *Atlas of Emotion* (2007), Giuliana Bruno brings to light film's affinity with architecture to suggest that cinema is as much a spatial as a temporal art. Her contribution belongs to a period of revision, from the 1990s onwards, of the post-structuralist and psychoanalytic theories that dominated film studies in the 1960s and 1970s. By dislocating the emphasis from *sight* to *site*, from *optic* to *haptic*, Bruno breaks with the notion of filmic space as an inheritor of Renaissance perspective and transforms the film spectator, traditionally seen as a *voyeur*, into a *voyageur*, one who embarks on an emotional journey through different sites.

I evoke Bruno's understanding of cinema because I believe it resonates with my first experiences of Taipei, a city on the other side of the planet from Brazil. The first time I felt transported to it was when I saw Tsai Ming-liang's *Vive L'Amour* (*Aiqing wansui*, 1994) in a cinema in São Paulo in the late 1990s. The film had been released commercially – albeit with a certain delay – to critical acclaim, and played for a few weeks in the city, during which time I had the chance to see it at least three times on the big screen. A few years later, in 2000, Edward Yang's masterpiece *A One and a Two* (*Yi yi*, 2000) was also released commercially in São Paulo, which meant that once again I embarked on an emotional journey through the streets, the houses, the hotels and the viaducts of Taipei. What I noticed was that, gradually, other films by Yang and Tsai started to produce in me a virtual memory of this urban space, so distant and yet so familiar on more than one level. If film viewing is indeed, as Giuliana Bruno says, 'an imaginary form of *flânerie*' (Bruno 2007: 17), my *flânerie* through Taipei, set in motion by the travelling medium that is cinema, created in me personal memories of a city to which I had never been.

Like me, many other film lovers living in São Paulo – Brazil's biggest and richest city and the country's cultural hub – became more and more aware of the talent coming from Taiwan from the 1980s onwards, when Brazilian audiences were able to see major works by Taiwan New Cinema (*Taiwan xin dianying*) masters Hou Hsiao-hsien and Edward Yang. The first Taiwanese film shown in Brazil was probably *Dust in the Wind* (*Lianlian fengchen*, dir. Hou Hsiao-hsien, 1986), during the São Paulo International Film Festival (Mostra Internacional de Cinema de São Paulo) of 1987, Brazil's largest and most prestigious film event, running since 1977. Since then, the 'Mostra' has been showcasing Taiwan cinema quite consistently, including *Daughters of the Nile* (*Niluohe nü er*, 1987) by Hou Hsiao-hsien and *The Terrorizers* (*Kongbu fenzi*, 1986) by Edward Yang, in its 12th edition in 1988; films by Ang Lee, Li You-ning, Chen Yu-xun, Lin Cheng-sheng, Yee Chih-yen in the 1990s; and by Sylvia Chang, Chen Singing, Cheng Fen-fen and Chi Y. Lee from 2000 onwards. Most notably, since 1997 Tsai Ming-liang's work has been fêted by the festival and by audiences, and his films *The River* (*He liu*, 1997), *What Time is it There?* (*Ni nei bian ji dian*, 2001), *The Skywalk is Gone* (*Tianqiao bujian le*, 2002), *Goodbye, Dragon Inn* (*Bu san*, 2003), *I Don't Want to Sleep Alone* (*Hei yan quan*, 2006) and *Stray Dogs* (*Jiao you*, 2013) have all been shown at different editions of the 'Mostra'. The work of Lee Kang-sheng as a director, including *The Missing* (*Bu jian*, 2003) and *Help Me, Eros* (*Bang bang wo, aisheng*, 2007), has featured in the same festival, and more recently the documentary *Flowers of Taipei: Taiwan New Cinema* (*Guangyin de gushi: Taiwan xin dianying*, dir. Hsieh Chinglin, 2014) and the restored version of *A Brighter Summer Day* (*Gulingjie shaonian sharen shijian*, 1991) by Edward Yang have also been shown.[1]

There is no doubt that the presence of Taiwan New Cinema films as well as other Taiwanese titles in the São Paulo International Film Festival and, more recently, in the Rio International Film Festival (1999–present), has a connection with their previously found prestige in European film festivals such as Cannes, Venice and Berlin. Most notably, the Venice Film Festival has nurtured a special fondness for Chinese-language films, and Taiwan cinema in particular, especially since 1989 when it awarded the Golden Lion to Hou Hsiao-hsien for *A City of Sadness* (*Beiqing chengshi*), and later in 1994 to Tsai Ming-liang for *Vive L'Amour*. The role of global film festival networks in establishing a certain number of films, sometimes with similar styles or displaying similar tendencies, as synonymous with a national cinema is well known and well discussed. The issue of national cinemas, however, has been quite contentious since the 1990s, seen perhaps as inadequate in our era of globalisation. It is worth pointing out that during the 1960s, the filmmaker from those countries considered to be 'peripheral' was frequently seen as a spokesperson for the nation as an 'imagined community', in Benedict Anderson's (2006) terms, engaged in a project of social transformation. Today we live in times of ebbs and flows, averse to totalising or binding notions and thus fomenting a critical spirit with little in common with the political thinking of the 1960s. One needs simply to observe how the prefixes 'trans', 'inter' and 'multi' abound and even seem mandatory in today's film and audiovisual studies, in what seems to be an effort to grasp the overarching effects of contemporaneity's preference for fragmentation (see, for example, Appadurai 1996; Naficy 2001; Shohat and Stam 1994; Durovicova and Newman 2009; Berry and Pang 2008; Higbee and Lim 2010). National cinema thus seems, all of a sudden, to be an anachronistic conception.

At the same time, the notion of national cinemas persists despite the current landscape of circulation and simultaneity. Its importance is repeatedly emphasised by international film festivals each year in their categorisation of films into different countries. It would thus be erroneous to do away with it completely; undoubtedly, any considerations of Taiwan cinema are indeed considerations of a national cinema, albeit in a global context. So how was this national cinema perceived in a country situated across the globe from it?

In the 1980s and 1990s, as I am sure was also the case with cinephile audiences elsewhere, Taiwan cinema became quite simply – and with a little help from Peggy Chiao, also known as 'the Godmother of Taiwan New Cinema' (Xu 2007: 9) – synonymous with the filmic movement that rejuvenated the cinematic landscape of Taiwan during those years, and secured its place on the world cinema map. This also meant that Taiwan was established as a separate entity from China in the cinematic world, seen as a different country producing a completely different cinema. In Brazil, it always appeared, and still does, as Taiwan in the national cinema framework of any film festival, and never in any connection with the People's Republic of China (PRC). This happens despite the fact that Taiwan and Brazil do not have official diplomatic relations, as Brazil recognises the PRC.[2]

As well as appearing in film festivals, Taiwanese films have occasionally been released commercially in Brazilian cinemas, as was the case with Yang's *A One and a Two*, Tsai's *Vive L'Amour, The River, The Hole* (*Dong*, 1998) and *The Wayward Cloud* (*Tian bian yi duo yun*, 2005), as well as many of Ang Lee's films made in and outside Taiwan. It was also the object of three retrospectives, the first in 2001 at the Centro Cultural São Paulo ('Cinema Taiwanês'), the second in 2008 at the Brazilian Film Archive ('Tesouros da Cinemateca de Taiwan'/'Treasures from the Taiwan Film Archive'), and the third in 2009 again at the Centro Cultural São Paulo ('Mostra do Cinema Taiwanês Contemporâneo'/'Contemporary Taiwanese Cinema Exhibition'). These were organised by Brazilian public cultural centres in conjunction with the Taipei Economic and Cultural Office in São Paulo, which opened in 1992 and has since been keen to promote Taiwan cinema and culture in Brazil. A fourth exhibition was organised at the Centro Cultural Banco do Brasil in 2004, entitled 'As Três Chinas'/'The Three Chinas', focusing on films from the PRC, Taiwan and Hong Kong.

Despite the more general approach to the notion of Taiwan cinema observed in these efforts, which often included more auterist films alongside commercial productions, animations and documentaries about Taiwan, or which focused on a historical perspective, Taiwan cinema is still seen as synonymous with Taiwan New Cinema as well as with its 'second wave' represented by Tsai Ming-liang, despite his, Hou's and Yang's highly idiosyncratic oeuvres. It is worth noting how these auteurs' reputation within the Brazilian cinephilic landscape has been reinforced by a full retrospective of Hou Hsiao-hsien's work, held in the Centro Cultural Banco do Brasil in São Paulo, Rio de Janeiro and Brasília in December 2010 and January 2011, and which was accompanied by a comprehensive catalogue containing articles, reviews and pictures of his films.

Yet, from Taiwan cinema's triumvirate, it is perhaps Tsai Ming-liang who has been more overtly embraced by Brazilian audiences and festivals since *The River* was shown at the 'Mostra' in 1997. Tsai has visited Brazil at least twice, once to attend the festival in São Paulo in 2003 alongside Lee Kang-sheng and Lu Yi-ching. On that occasion, they presented *The Skywalk is*

MOSTRA DO CINEMA TAIWANÊS CONTEMPO RÂNEO 9 a 18 janeiro 2009

Figure 2.1 Contemporary Taiwanese Cinema Exhibition in São Paulo, 2009
(Every effort has been made by the author to obtain copyright permission)

Gone, Goodbye, Dragon Inn and *The Missing*, and Tsai made a short film, *Aquarium*, for the portmanteau effort *Welcome to São Paulo* (*Bem-vindo a São Paulo*, 2004), produced by the festival's head, Leon Cakoff (Mello 2013). His second visit happened in 2010, when he attended a full retrospective of his work organised in São Paulo and in Rio de Janeiro at the Centro Cultural Banco do Brasil, offering talks and interviews to faithful fans. Today, Tsai, but also Hou and Yang, as well as the chameleonic Ang Lee, can be considered quite well known in the country, especially amongst students, cinephiles and academics who, in many ways, are also inheritors of a French cinephilic tradition dating back to the 1960s.

Japanese cinephilia in São Paulo

As well as relating to the global festival network and its impact on the exhibition and distribution of films around the world, I would like to suggest that the prestige of Taiwanese cinema in Brazil can also be explained by a long tradition of consistent distribution, reception and critical appreciation of Japanese films in the country. The reason for this is that Brazil is home to the largest Japanese population outside Japan, totalling around 1.5 million *nikkeis*, [3] and thus has always had a special relationship with Japan and its culture. Japanese immigration in Brazil started officially on 18 June 1908, when the ship *Kasato Maru* harboured in the port city of Santos with the first 781 immigrants from Japan, destined to work the farms of the state of São Paulo. This migratory influx was quite steady throughout the first half of the twentieth century, but came to an almost complete halt in 1973, with the arrival of the last official Japanese immigration ship in Brazil (see Motoyama 2011; and Carneiro and Takeuchi 2011). Interestingly, the city of São Paulo, unlike most other Western cities with a considerable population of immigrants, never had a Chinatown. Rather, its Asian neighbourhood, known as Liberdade, is full of Japanese restaurants, shops and temples, where most immigrants and their descendants lived and worked.

The city of São Paulo experienced something peculiar in relation to Japanese cinema from 1953 to 1988: whilst in other parts of the Western world Japanese cinema was seen by the public and critics only after the 1960s, here cinemas began to show them almost a decade earlier. In Liberdade there were four film theatres dedicated exclusively to Japanese cinema, namely Cine Niterói, Cine Jóia, Cine Tokio and Cine Nippon, exhibiting the works of each of the main Japanese film studios, respectively Toei, Toho, Nikkatsu and Shochiku (Kishimoto 2013). These were genre films such as samurai epics, musicals, monster films, comedies, animation, crime films, dramas etc., as well as the works of Japanese masters Kenji Mizoguchi, Yasujiro Ozu, Mikio Naruse and Akira Kurosawa, amongst others. As Lúcia Nagib explains, 'thanks to this relationship, which also echoed in other parts of the country, Brazilian people were able to see, for instance, Yasujiro Ozu's masterpieces almost a decade before the filmmaker became an icon of modern cinema in other parts of the world, celebrated by critics such as Noel Burch and David Bordwell'. Nagib further recalls that 'during the 1950s and 1960s, classics by Ozu, Kurosawa, Mizoguchi and Naruse were shown in Liberdade alongside films from rebels such as Imamura, Oshima and Yoshida, in mixed and unequal bills, but which influenced lots of cinephiles and filmmakers, including those of Brazilian Cinema Novo' (Nagib 2004).

After the 1960s, and following the increasing decline of Japanese film studios facing stiff competition from television, the film theatres at Liberdade gradually began to include 'foreign films' in their listings, and finally started to close down one by one until the 1990s. However, the love affair between Japanese cinema and Brazilian audiences, made up of faithful *nikkeis* as well as of cinephiles, critics and filmmakers, was already well cemented, and from the 1980s onwards there have been numerous film exhibitions of the work of Japanese filmmakers, retrospectives of Japanese cinema as well as dedicated slots in the São Paulo 'Mostra' about the cinema of Japan, with no signs of a decline. There have also been numerous academic studies of Japanese cinema in Brazil, led especially by Lúcia Nagib during the 1980s and 1990s, a pioneer of Japanese film studies and world authority in the field.

It seemed important, therefore, to point out this peculiarity of Brazilian/São Paulo society as Taiwan New Cinema directors such as Hou, Yang and later Tsai have been seen as inheritors of a certain Asian cinema aesthetic and prestige previously located and recognised in Japanese filmmakers such as Kenji Mizoguchi and Yasujiro Ozu. Hou has perhaps pride of place in this line of hereditary succession; in 2003 he made a film entitled *Café Lumière*

Figure 2.2 Cine Niterói, Liberdade, São Paulo
(Source: Norma Albano/Midia Agencia Estado)

(*Kafei shiguang*) for Shochiku as homage to Ozu, with direct reference to his masterpiece *Tokyo Story* (*Tokyo Monogatari*, 1953), and the degree of his indebtedness to Ozu's highly original style has been debated quite extensively (see for instance, Udden 2009; Phillips and Stringer 2007; Bordwell 2005). The love affair between Brazilian audiences and Japanese cinema could thus be seen as having travelled south across the East China Sea since the appearance of Taiwan New Cinema. Only this time this peculiar movement was not related to immigration: the Japanese were, by the 1980s, already integrated into Brazilian society, and while the Taiwanese started settling in Brazil in the 1960s, their community, totalling approximately 100,000 as of 2015, never had a similar cultural impact in the country.[4] Rather, it was led by Brazilians who learned to love Japanese cinema before the rest of the world.

Another Taiwan: *Cape No.7* and Wei Te-sheng

In 2010, I had the chance to be received as Visiting Fellow at the School of Film and New Media of Taipei National University of the Arts (TNUA), during a period of post-doctoral research.[5] My project then was broadly concerned with the relationship between cinema and the city, and issues of realism, space and memory in contemporary world cinema. The films of Tsai Ming-liang were central to my investigation for their privileged engagement of space and architecture, and for their indissociable rapport with the urban space. As mentioned before, this urban space is mostly the city of Taipei, and it is no surprise that, as a faithful spectator of Tsai's singular body of work, built from a web of related themes, characters and spaces, I felt intimate with this onscreen world. When I first arrived in Taipei in 2010, the streets, the viaducts, the trains, the buildings, everything reminded me of films by Tsai Ming-liang and also by Edward Yang.

I would like briefly to recall two episodes that now seem emblematic of what I came to perceive as a gap between an idea I had of Taiwan cinema and another side of this national cinematography, until then unbeknownst to me after years living in Brazil and in the UK. The first anecdote concerns a conversation with Professor Peggy Chiao during the first week of my stay at TNUA. Knowing I was going to be talking to the godmother of Taiwan New Cinema made me anxious and keen to express my love affair with those films and filmmakers she had once promoted around the world. Peggy was very welcoming, but she was quick to point out that Taiwan cinema was now moving in different, more commercial directions, and that the days of art-house cinema were gone. This seemed somehow discouraging to me at first, as I never really had a serious research interest in commercial cinematic practices. It was also during this stay that Peggy gave me a DVD copy of the film she had just produced, *Hear Me* (*Ting shuo*, 2009), directed by Cheng Fen-fen, and which I took to her friend Leon Cakoff of the São Paulo International Film Festival so that it could be considered for inclusion in its 34th edition in 2010. On Peggy's recommendation, I also watched another film, entitled *Zoom Hunting* (*Lie yan*, dir. Cho Li, 2010), and despite truly enjoying both films, they had a different personal impact from my previous experiences with Taiwan cinema.

The second anecdote I will briefly recall here concerns the fact that in the first week of my stay at TNUA all I was asked by students and members of staff was whether I had seen the film *Cape No.7* (2008). Frankly speaking, I had never heard of such a film, let alone of its director, Wei Te-sheng. So my new friends were quick to arrange a special screening of *Cape No.7* in the school's auditorium, where I sat alone and enjoyed the experience of watching my first Taiwanese romantic comedy, all the while admiring the beautiful scenery of the Taiwanese subtropical south coast. What I was then quick to realise was that a more 'commercial' Taiwanese cinema seemed to be on the rise after a period of relative decline of its arthouse film production in the 2000s. I also realised that this production was virtually unknown in Brazil, and that Wei Te-sheng was a name that did not ring any bells with a cinephile crowd, let alone a bigger public. Later, I found out that his only works to have been shown in Brazil were his contribution to the portmanteau film *10+10*, made of 20 short films by 20 different Taiwan directors and shown at the 36th São Paulo International Film Festival (2012), and, as producer, *Warriors of the Rainbow: Seediq Bale* (dir. Umin Boya, 2011), screened twice during an Asian Film Festival in São Paulo ('Traffic – 1° Festival de Cinema e Cultura Asiática de São Paulo') in 2012, alongside works from various others Asian film directors. The repercussions of these rare screenings of Wei Te-sheng's works in Brazil were minimal.

If Wei Te-sheng's international reception has proven quite challenging to the point that it does not stand any comparisons with previous reception of Taiwan New Cinema and of Tsai Ming-liang's work, it also seems undeniable that a phenomenon such as *Cape No.7* speaks volumes about how the Taiwanese cinematic landscape has been changing in the new millennium, pointing in new directions and to new ambitions. It was quite clear that films such as *Cape No.7*, *Hear Me*, *Zoom Hunting*, as well as other commercial successes of the time such as *Au Revoir Taipei* (*Yi ye Taipei*, dir. Arvin Chen, 2010) and *Taipei 24H* (*Taipei yi xiang*, dir. An Jie-yi, Chen Ying-jung, Cheng Fen-fen et al., 2009), seemed to appeal to the demands of a local audience and also to a larger Chinese market, but often failed to achieve international recognition. This does not mean that they were absent from film festivals completely, but their screenings did not seem to award them any significant prestige among global audiences or with film critics and academics. Could this be a matter of an 'arthouse' cinema being able to find an international public, whilst more 'commercial' experiences become easily trapped within the constraints of a specific culture, thus unable to 'travel' so well? Or could the issues of distribution, exhibition and reception of Taiwan cinema be related to other, more specific and perhaps more hidden, commercial, political and artistic forces? Finally, what are the main reasons for the disparity between a persistent idea of what Taiwan cinema is and the country's current film production landscape? These are tough questions to answer, but rather than attempting to do so in a straightforward way, I will now venture a tentative hypothesis and a vague prognosis.

The general appreciation of how Brazil has received Taiwanese films offered in the first part of this chapter privileged, as might have been expected, the work of three artists connected to the specificity of Taiwan national identity in relation to cinema: Hou Hsiao-hsien, Edward Yang and Tsai Ming-liang. Not by chance, their emergence in the cultural landscape of the country coincided with the years of gradual opening and the consequent lifting of martial law in Taiwan in 1987. Since then, cinema has been playing a crucial part in what could be described as a search for an identity within Taiwanese society, and such issues have been discussed widely in contemporary English-language scholarship on Taiwan cinema (see for instance Yip 2004; Hong 2011; Berry and Lu 2005; Davis and Chen 2007). Taking these observations into consideration, a quick glance into these filmmakers' own issues of national identity could perhaps offer an insight into the way of differentiating their work from that of Wei Te-sheng.

Hou, a Hakka, was born on 8 April 1947 in Guangdong. He and his family fled the Chinese civil war to Taiwan in 1948, and he grew up on the island where he later developed his longstanding and highly influential career as a filmmaker. Yang was born on 6 November 1947 in Shanghai and, just like Hou, fled with his family to Taiwan during the civil war, growing up in Taipei. Tsai Ming-liang, a Chinese-Malay, was born on 27 October 1957 in Kuching, Crown Colony of Sarawak, Malaysia. He moved to Taiwan in his twenties, where he developed his prestigious artistic career. What these three Taiwan-based film directors seem to share are the fluid borders of their national identities, and their positionality as both inside and outside a certain notion of Taiwaneseness, which remains a fluid concept in itself, referring to something foreign, out of place, dislocated. These are, not by chance, the types of social, cultural and personal experiences often depicted in their films, albeit through different angles of approach.

On the other hand, Wei Te-sheng comes from a younger generation of Taiwanese filmmakers, and contrary to Hou, Yang and Tsai, he was born in Taiwan, in Yongkang City, Tainan County, now part of Tainan City. This biographical detail is relevant to this hypothesis insofar as it relates to his politics of representation, especially in connection with *Cape No.7*, arguably his most successful film to date. In its presentation of a twin love story between a Japanese and a Taiwanese, referring nostalgically to the period of Japanese colonisation of Taiwan (1895–1945), *Cape No.7* is, according to Mark Harrison (2012), notable for its inclusion of Japan and exclusion of mainland China (also see Berry in this volume):

> As part of the localist cultural movement that has flourished since the 1990s, *Cape No.7* can be located within the post-martial law reaction against the sinicization of politics, education and culture in the KMT

[Kuomintang] era [...] *Cape No.7* [...] produces a Taiwanized cultural product representing the aspects of Taiwan left out by the politics of sinicization, such as the lives of working-class Taiwanese outside of Taipei and the memory of Japanese colonization.

(Harrison 2012: 93)

In its connection with the nativist and localist cultural movements in recent Taiwanese history, *Cape No.7* also promotes a type of character representation based on the exploration of Taiwanese archetypes, which explains in part the film's popularity in the country. As Harrison further suggests, 'the character archetypes offer the appeal of self-representation in which a key pleasure of the film is its articulation of a distinctively Taiwanese form of social knowledge that allows Taiwanese viewers to, as it were, know themselves as Taiwanese as much as know the characters in the film' (Harrison 2012: 93). The use of archetypes in character representation, the narrative closure provided by the romantic ending, the genre conventions in place and the film's overtly commercial appeal – despite its at times clunky narrative and rhythm – all point towards 'social integrity':

In its narrative content and history writing, *Cape No.7* becomes an instance of a response in the politics of culture to the 'crisis of representation' highlighted earlier in the field of political rhetoric and the broader instability of Taiwan's identity formations as a nation state. Against Taiwan's lack of global recognition and the limits and failures of its domestic politics, it proposes a security of vision about the nature of Taiwanese society, as 'naturally' or 'self-evidentially' Taiwanese and not something else.

(Harrison 2012: 94)

Harrison's observations about *Cape No.7*'s search for coherence and closure at the heart of an essentially fragmented and fluid national identity such as that of Taiwan should be read in relation to previous cinematic experiences in which the notions of identity instability and unknowability were embraced and incorporated into the very cinematic form of Taiwan New Cinema and Tsai Ming-liang's oeuvre. Think of the beginning of Yang's *The Terrorizers*, with its kaleidoscopic and enigmatic presentation of multiple stories – real or not – in what Jameson saw as the quintessential post-modern city, Taipei (Jameson 1989). Or of the absence of a home in Tsai's *Vive L'Amour*, where characters occupy empty apartments, roam the streets at night and live their lives in a state of flux. Or of the rootlessness of the boys from Fengkuei trying to make a living in Kaohsiung, as depicted in Hou Hsiao-hsien's *The Boys of Fengkuei* (*Fenggui lai de ren*, 1983). These are human conditions which, despite being localised, are easy to identify with, and the sophistication of their filmic treatment also earned these filmmakers their place in the cinematic world pantheon. Wei Te-sheng's work, on the other hand, seems to offer little in comparison, and despite its East Asian commercial success it has failed to attain universality, perhaps by remaining both too local and too conventional.

Sylvia Chang in Araguari, or the other face of cinephilia

Regardless of the crucial differences between *Cape No. 7* and previous experiences in arthouse cinema in Taiwan, it is also quite possible that I am incurring a gross simplification when suggesting that Wei's work can never resonate with an international audience in the way both Taiwan New Cinema's and Tsai's works have done in the past. In fact, this assumption perhaps disguises a rather nostalgic view of Taiwan cinema and, ultimately, of cinephilia, seen as weathered or even absent in an era of digital files and of small, portable screens. I will therefore recall a final anecdote in order to question certain assumptions and suggest a different prognosis on the international reception of Taiwan cinema.

I was recently in the town of Araguari, located 624 km from São Paulo in the west part of the state of Minas Gerais, Brazil. Araguari is a small town by Brazilian standards, whose main source of income derives from agriculture and livestock farming. One night, I went into the local DVD rental store which still survives in the town (most in São Paulo have shut down in recent years), and there I found Sylvia Chang's romantic comedy *20 30 40* (2004). I had not heard much about the film, but as a Taiwan film lover, I diligently rented and watched it. Why was this film available in this particular shop? What mysterious cinema circulation forces had brought Sylvia Chang to Araguari? How many people had seen her film and enjoyed it? I suspect that those who did had not heard of Hou, Yang and Tsai before, all conspicuously absent from the rental store's collection. At the same time, could this indicate that there is, after all, a place for a more commercial Taiwanese cinema within an international/Brazilian audience, ready to identify with its light comic and romantic tones?

Yet, rather than persisting in dualisms such as arthouse cinema versus commercial cinema, there may be a third way into this equation. I was recently approached by the Taipei Economic and Cultural Office in São Paulo, who expressed their interest in organising another retrospective of Taiwanese films in the city, following the previously mentioned experiences of 2001, 2008 and 2009. This time, they offered a selection from the so-called Taiwan Cinema Toolkit,[6] a collection of DVDs that is part of the Taiwan Cultural Toolkit project, a 2014 initiative of the Ministry of Culture of Taiwan in conjunction with the Taiwan Film Institute (formerly Chinese Taipei Film Archive). The package – an ongoing project hoped to grow each year – comprises around 113 titles at the time of writing in June 2016, dating from different moments of Taiwan cinema history, and is destined for non-profit screenings at the Taipei Offices and other cultural centres around the world. Interestingly, this collection is divided into themes such as 'Youth',

'The City', 'Cultural Conflict', 'Gender', 'Literature', 'History', 'Society', 'Indigenous Peoples', 'The Environment', and includes films by Hou, Tsai and Yang, as well as more recent successes such as *Monga* (*Mengjia*, dir. Doze Niu, 2010) and Wei Te-sheng's *Cape No.7* and *Seediq Bale*. In this cinema toolkit, therefore, auteurs of high international prestige exist on an equal footing with more commercial or less established Taiwanese directors virtually unknown to Western audiences. Moreover, their films are presented as DVDs, a format that is the epitome of home viewing, practically averse to a more traditional love of cinema associated with post-war French cinephilia, and which still subsists in international film festivals, film theatres and archives all over the world. This initiative of the Taipei Economic and Cultural Office in São Paulo, therefore, seems to open new forms of reception of – and affection for – Taiwanese cinema by Brazilian audiences.

Conclusion

In this chapter I have tried to give an overview of the reception and perception of Taiwanese cinema in Brazil from the 1980s to the 2010s, through a combination of facts, impressions and personal anecdotes. I believe that this particular case highlights how the complex notions of cinephilia and national cinema, despite being in flux, remain intertwined in the new century. The first has been made up of different layers since it became established as a notion in France in the 1950s and 1960s. It concerns the global role played by (especially European) film festivals and film magazines in dictating what films and what directors to watch at a particular time. However, it is also related to migratory forces and their cultural, artistic and academic impact, as the example of Japanese immigration to Brazil clearly demonstrates. It is also related to the force of film schools and film students, who will go on to organise film events or to write about cinema, thus influencing new generations of cinephiles. Finally, cinephilia has been considerably reshaped in recent decades by the new possibilities afforded by the internet, with online film journals, forums, downloads and file sharing constantly influencing people's tastes and impressions, as well as imposing new and independent film distribution channels. This new cinephilic landscape has a direct impact in what any national cinema means in the twenty-first century. Within it, it seems too soon to venture further propositions, but there is a chance that new generations of Brazilian film lovers will have a different, more plural understanding of what Taiwan cinema is.

Notes

1 Data retrieved from Mostra website: 39.mostra.org/br/arquivo/ (accessed 6 June 2016).
2 Brazil and Taiwan maintain unofficial diplomatic relations via economic and cultural offices in each other's major cities.

3   A *nikkei* is a Brazilian citizen, national or natural of Japanese ancestry, or a Japanese immigrant living in Brazil.

4   In 2015 there were approximately 100,000 Taiwanese and Taiwanese descendants in Brazil, and around 150,000 mainland Chinese. See IBGE website: www.ibge.gov.br/english/ (accessed 6 June 2016).

5   At TNUA I was received by Professor Daw-ming Lee and Professor Peggy Chiao, as well as by members of staff and students who provided me with an ideal research environment.

6   See the Republic of China (Taiwan) Ministry of Culture website: www.taiwanaca demy.tw/toolkit/index.php?option=com_cinema&view=home&Itemid=171 (accessed 6 June 2016).

3 Variables of transnational authorship
Hou Hsiao-hsien and Wei Te-sheng

Valentina Vitali

Introduction

In 2008 I published an essay that examined journalistic discourses about Taiwanese filmmaker Hou Hsiao-hsien's films (Vitali 2008). I observed that the proliferation of reviews of Hou's films in the European and US trade press since the mid-1980s was surprising because the films, featuring exclusively at a handful of film festivals, were barely visible. I analysed the reviews and argued that these promoted not Hou's films, but a particular mode of relating to cinema, including to art films, which until then had been deployed only for big commercial releases. *Empire*'s approach to cinema – the kind of hollowed-out cinephilia and vacuous formalism mobilised to appeal to the mass market for blockbusters like Spielberg's productions – was being adopted to review Hou's work even as Hou was presented as a film auteur and his films discussed as art or avant-garde films. This was new; in the past art and auteur films had never been promoted in this way. This shift occurred at a time when French, British and other European national cinemas began to be challenged by, and eventually capitulated under a new phase in the American film industry: the dominance of finance capital, and with it the phenomenal rise of increasingly aggressive marketing and blanket release worldwide for faster capital realisation. In this context, even as a new film-reading manual conducive to mass appeal was being sold in the reviews, Hou's films, perhaps precisely because invisible, also served as a terrain onto which were projected anxieties about the precarious state of European national cinemas and film industries.

My 2008 essay examined reviews of Hou's films made and/or released between 1983 and 1998, from *The Boys of Fengkuei* (*Fenggui lai de ren*, 1983) to *Flowers of Shanghai* (*Hai shang hua*, 1998), with but a cursory look at reviews of *Millennium Mambo* (*Qianxi manbo*, 2001). When the editors of this anthology asked me to extend my analysis to the films that Hou has made since the millennium and, from the treatment these films received, to extrapolate about the reception and possible fortunes of a new generation of Taiwanese filmmakers like Wei Te-sheng in the same markets, I hesitated to accept, for three reasons. First, the ground has changed so radically since 1998 that a whole new set of considerations is in order. Since the mid-1990s

Taiwanese films, like other national cinemas, have gained much greater exposure on the international film market than they had earlier – including Hou Hsiao-hsien's work, especially after his *A City of Sadness* (*Beiqing chengshi*, 1989) won the Golden Lion at the Venice Film Festival (see Chen 2006). As Chen points out, Taiwan New Cinema's strategy 'to first win international fame before coming home', coincided with 'the Taiwanese state's ideological project to join the United Nations' and the discovery of 'the marker of [Taiwan New Cinema] to register the name of "Taiwan" in the American mind, hoping to win US support' (Chen 2006: 143). Indeed, the greater circulation of Taiwanese films within the international market went hand in hand with crucial changes in the country's political situation, developments in which Hou was directly involved (see Yang 2001; and Hou et al. 2004).

Second, with regard to the global film industry, perhaps one of the most relevant factors for the matter at hand has been the US studios' adoption of a new production strategy geared at their further expansion into regional markets. The strategy has involved incorporating prominent filmmakers of foreign national cinemas into the Hollywood system and distributing worldwide the films they make as 'native' product, even if such films are made with US funding and under conditions imposed by the studios. So, while John Woo's *Hard Target* (1993) and *Broken Arrow* (1996) were conceived and marketed as films that signalled the Cantonese director's move to the US industry, Ang Lee's *Crouching Tiger, Hidden Dragon* (*Wo hu cang long*, 2000), released worldwide in Mandarin with subtitles, was sold as a Chinese or Taiwanese film, even if, as Chan (2003: 58) points out, 'the film's only links to Taiwan are the director's own ethnic origin as well as those of his Taiwanese actors, Chang Chen and Cheng Pei Pei'.

Third, Hou Hsiao-hsien and Wei Te-sheng are very different filmmakers. If my 2008 essay is anything to go by, Hou Hsiao-hsien was selected, constructed through specific industrial procedures and packaged by discursive strategies that translated for the European and US public the person and work of Hou Hsiao-hsien into the film auteur Hou (or HHH, as he is also referred to after Olivier Assayas's film *HHH: un portrait de Hou Hsiao-Hsien*, 1997). I say translated, in the Latin sense of 'carried across', because in addition to the typical characteristics of film authorship (such as continuity of theme and style across his work), attached to Hou's auteur status was then a sense of (other-)national specificity and of 'authenticity': his representativeness of a national culture (Taiwan is given as Hou's country of origin by most reviewers), of a Taiwanese new cinema wave, and the capacity to speak for Taiwan to an international audience. Unlike John Woo, who has come to be seen as a 'global' figure who has 'sold-out', or Ang Lee, whose work is seen as marked by a high degree of mobility and duality (a 'back-and-forth' between the United States and Taiwan), Hou remained first and foremost a national auteur well into the early 2000s.

This is not the way HHH is presented today. Post-2000 reviews indicate that over the last ten years, the auteur Hou Hsiao-hsien has become a figure who is international, though not quite like other, equally international film-makers. Unlike, say, Otar Iossellani or Atom Egoyan, HHH's internationality is entirely dependent on his status as 'authentic' national auteur. He has become a transnational auteur, in the sense that his capacity to make films in Japan and France that circulate internationally is reliant on his Taiwanese-ness, on his films' locality and on Hou's own foreign-ness in relation to Japan and France.

I return to this point below. For now it is enough to say that I am not concerned here with what makes Hou's films national, transnational, inter-national or global. In fact, I will not discuss the films at all. What interests me are the procedures and the strategies that, from 2001, have been put to work to transform what had been originally sold to the US and European audi-ences as a (if not *the*) 'authentic' Taiwanese filmmaker or auteur,[1] into a transnational auteur. In 2005 a review of *Three Times* (*Zuihao de shiguang*, dir. Hou Hsiao-hsien) claimed triumphantly that Hou 'can do anything' (Taubin 2005: 6). This is of course not true. What attaches precisely to the transnationality gradually acquired by Hou Hsiao-hsien? In the third part of this chapter I examine the discourses by which Hou was transformed into a transnational auteur.

As was the case for Hou's early work, Wei Te-sheng's films were also not to be found in European and US cinemas. Unlike Hou's, however, neither were Wei Te-sheng's films reviewed in the European press. In the fourth and fifth sections of this chapter I consider the circulation and reception of Wei Te-sheng's better known films, their invisibility within the European theatrical market, and the obstacles to this filmmaker's acquisition of the same degree of transnationality that, as I show below, is now being enjoyed by Hou Hsiao-hsien.

However, before I proceed with the analysis of the films' reviews, some practical considerations are in order. A look at the routes taken by the two filmmakers shows that we are dealing with crucially different channels of production, distribution and exhibition. To outline these trajectories without lengthy detours into the meandering complexities of the global film industry, I will rely here on the three categories employed by Chris Berry and Mary Farquhar in their *China on Screen* (2006). To be precise, more than cate-gories, these are patterns that Berry and Farquhar identify in their discussion of the interaction of the national and the transnational in Singapore film: the local popular film, the modernist (international) festival film, and the commercial international (art) film:

> First, there are films that are limited to a local population by virtue of the high level of specific local knowledge required. These films are necessarily mass market [...] because only they can find a large enough local box office to be economically viable. Second, there are low-budget, modernist films that are artistically avant-garde and socially and politically critical. These films circulate on the international festival circuit [...] Finally, there

is a group of films made with an international crossover market in mind – the new international commercial art cinema.

(Berry and Farquhar 2006: 214)

At a glance, and as far as production is concerned, Hou Hsiao-hsien and Wei Te-sheng seem to have started their careers from essentially the same place: with local productions addressed to the local population.[2] Some 20 years separate their respective debuts in cinema, and yet at the time of writing, four years after Wei's *Warriors of the Rainbow: Seediq Bale*'s (2011) screening at the Venice Film Festival and only months away from the much-awaited general release of Hou's *The Assassin* (*Nie yin niang*, 2015), the two filmmakers could be said to have also ended up in the same place, this time around a very different place from where they started: the commercial international (art) film. However, this is where the similarities end. Whereas by early 2016 *The Assassin* was to be released theatrically worldwide, *Seediq Bale* was released theatrically only in parts of Asia, with a very limited release in the United States, on television in Hungary, Poland and Canada only, and for the rest as home entertainment (as download or DVD).

It is possible to argue that this has to do with the films' and, more generally, with the two filmmakers' different modes of address, and that Wei's films failed to be picked up for worldwide theatrical release because of 'the high level of specific local knowledge required' (Berry and Farquhar 2006: 214) to appreciate them. However, could not the same be argued of Hou's Taiwan trilogy films?[3] Paul Willemen (1994: 206–222; Willemen 2006) argued that the national is a question of mode of address. As he also emphasised, that address is itself the result of historically, geographically and industrially specific interests – very real pressures that orchestrate the cinematic substance available to the filmmaker. The same must be true of the transnational, where the pressures and substance at work are no longer limited to those within the national constellation, however hybrid this is conceived. From this theoretical perspective, it becomes impossible to maintain that a film like Wei's *Cape No.7* (2008) failed to make it into the international market because its address is beyond the pale of the European (high-brow) public.

New technologies notwithstanding, the circulation of cultural commodities (and not only of those) across national borders continues to be policed by myriad regulatory measures, precisely because of the phenomenal increase in the amount of circulated goods and the rapidity with which they are made to move. Studies of the transnational in cinema take as their starting point such increase and tend to focus on films' cross-border positionality and mobility. Here my concern is as much what moves across national borders as what is left behind, not carried across. Few would doubt that increasingly monopolistic channels of distribution and exhibition impact greatly on a film's mode of address, often to the point of defining it. Which precise channels were involved in the making and circulation of Hou and Wei's films, and which discourses were mobilised to modulate the ways in which audiences would relate to the films' address? A closer look at the trajectories followed by Hou over a period of 35 years and by Wei over just seven years will enable us to identify more precisely the industrial specificities that mark our three categories or patterns when applied to these two Taiwanese filmmakers. It will enable us, in other words, to identify the particularity of each moment of the films' production cycle and their geography: the nationality of the main production company or source of funding, the range and scope of distribution, and the range and type of exhibition.[4]

The production and distribution of Hou Hsiao-hsien films since 2000

Up to and including *The Puppetmaster* (*Ximeng rensheng*, dir. Hou Hsiao-hsien, 1993), Hou relied on local (Taiwanese) production and, presumably, funding, while from *Good Men, Good Women* (*Hao nan hao nu*, dir. Hou Hsiao-hsien, 1995) to *Flowers of Shanghai* (1998) on regional (partly Japanese) production. International (French) production kicked in in 2001 with *Millennium Mambo*. *A Summer at Grandpa's* (*Dongdong de jiaqi*, dir. Hou Hsiao-hsien, 1984) marks the breakthrough at European and US film festivals, and Hou's films circulated nearly exclusively on the international film festival circuit until *Café Lumière* (*Kôhî jikô* [in Japanese] or *Kafei shiguang* [in Mandarin], dir. Hou Hsiao-hsien, 2003). *Café Lumière*, made entirely with Japanese production money, was shown at many international film festivals and was on general (though limited and often arthouse-only) release in Europe, the United States, East Asia and parts of Latin America. The same is true of *Millennium Mambo* and *Three Times* (partly French-produced). Things began to change with *Flight of the Red Balloon* (*Le voyage du ballon rouge*, dir. Hou Hsiao-hsien, 2007), which was produced mainly with French funding and which, in addition to receiving international film festival exposure, was released theatrically and widely across Europe, parts of East Asia and, in a limited way, in the United States. With *The Assassin*, Hou has come back to local (or at any rate regional: Taiwan and Hong Kong) production, but this time around on worldwide theatrical release (as well as international film festivals). Importantly, *The Assassin* has been picked up for theatrical release by Well Go USA Entertainment, the same US company that distributed (though not theatrically) Wei Te-sheng's *Seediq Bale*.

Reviewing Hou Hsiao-hsien in the new millennium

Within this production-to-distribution cycle, trade press reviews play a crucial role. Whether from *Variety*, which in its characteristic short-hand language addresses potential distributors and exhibitors directly, or from *Cahiers du cinéma*, which speaks primarily to and for the European cinephile, reviews determine quite directly whether a film is watched or not, by whom and how.

Reviews have, first and foremost, a temporal dimension. They built Hou Hsiao-hsien up over 30 years as a regular presence at international (read

'European') film festivals and arthouse cinemas. They lent to the filmmaker and his work a past and a future, a temporal continuum (from festival to festival, year to year) within which Hou's work came to be seen as something that remained constant (for example, in its quality and, more crucially here, in its Taiwanese-ness and deployment of specific formal strategies), while acquiring maturity and a certain malleability. Hou's films have always been seen as as suitable for one festival as for another, however different the festivals and the films are perceived to be.

In my 2008 essay I showed that, over a period of 15 years, Hou was constructed as a film auteur whose national specificity (Hou's and that of his films) was a constitutive dimension. Some knowledge of Taiwan's history was deemed necessary to appreciate his films fully. At the same time reviews passed on the very clear message that Hou's films could be enjoyed also without that knowledge, partly because they addressed universal themes and partly because they appealed to any cinephile, to anyone who could 'groove' in their purely sensorial qualities. In other words, in the construction of HHH the film auteur, national or historical specificity functioned essentially as a sales point, a marketing exoticism of sorts. This continues to be the case also for reviews of films Hou made after 2000. For instance, Emmanuel Burdeau (2005: 24–26), in his review of *Three Times*, speaks of 'anachronism', of 'historical short-circuit' ('*court-circuit historique*') and of 'obliterating distances' ('*annulant les distances*') simply because the film's three episodes are not in chronological order. For Alain Masson (2005) the historical specificity of the three episodes is irrelevant: the three episodes refer not so much to three moments in the history of Taiwan, but to Hou's earlier work; they are instances of authorial self-reflexivity. Masson claims so in spite of Hou (2005: 17) explicitly denying it in the interview that follows Masson's article in the same journal. Indeed, most reviewers presented *Three Times* as a self-referential film, a 'kind of summation' (Ryans 2006: 17), 'synthesis' (Masson 2005: 13) or '"best of" primer' (Hampton 2006: 34) of Hou's body of work up to that point, a 'retrospective' film (Burdeau 2005: 26) that made Hou's work and the filmmaker himself more 'accessible'.

In reviews written up to 2000, knowledge about Taiwan history and/or historical specificity functioned as a sales point, but an important point nevertheless. This remains the case in reviews written after 2000 (from *Millennium Mambo*), though from that point onwards the nature of such historicity began to be presented not simply as knowledge of Taiwan's history, but rather as politics – something that marks Hou's work as political filmmaking of sorts. To be clear, the details and specifics of those politics are seen as irrelevant to European and US audiences and no reviewer offers information on the subject. All we need to know, we are told, is that something about Hou's films has political relevance in Taiwan, a factor that makes Hou an *engagé* (politically committed) director (for instance, Frodon 2005b). Parallels with other *engagés* authors follow suit: with French Nouvelle Vague director Robert Bresson, with Federico Fellini as heir of Italian Neo-realism, with

Wong Kar-wai as representative of the Hong Kong new wave (Ryans 2006). By 2009 Hou is included in a very select group of film auteurs consulted for a special feature of *Sight & Sound* (May 2009) on 'The New Wave at 50'.

Post-2000 reviews present Hou as a filmmaker who moves or can move across national borders and even class divides – from festival to festival, region to region, and from arthouse to more popular sectors of the market. What enables him to move, it is suggested, is Hou's status as an auteur on a par with Yasujirô Ozu (Taubin 2005; Ryans 2005). That Hou had to move because it has become difficult to make films in Taiwan is mentioned only once by Tony Ryans (2006). This critic's review of *Three Times* (Ryans 2006), retracing as it does Hou's emergence from local filmmaker to international auteur, is exemplary of the way journalistic discourses on HHH have changed during the last ten years. Taiwan's history remains a consideration (even if still mentioned only in brackets, that is, as 'optional'), but Ryans (2006: 16), like other critics, writes of 'archetypal' memory, universal concerns, 'international polls' (Ryans 2006: 16), wide distribution. Hou, we are told, deserves to be known in the UK like Wong Kar-wai. The 'popular success' (Ryans 2006: 17) of *Three Times*, which, it is claimed, is more accessible than Hou's earlier films yet (somehow) no different from them, is a clear indication that the whole of Hou's work should be accessible across nations and classes. By providing biographical information critics present Hou as local (Taiwanese) 'talent', but of migrant stock and exposed to British cinema. It is 'talent' that, in the critics' view, enables Hou to move 'forward' from the local (Ryans 2006: 17).

From 2001 Hou Hsiao-hsien is thus constructed as an auteur who moves but whose style seems impermeable to change. Continuity, if not of themes certainly of style, within the auteur's body of work remains an important critical consideration. In fact, it is continuity within the work that is deemed to enable Hou to be mobile, to operate across national borders and still be 'HHH'. The way he uses specific filmic forms, how he combines them into a Hou *mise en scène*, as it were, is, we are told, unique to him, but as forms (for instance the long take or *plan-séquence*, or the play-back) they are also used in the reviews to draw parallels and associations with other, mostly non-Chinese directors and artists: Akira Kurosawa, Wong Kar-wai, Jim Jarmusch, Robert Altman, Francis Ford Coppola, Chris Marker, Keith Jarret, Eric Satie (Hampton 2006). A modernist use of form is assumed to unite across national and regional borders. By that recourse, as well as by his presence at film festivals, Hou is made to become a central figure of an international circle of film auteurs.

Although international funding was already there with *Café Lumière*, it is with *Three Times* that reviews switch from a discourse of national specificity to one of internationality. It is as if it was the wider distribution, the perceived greater accessibility and thus the perceived or potential success of *Three Times* (see Frodon 2005a), and not the funding itself, that made Hou eminently suitable to be internationalised. Thus Howard Hampton's review of this film speaks of 'human interest', 'deeply intuitive' (read: no ulterior knowledge required to appreciate the film) and of 'emotionally transparent texture' (Hampton 2006: 32–36). If the critic is to be believed, with *Three Times* we inhabit nothing more specific than 'environments', 'ecosystems', 'human habitats', while the silent section of the film, which is actually set in 1911 (when the Xinhai Revolution of 1911–12 was about to bring an end to the Qing dynasty and establish the Republic of China), is seen by Hampton as 'time-bound yet timeless'.

Similarly, for Alain Masson (2005) *Three Times* deals with the universal theme of love. This may well be love at three different historical times, but from the critic's tone we would be forgiven for taking Hou's films to be saying that with love the same joys and sorrows apply, no matter when or where. Failing to spot that each of the episodes is set in Taiwan, Masson even argues that Hou forsakes two of the three rules of classic theatre (unity of time and of place) to focus instead on unity of action (love relations). From this it is one small step to include Hou in a selection of world auteurs (as in the port-manteau film *Chacun son cinéma/To Each his Own Cinema*, dir. Theodoros Angelopoulos et al., 2007) who have the capacity to work away from home. That same year *Flight of the Red Balloon* (2007) confirmed that Hou can speak of '*la capitale*' (Paris) and of a 'foreign culture' ('*culture étrangère*'), where said culture is understood as 'foreign' not in relation to the critics and their intended public, but to Hou's own 'foreign-ness', his Taiwanese-ness. As the critique of Cahiers du Cinéma (2007: 34, my translation) put it in a short preview of *Flight of the Red Balloon*:

> Après Tokyo (*Café Lumière*), cette deuxième immersion du cinéma de Hou Hsiao-hsien dans une capitale étrangère est une étrange et désirable promesse.
>
> [After Tokyo (*Café Lumière*) this second immersion of Hou Hsiao-hsien's cinema into a foreign capital is a strange (foreign) and desirable promise.]

By 2008, in an interview with Jean-Michel Frodon (2008a), Hou himself admitted that he now felt capable of operating internationally:

> I had no idea that one day I would make a film in France, especially before making *Café Lumière* in Japan. I did not think I would make films abroad because for me the reality of a place is much too important to 'internationalise' myself. [The reality of a place] is at the basis of every-thing I do. After I was offered the opportunity to make a film in homage to Ozu in 2003 I understood that it was totally possible, and I therefore welcomed the offer of the Musée d'Orsay with open arms.
>
> (Frodon 2008a: 30, my translation)

However, this new-found capacity did not make Hou a transnational auteur. On the contrary, what could have loomed large at this point in Hou's career is the danger of invisibility or at any rate the lack of differentiation amidst myriad equally mobile, 'internationalised' filmmakers. A review of the DVD of *Café Lumière* in *Positif* hints at that possibility by talking of Hou's cinema as a cinema of 'errance', of wandering (Gombeaud 2005: 19). From this perspective, the reviews' push-and-pull between Hou's Taiwanese-ness (or national specificity) and universality (Hou's capacity to move and appeal beyond his locality or specificity) is crucial. While such push-and-pull is a constant feature of articles on Hou, with critics juggling a careful balance between these two perceived characteristics of his work, from the second half of the 2000s a change in directionality occurs nevertheless. Gradually the balance began to tilt towards internationality and universal appeal. That said, national specificity continued to be seen as crucial: the national dimension of Hou's work remains and it is that which, in the eyes of critics, allows him not to get lost in the over-populated world of the global film industry. So, as Hou started getting international (Japanese and French) funding *and* shooting films in these countries, one question began to loom in the reviews, even if it was never quite explicitly asked: can Hou Hsiao-hsien, under these new conditions, remain a Taiwanese auteur? The answer, it seems, is yes: Hou has become not a global filmmaker (à la John Woo), or an international one (à la Atom Egoyan or Otar Iossellani), but a transnational auteur, one in whose films, no matter where they are made, the national continues to be at work.

Reviews of *The Assassin* in *Sight & Sound*, *Variety* and *Cahiers du Cinéma* confirm my original hypothesis: *Empire*'s approach to cinema is mobilised for Hou's films even as Hou is presented as an auteur. Yet not without a degree of tension because, even in this day and age, this film's genre (*wuxia* or martial arts) militates not so much against the auteur side of the balance, but above all against a sense of national (as opposed to regional) specificity. So, while in reviews of *The Assassin* parallels are made between Hou's *wuxia* and those of other regional directors, great efforts are also made by the critics to underline the authorial elements of *The Assassin* – an authorship a fundamental component of which is Hou's and his films' national specificity.

The national is seen to continue to be at work in Hou's international work in quite literal ways. Hou himself is reported to have said that he transferred local concerns onto his new place of work, be it Japan with *Café Lumière* – for instance the theme of single mothers, an issue in Taiwan that Hou adapted to the Japanese context,[5] or France with *Flight of the Red Balloon* – for instance the Taiwanese au-pair. However, the historicity or national specificity of Hou's films is mobilised also in less direct and more interesting ways. As the sales points of national specificity and historicity were made to tally, in the reviews, with Hou's newly acquired mobility, their function also began to change. Until roughly the mid-2000s it was seen as the job of the critic to provide (or not) the relevant historical information deemed necessary (or not) to appreciate Hou's films fully. As Hou became more and more of a regular and known festival presence, and more and more interviews appeared, he also began to be made to provide that information himself, often directly and explicitly (see, for instance, the interview with Jean-Michel Frodon, 2005b). In these reviews and interviews Hou emerges not as someone to be 'understood', as was the case in the first half of the 2000s, but as a source of knowledge himself: knowledge about his films, as any filmmaker is assumed to have, but also and above all knowledge about Taiwan. While before the mid-2000s historical information, proffered by the critic, was used as a means to underline Hou's (national or local) 'authenticity', now it is Hou himself who tells us what we need to know about Taiwan to understand his films (which is different from offering the authentic perspective on Taiwan). By the time of *Three Times* the discourse of historical knowledge in reviews of Hou's films has changed fundamentally: Hou has become an interpreter, a translator of Taiwan across the cultural divide. He interprets Taiwan for the European and US audiences and tells them about the changes the country has undergone over the years.

The final stage in the transformation of Hou's authorial persona as it emerges from the reviews is the perception that Hou can transfer or project his interpretative look onto the temporarily adopted country (see, for instance, Ryans 2006; and Frodon 2008b). This is a capacity that is understood in the reviews to depend entirely on Hou's status as a 'non-national', as an outsider to the countries in which the films are made, and thus dependent on Hou's Taiwanese-ness. For it is precisely Hou's locality, his Taiwanese perspective, that he is seen to bring to France and Japan. We are told this is a perspective that makes Hou's cinematic rendition of these countries all the more sensitive, objective and ultimately more realistic. It is not surprising that this is an assumption rooted in eighteenth-century ideas of empirical truth – ideas that nineteenth-century European Realism partly incorporated – given the historical specificity of the criteria underpinning European and US critics' aesthetic judgements. What is more puzzling is that such criteria be applied to discussions of Hou's films even as he is presented as a Taiwanese filmmaker. However, contradictory discourses are the bread and butter of film journalism. In this particular case they enable critics on the one hand to acknowledge that foreign funding and foreign production circumstances do shape Hou's address and, on the other hand, to continue presenting Hou as a quintessentially Taiwanese filmmaker – a director whose authorial look on the locality, on the reality at hand, takes on a transferrable function, movable from one nation to another, where transferability and thus trans-nationality are conditional on rootedness in an 'other' local, an 'other' (national) specificity.

The production and distribution of Wei Te-sheng's films

Unlike Hou Hsiao-hsien, Wei Te-sheng mostly bypassed the international film festival circuit. *Cape No.7* was made with small, local production money. It featured at less than a handful of minor (thematic) European film festivals, as well as at East Asian festivals, and was released theatrically regionally, including by no less than Buena Vista International. Despite this distributor's weight on the global market and the film's enormous success locally and regionally, *Cape No.7* remained there. By contrast, Wei's third feature was clearly meant for the international market. A major Central Motion Picture (Taiwan) investment headed by John Woo and Terence Chang (the film's producers), *Seediq Bale* did, however, eschew once again or was simply not picked up by European film festivals with the exception of Venice. Significantly this is the same festival that awarded the top prize to Hou's *A City of Sadness*, but *Seediq Bale* received no such award, in Venice or in New York, where it was submitted as a contender for nomination in the Foreign Language Film category of the 84th Academy Awards. It was released theatrically regionally as well as in a limited way in the United States. Well Go USA Entertainment, which specialises in action films, picked it up for home entertainment release, as did a few Eastern European and one Canadian television distributors.

Reviews of Wei Te-sheng's films

Few in the US and European trade press picked up Wei Te-sheng's films – a factor that has partly to do with the films' absence at European film festivals. The only review I could find of *Cape No.7* in major European and US trade journals was in *Variety*, and was written by Richard Kuipers (2008) reporting from the Taipei Film Festival. Kuipers's tone in that review is condescendingly positive, but then most *Variety* reviews of newly emerging independent filmmakers' works tend to be condescending in one way or another. More importantly, Kuipers shows no qualms in restricting *Cape No.7*'s potential to the regional market: 'This charmer has remake potential and strong regional prospects, though chances of a big bust-out in Western markets look slim' (Kuipers 2008: 46).

Kuipers's message to US and European distributors, *Variety*'s main addressees, is clear: *Cape No.7* is not suitable fare for international distribution, though script and filmmaker could turn out to be fertile ground should producers and distributors want to exploit the film's and/or the filmmaker's regional success as tools to increase their share in that market.

Seediq Bale did feature at the Venice Film Festival, but reviewers were on the whole very dismissive, if not worse. For Cahiers du Cinéma (2011: 49) *Seediq Bale* was simply an 'odieux film taïwanais de Wei Te-Sheng produit par John Woo' (a detestable film by Wei Te-sheng produced by John Woo), while *Variety* defined it as a 'wildly ambitious rumble-in-the-jungle battle epic' (Chang 2011). Characteristically, *Variety*'s critic praised the film condescendingly for its 'raw physicality and crazy conviction', but ultimately condemns it:

> the primitive warfare in *Warriors of the Rainbow* recalls that of *Apocalypto* minus Mel Gibson's sense of pacing and technique … the physical

production evinces little sense of discipline at any level. The chaotic combo of hard-slamming edits, gory mayhem and Ricky Ho's forever-hemorrhaging score makes the picture simply exhausting to watch over the long-haul ... [the film] doles out setpieces and narrative details with an often clumsy hand ... much needed complexity ... the occasional shots of CGI rainbows ... send the film momentarily spiralling into camp. F/x work is generally substandard throughout ...

(Chang 2011)

Variety condemned Wei Te-sheng's national epic as immature filmmaking, where the assumed criteria of 'maturity' or competence are conformity to the generic model not of just any epic, but of the epic film as developed and exploited by the US industry (the reference to Mel Gibson). The review of *Cape No.7* condemned that film to remain exclusively for 'local' consumption but, precisely because of that, potentially exploitable. By contrast, reviews of *Seediq Bale* took this film to be more suitable than *Cape No.7* for international circulation (e.g. the epic genre), and yet, precisely because it was liable to be seen globally, *Seediq Bale* was ultimately seen as not being up to the task and thus not exploitable. By embarking on a far more generic production than he had done with *Cape No.7*, probably hoping in this way to appeal to the international and even the global markets, Wei Te-sheng also exposed himself to the kind of short-sighted, parochial criticism meted out in the reviews above, and clearly not to his advantage.

Conclusion

Although Hou and Wei seem to have started and ended in the same place – from small to large local funding and international distribution – the channels by which they arrived at their destination marked in a very fundamental way the position they came to occupy by the mid-2010s. The spheres that Hou was able to cultivate with years of presence on the international and, above all, the European film festival circuit have enabled him to command international as well as local funding *and* to have a solid footing in every section of the global exhibition market (arthouse and commercial, theatrical and home entertainment). The fate of *Seediq Bale*, at the time of writing confined to a niche of the home entertainment market, suggests that the film's generic choice (historic/epic action) was actually not the decisive factor. Far more determining were European film festivals and the gatekeepers who make it possible to access them. While the latter enable a film's transition from local and regional festivals to European festivals, where the film may or may not be picked up for European and US (mostly arthouse) distribution, the festivals themselves make or break European funding. As *The Flight of the Red Balloon* shows, more often than not such funding also guarantees a margin of international distribution and exhibition beyond the film festival circuit.

In the 2000s, major Hollywood producers invented the 'native' (foreign) director to further their expansion into regional markets. In the seminal case of *Crouching Tiger, Hidden Dragon* this strategy worked: it sold to those markets, to the US domestic and to Hollywood's more traditional foreign markets (e.g. Europe) a sensational imaginary if not of the region, then certainly of the region's cinema. An essential element of that strategy, indeed a condition *sine qua non*, is that the 'native' filmmaker conforms to the US studio's mode of operation. Just how essential that is became clear to, for instance, Tsui Hark and Guillermo Del Toro, both of whom found working under the US studio's imposed conditions unacceptable, so much so that Tsui Hark went back to Hong Kong while Del Toro took to making films elsewhere. Irrespective of what one may think of Hou's films, of what they actually are and do, I suspect that a process parallel to this US strategy may be at work in Hou's case – aspects of which surface in the reviews. Could HHH be national cinemas' response to Hollywood's 'native' director? Second cinema's retort to first cinema's new expansion stratagems?[6] Hou Hsiao-hsien has become a transnational auteur whose capacity to be international while remaining national rests not necessarily or exclusively on his capacity to give audiences a vision of Taiwan deemed 'true' or 'authentic' (as the pre-2000 Hou was constructed). It also depends on his capacity to be adaptable to and incorporated into the (non-Taiwan) national as an outsider, as an 'other-national', someone who can reflect back to non-Taiwanese audiences a 'truer', more 'realistic' image of themselves from the outside. Adaptable and incorporated into other nations' film industries but, crucially, not assimilated or conforming to any of them, for that would simply render HHH 'le maître taïwanais' (Malausa 2015: 19), unsuitable ground for such 'objective' back reflection. As for Wei Te-sheng, the pressure is clearly on the 'Taiwanese helmer' (Kuipers 2008: 46) to conform to the US model, certainly as far as *Variety* is concerned. I am not in a position to say whether Wei Te-sheng will capitulate to this pressure or whether he will pursue the trajectory he embarked on with *About July* (*Qiyue tian*, 1999) and *Cape No.7*. However, if the career of Hou Hsiao-hsien and the treatment meted out to *Seediq Bale* are anything to go by, it seems to me that Wei will be better off staying within small, local production, at least for now, for this may just be precisely what will enable him, in the long term, to keep making films that are and will be seen as distinctly his own.

Notes

1 Possibly more so than Edward Yang, who studied cinema in the United States, and perhaps also more than Tsai Ming-liang, whose work has addressed questions of Taiwanese history less explicitly than Hou's.
2 Whether *Cute Girl* (*Jiu shi liu liu de ta*, dir. Hou Hsiao-hsien, 1980), *Cheerful Wind* (*Feng er ti ta cai*, dir. Hou Hsiao-hsien, 1981), *About July* (*Qiyue tian*, dir. Wei Te-sheng, 1999) and *Cape No.7* (*Haijiao qihao*, dir. Wei Te-sheng, 2008) were aimed at a working-class, lower-middle-class or educated middle-class public is not

something that concerns me here, partly because my focus is on questions of locality and geographical mobility.

3 The trilogy here refers to HHH's *A City of Sadness* (1989), *The Puppetmaster* (1993) and *Good Men, Good Women* (1995).

4 What follows is based on the best, most reliable information available at the time of writing, including the Internet Movie Database (IMDb), film festival catalogues, trade journals like *Variety* (US), and other specialist magazines, such as *Cahiers du cinéma* (France) and *Sight & Sound* (UK). For the sake of consistency, I have used the films' date of release.

5 See the interview in *New Left Review* (Hou et al. 2004), which is referenced by Tony Ryans (2005) in his review of *Café Lumière*.

6 My use of the terms first and second cinema here refers to Stephen Crofts's (1993) seminal essay.

4 Taiwan cinema at the Venice Film Festival

From cultural discovery to cultural diplomacy

Elena Pollacchi [1]

The changing landscapes of European festivals and Taiwan cinema

The 2011 presentation of Wei Te-sheng's *Seediq Bale* in competition at the Venice Film Festival demonstrated how times have changed since the late 1980s and 1990s. It was during these decades that European film festivals brought new directors and unexplored territories, including Taiwan, to the world's attention. The Golden Lion for Hou Hsiao-hsien's *A City of Sadness* (*Beiqing chengshi*), as the first major award given in 1989 to a Chinese-language film, paved the way for a successful relationship between the Venice festival and Chinese-language films. The 1990s were years of cultural discoveries for film festivals. Films from mainland China and Taiwan established a prominent position within major festivals whereas Hong Kong cinema had an earlier circulation in Europe, particularly with martial arts films (Law et al. 2004). In 1994, the Golden Lion awarded to Tsai Ming-liang's *Vive L'Amour* (*Aiqing wansui*) confirmed the Venice festival's special attention to auteurs from Taiwan. Moreover, thanks to the European arthouse distribution system, which was well in place at that time, Taiwanese films received theatrical distribution and this helped establish a certain line of Taiwan cinema that came to be identified mainly with such directors as Hou Hsiao-hsien, Ang Lee and Tsai Ming-liang. Within the Italian media landscape of the 1990s, these three filmmakers, together with the Fifth Generation of mainland Chinese directors, first and foremost Zhang Yimou and Chen Kaige, composed the emerging image of 'Chinese cinema'. The distinction between productions from Taiwan, Hong Kong and the People's Republic of China (PRC) was principally specified in festival catalogues, occasionally sparking some debate on the way countries were listed, in particular Taiwan and Hong Kong prior to the 1997 handover.

In fact, when looking at the Venice Film Festival, films from Taiwan have been labelled in different ways since 1960, when the 26-minute art documentary *A City of Cathay* (*Qingming shang he tu*, dir. Loh I-cheng, 1960)[2] was presented in the documentary section as the first Taiwanese title in Venice. The archive of La Biennale di Venezia (ASAC) has been an essential source of information for all historical data related to the Venice Film Festival included in this chapter. The Venice Film Festival is one of the activities of the cultural foundation La Biennale di Venezia, which also includes the world-renowned biennial visual art exhibition and activities in theatre, music, dance and architecture. Archival information is here combined with my own first-hand observations as a festival correspondent and programmer.[3] According to archival data, the frequency of use of the term 'Taiwan' to indicate the country of origin has gradually decreased in favour of the more controversial 'China, Taiwan'. Since 2012, the label 'Chinese Taipei' has been officially adopted in festival catalogues in line with international events such as the Olympic Games. Regardless of the national label, Hou Hsiao-hsien, Ang Lee and Tsai Ming-liang remain the few Taiwanese names known to the Italian general audience thanks to their regular presence at the Venice Film Festival and to the theatrical circulation of their films until the early 2000s.[4]

With the impact of the economic crisis of 2008 on the cultural sector and on the arthouse distribution system, the circulation of Taiwanese films in Italy has stopped, while the distribution of any films other than domestic and Hollywood productions has drastically diminished.[5] Moreover, since the early 2000s and even more so after the collapse of the arthouse distribution circuit, international film festivals have increasingly turned into platforms for film circulation. Major festivals such as Cannes, Venice and Berlin, with their requirements for world and international premieres, have thus come to serve as crucial nodes in the festival circuit which, in turn, has become an essential element in the global film business.

The 'discovery paradigm' that Nichols described in 1994 as the festival's practice of bringing to prominence unknown names and national film traditions has almost been reversed (Nichols 1994). In the last decade, a shrinking number of new directors have featured in the main competition of major festivals with more chances given to established filmmakers. An overview of Cannes and Venice since 2000 confirms that all the full-length feature films of Hou Hsiao-hsien and Tsai Ming-liang have featured in the main competition. All young and up-and-coming filmmakers have presented their works either as special screenings out of competition or in the festivals' independent sections.[6] Cannes has made no exception to the rule of the masters, as the only other Taiwanese film in competition has been Edward Yang's *A One and a Two* (*Yi yi*) in 2000. Venice has had a few exceptions with Chang Tso-chi's *The Best of Times* (*Meili de shiguang*) in competition in 2002, Lee Kang-sheng's *Help me, Eros* (*Bangbang wo, aishen*) in 2007 – a title closely connected to Tsai Ming-liang – and Wei Te-sheng's *Seediq Bale* in 2011.[7]

Among recent titles screened outside the official selection, two peculiar omnibus films supported by Taiwanese state offices are worthy of attention.[8] These are *Taipei Factory*, which opened the Directors' Fortnight in Cannes 2013, and *Taipei Factory II*, the first Italian-Taiwanese co-production, a 'special screening' at the Venice Film Festival in 2014 (more details about both projects will be discussed later in the chapter). These two titles, which featured mainly young Taiwanese filmmakers, were part of a state-driven project for the international promotion of Taiwanese cinema and as such would be rarely part of the official selection of a major festival. However, despite their nature of commissioned works, together with the competition entry *Seediq Bale* in 2011, they point to the changes both in Taiwan's film environment and in the festival's reception of Taiwanese films. When the festivals – traditional sites for cultural exchange – were expanding their range of activities by including more market-related activities, these screenings can be seen as examples of the dialogical process between festivals and the Taiwan film industry. How did the presentation of *Seediq Bale* and the *Taipei Factory* project resonate with the Venice festival audience and media? How do Taiwanese titles connect to the global film scene via the festival context?

Through a brief discussion of the presentation and reception of *Seediq Bale* and *Taipei Factory II* within the context of the Venice festival, this chapter will shed light on the dynamics that currently engage major festivals, cultural policies and global film industries. Although scholarly research has approached film festivals from many different perspectives, attention given to the specific interplay between screenings of Chinese-language films, international politics and festivals' cultural practices remains limited. Taiwanese productions such as Wei Te-sheng's *Seediq Bale* and the state-funded *Taipei Factory II* provide two interesting entry points for such a discussion, as they encourage a broader understanding of the presentation of a certain line of national cinema as part and parcel of practices of cultural diplomacy. Furthermore, a discussion of the Venice festival and Taiwan cinema in the light of cultural diplomacy takes into account international, regional and domestic dynamics, and the diverse sets of interests converging into the festival context.

Cultural diplomacy has been approached as a relevant aspect of the broad and largely discussed field of public diplomacy (Cull 2008). Its definition spans from the promotion of a state's cultural achievements to the deliberate projection of a nation's culture and values in order to promote and improve a country's image (Arndt 2005: 553). Other studies have observed an increasing relevance of cultural diplomacy in a world where images and symbols as well as brands are used as significant components of international, regional and domestic policies (Villanueva 2007: 19). Moreover, practices of cultural diplomacy imply a dialogical participation of both government actors and private firms for state promotion purposes and in relation to the increase of economic exchanges and cooperation among countries. Therefore, they have been connected to practices of nation branding (Anholt 2002) and soft power, defined as the positive ability to attract and persuade in the realm of international policy (Nye 1990, 2011).

This approach seems particularly poignant in relation to current film market dynamics in Chinese-speaking territories. In fact, the rapid expansion of the Chinese film market has strongly affected film industries both on regional and global levels. Not incidentally, screen cultures have also been studied in their complex relation to practices of China's 'soft power' (Voci and Hui 2017) and so have media and broadcasting in the context of Taiwanese diplomacy and propaganda (Rawnsley 2000, 2015). In the so-called Greater China region, the Hong Kong film industry has, since the early 2000s, increasingly served the needs of mainland Chinese cinema by providing skilful film professionals to Chinese productions, while Taiwan cinema has seen a growing number of co-productions with the PRC.[9] In the global context, the growing impact of China on the film and entertainment sector is strictly connected to the rise of China as a political and economic superpower. Furthermore, against the backdrop of 'China's peaceful rise' during Jiang Zemin's presidency between 1993 and 2003, the embrace of the soft power of the 2008 Beijing Olympics, and Xi Jinping's 'China Dream', a term popularised after 2013, screen cultures have made a significant contribution to the projection of China's national image.[10] With the rapid growth of the Chinese film market into the most appealing target for film productions, not only PRC-HK-Taiwan co-productions have mainland China as their primary goal, but also Hollywood aims to reach the vast Chinese audience. The studios have approached the Chinese market in many ways through locations, storyline and casting, as well as through partnerships and film financing deals.[11]

In this global framework, Taiwan-based productions such as *Seediq Bale* and the *Taipei Factory* project articulate a complex discourse, in which responses to China's soft power strategies are intertwined with attempts at international promotion. If *Seediq Bale* revolves around events of Taiwanese national history that are little known to the festival audience and seems to target mainly the regional audience, *Taipei Factory* and *Taipei Factory II* address international film professionals by presenting opportunities for investment and collaboration.

Seediq Bale: *Wei Te-sheng's 'exotica' and national concerns*

> Stunning to look at, authentic to a fault and a little tedious to follow for over two and a half hours, the Taiwanese action saga *Warriors of the Rainbow: Seediq Bale* tells the true story of Taiwan's aboriginal people [...] This big-scale actioner coproduced by John Woo will check in as a strange sort of exotica for very specialized audiences, read festival and serious action fans.
>
> (Young 2011)

Seediq Bale had its world premiere on 1 September 2011 during the first day of the 68th Venice festival alongside the long-awaited *Carnage* by Roman Polanski. The Italian press release announced the film as the first and biggest Taiwanese epic title, with a budget of US $25 million, ten years of preparation and 15,000 people involved in the cast (most of them aborigines). It also referred to the co-producer John Woo, who had received the Lifetime Achievement award in Venice the previous year and was better known to the international media and festival audience than director Wei Te-sheng (ANSA 2011). Far from the well-known Taiwanese auteurs beloved in Europe, Wei Te-sheng had proven successful in the local and regional market but not among Western audiences and European festivals. His films have dealt not only with Taiwanese national history, but also with local stories with the domestic and regional audiences as their main target. His debut film, *Cape No.7* (2008), took the Asian market by storm, but as Sheng-mei Ma (2015b: 3) noted in her discussion of Taiwan cinema, 'that which strikes a chord in Taiwan fails to resonate elsewhere'. Ma defined a number of titles as 'unglobalizable'; Wei Te-sheng's *Cape No.7* provides a perfect example of this with its record-breaking box office performance in many Asian territories, but very limited visibility in Europe (Ma 2015b: 3).[12] Similar fortunes followed the Venice premiere of *Seediq Bale*. Its circulation in Europe with some theatrical distribution after the Venice premiere did not contribute to establish Wei's position in the festival circuit and Venice's attention returned to Tsai Ming-liang, recipient of the Grand Jury Prize for *Stray Dogs* (*Jiao you*) in 2013. How could a film conceived as an action movie and for a broader audience such as *Seediq Bale* have less resonance than the audacious, yet challenging works of Tsai Ming-liang?

Despite the bombastic promotional lines, *Seediq Bale* went either unnoticed or received mixed reviews upon its Venice premiere. In line with *The Hollywood Reporter*, the trade magazine *Variety* praised *Seediq Bale*'s action sequences, as well as its attention to anthropological detail and meticulous historical references related to the Wushe Incident of 1930. However, it also noted sub-standard special effects and a chaotic combination of 'hard-slamming edits, gory scenes and Ricky Ho's forever-hemorrhaging score' (Chang 2011; also see Rawnsley's interview with Wei in this volume). Although such trade magazines mainly focus on production values and discuss the market potential of a film, their reviews are relevant within the festival environment and often provide a preliminary perception of the response of the general media. An overview of the Italian press in reaction to *Seediq Bale* confirmed the mixed reaction and revealed how the aesthetic features rather than the narrative line puzzled most reviewers.[13]

Revolving around the fight of the Taiwanese aborigines against the Japanese colonisers, *Seediq Bale* is a blend of war action scenes, melodramatic moments and several gore sequences. If such a variety of modes found a positive response among the Asian audience, festival attendees felt quite unprepared for such a combination of film genres. The historical events, which were little known to European audiences, should not necessarily be seen as a limiting factor. Sheng-mei Ma (2015b) emphasises content, storylines and narrative structures as a primary reason for the successive failures of recent Taiwanese films abroad. However, it was mainly aesthetic features that impinged on the festival success of *Seediq Bale*, which better resonated in the Asian film environment. Some blog comments pointed to the fact that warriors never succumb in *Seediq Bale*. However, such episodes were not read as a narrative of extreme bravery, but as an odd feature that in its cinematic insistence escapes any verisimilitude or empathy with the character. Even if the hero Mona Rudo epitomises the strenuous fight of the aborigines, some reviewers noted how his above-the-line resistance suggests a certain film naivety (Pontiggia 2011). Other critics pointed to the incessant series of battles that never reach a climax and ultimately fail to transform the film into either an action or a war epic (Capolino 2011).

In addition to the combination of film genres, variations in the editing pace and an over-abundance of music turned *Seediq Bale* into an odd presence in a major festival's competition. Many Italian film critics raised the question of why the film was screened in the main competition rather than at a special screening, which would have still testified to the grand scale of the Taiwanese production yet without forcing a comparative judgement with other competition films. A significant distinction between Wei Te-sheng's festival participation and that of the earlier masters is connected to the changed festival paradigm where newcomers are rarely included in the main competition. Hou Hsiao-hsien, Ang Lee and Tsai Ming-liang carved their reputations alongside the development of the festivals and shaped their own audience regardless of the scale, genre and commercial potential of their works. Wei Te-sheng's *Seediq Bale* entered the Venice competition as a newcomer in Europe even if his profile was already established in Taiwan and other Asian territories thanks to the success of *Cape No.7*. As explained earlier in the chapter, by reason of the changed festival paradigm from cultural discoveries to recognised auteurs, unless large scale productions by emerging talent are framed within gala screenings and introduced as epitomes of the current trend of world popular cinema, they remain too distant from what is expected of a main competition entry. Here, the divergence between the different audiences emerges as a major limitation for the international circulation of the film. On the one hand, the festival audience – mainly composed of Western film professionals and film-goers – found it difficult to connect to Wei Te-sheng's stylistic features. On the other hand, Taiwanese and, in general, Asian audiences enjoyed revisiting a well-known historical episode through the lens of an action-epic film, which was in line with the aesthetic tendencies and the standards of commercial popular films of the time.

We should also note that the increasing divergence between festival entries and popular productions from outside Hollywood and Europe was a further limitation on the impact of *Seediq Bale* in Venice. Films featuring popular actors and commercial productions have regularly been included in the line-ups of major festivals as they guarantee significant media coverage and popular appeal. Furthermore, they increase the visibility of the festivals' sponsors who are a vital support for major film events.[14] Nonetheless, commercially popular films are more frequently screened out of competition and Chinese-language productions are outnumbered by European and American titles. There were attempts to include certain Asian mainstream productions in the most prominent sections of Venice in the early 2000s, as demonstrated by Tsui Hark's opening title, *Seven Swords* (*Qi jian*), in 2005, and Ang Lee's Golden Lion *Lust, Caution* (*Se jie*), screened in the main competition in 2007. However, these films had potential on the international market on the basis of their well-known directors. There are several reasons why the festival circulation of Chinese-language mainstream productions was limited in the following decade. First, most Asian productions feature a cast that is mainly unknown to Western media and audiences, so they are less appealing than Hollywood or European productions. Second, their distribution schedule and release dates often prioritise the Chinese domestic market and this schedule is not always compatible with a festival's requirements for a world premiere. Finally, and more significantly, such Asian productions often target and appeal to a regional audience so that European audiences and festivals are less relevant for most commercial titles than a favourable release date which might better serve the vast Chinese-speaking audience.

The limited impact of Wei Te-sheng's *Seediq Bale* as an official competition entry is emblematic of the changed scenario of the first decade of the 2000s. The reception of Wei Te-sheng's style of Taiwan cinema was modest, but the festival served different purposes for a film such as *Seediq Bale*. From the perspective of Taiwanese investors and film crews, the Venice festival offered the ideal venue for launching the marketing of the film. Although his participation in the festival failed to elevate Wei's profile from regional to international, the announcement that the premiere would take place within the main competition circulated in Chinese-language media (in both mainland China and Taiwan). What took Taiwanese media by surprise was the listing of the film as a 'Taiwan, China' production. The English-language *Taipei Times* reported that the festival labelled the film as such in response to pressure from Beijing, as *Seediq Bale* had no PRC funds or actors involved so as to justify the listing of China (Shih 2011). In spite of the controversy, the presentation of the film in the main competition helped confirm Wei Te-sheng as a recognised and established film director who is able to compete with the world's most talented filmmakers.

From a broader perspective, Wei Te-sheng's competition entry also testified to the healthy status of the Taiwan film industry at a time when the PRC productions were becoming more competitive. Therefore, by showing an understanding of the regional perspective according to which the presentation of *Seediq Bale* in competition had a different meaning to a presentation as an out-of-competition film, the Venice festival contributed to cultural diplomacy, by giving it an elevated status. A Chinese obsession for having films screened in the main competition might be difficult to grasp by other international players. For Chinese and Asian companies in general, an entry into the main competition is a sign of prestige. Pictures on the festival's red carpet and with its logo serve to 'brand' a film as a high-quality product, but the main competition has an even higher value. Nowadays, all these elements are then used as promotional tools in the extremely competitive Asian market. Thus the dynamics of festivals reverberate in different ways for European and Asian players, as the competition in the Asian region has become tighter. The rapid expansion of the mainland Chinese market since 2011 has certainly played a significant role, but it is interesting to note how economic interests in the region are strictly connected to issues of international visibility and promotion of the country's image. As China is concerned with the country's image that circulates via screen cultures (Voci and Hui 2017), so is Taiwan with state-financed projects such as *Taipei Factory*.

The *Taipei Factory* project: cross-cultural experiment and promotion of Taiwan cinema

> There is unquestionable budding talent on show here, but overall *Taipei Factory* feels like a worthy cross-cultural experiment that gets lost in translation.
>
> (Dalton 2013)

The *Taipei Factory* project can be seen as a joint state-industry strategy to increase the visibility of Taiwan film activities at major film festivals. In 2013 and 2014 the two instalments of the *Taipei Factory* project were screened at the Cannes Directors' Fortnight and as a Special Screening at the Venice Film Festival. The project's main sponsor and organiser was the Taipei Film Commission, the semi-governmental office for film activities under the leadership of the city mayor and different film commissioners from the film industry. In the three years during which the project was conceived and developed, the Taipei Film Commission was also very active in the promotion of Taiwan film activities at international film festivals. In addition to its institutional role of supporting films shot in Taipei and promoting the capital city as a film location, the Taipei Film Commission regularly organised social events during all major festivals to celebrate talents from Taiwan and make them visible to international press and festival guests.[15] The *Taipei Factory* project was conceived as a series of omnibus films directed by up-and-coming Taiwanese filmmakers in collaboration with international directors and actors. This set of works should premiere at major international festivals, as international visibility and promotion of Taiwan as an attractive film business partner would balance the significant state investments. The project was quite ambitious since it aimed at securing the festival premiere slots during the early stages of production by means of agreements with different festivals. The two completed omnibus films provide an interesting attempt to guarantee visibility for Taiwan cinema while profiling Taiwan as a site for international collaborations.

In 2013, the international collaboration took the shape of a co-direction project entitled *Taipei Factory*. Four young Taiwan-based filmmakers worked with directors from outside the island, with each pair of directors making a 15-minute film set in Taipei. The project was developed as a joint enterprise with the Directors' Fortnight, an independent section of the Cannes Film Festival, and it was screened as the opening film on 16 May 2013.[16] The following directors worked in pairs: Singing Chen from Taiwan and Jero Yun from South Korea; Taiwan-based filmmaker Midi Z and French actor-director

Joana Preiss; Taiwan's Shen Ko-shang and Chilean director Luis Cifuentes; and Taiwan's Chang Jung-chi and Iranian director Alireza Khatami.[17] Director Midi Z described the project in positive terms as it provided him with an opportunity to work and communicate with people of different cultural and film backgrounds. Midi Z was also offered the opportunity to identify a French filmmaker of his choice as his partner and he decided to co-direct with Joana Preiss, an artist with a very different approach to cinema from himself.[18]

Although the project claimed that its main purpose was the international promotion of young Taiwan film directors, political agendas appeared equally strong. The first lines of the press note circulated by the Taipei Film Commission upon the first screening disclose the broader political significance of the project:

> The *Taipei Factory* initiated by the Taipei Film Commission and the Cannes Directors' Fortnight made its world debut at the prestigious Cannes Film Festival on May 16. The screening enjoyed a very well-received response at the Theatre Croisette and generated an energy and interest for Taiwan Cinema. *Taipei Factory* is the only Taiwanese film that is officially selected to screen at this year's Cannes Film Festival. The film marks the first time Taipei Film Commission joined hands with an international film festival to present a film project.
>
> (Taipei Film Commission 2013)

Both the promotion of Taiwan cinema at Cannes and the role of the Taipei Film Commission in Taiwan's international activities are here highlighted. It is also interesting to note how the film is framed within the Cannes Film Festival even if the Directors' Fortnight is an independent section. Such sections still allow a film to be framed within the festival, although they do not provide the most prestigious logo of the 'Official Selection'.[19] In fact, all major European festivals have strict regulations and films can be selected in the official selection only upon regular submission of a completed or nearly completed work. There might be exceptional circumstances for inviting films that do not go through the regular submission process such as awards, commemorative events and other special occasions which most frequently fall in the category of 'special screenings'. However, such circumstances do not include agreements with national institutions or state/corporate sponsorships whose aim is to showcase their film products. Showcasing activities as well as the results of state/corporate sponsorships tend to fall within film market screenings which are managed and regulated in a different way from the festival's official selection.

The second instalment of the *Taipei Factory* project took a different direction. *Taipei Factory II* was conceived from the start as the first Italian-Taiwanese co-production and targeted the 2014 Venice Film Festival. The co-production protocol between the Italian RAI Cinema and the Taipei Film Commission was signed during the 69th Venice Film Festival in 2012 and included film and TV co-production agreements and various forms of support for shooting in both territories. *Taipei Factory II* was conceived as three 20-minute short films, each of them directed by a Taiwanese filmmaker with the participation of Italian actors. The cinema section of the Italian public television RAI contributed the casting of young Italian actors, while the Taipei Film Commission financed the project and provided production and post-production support. Due to the productive structure of the project, the Taipei Film Commission and RAI Cinema aimed to screen the film in the official selection and not in one of the independent sections. However, due to the festival submission policy it was not possible to secure a slot in the official selection before the work was near completion, and once completed, the major significance of the work remained within its productive/collaborative structure. Therefore, the project was presented as a 'special screening' which highlighted the first Taiwanese-Italian co-production and testified to the increasing collaboration between the two countries. *Taipei Factory II* was then screened at the Golden Horse Film Festival in Taipei in November 2014 and received a limited theatrical circulation in Taiwan.

The nature of the *Taipei Factory* project was rather a promotional nature from its start, with the aim of encouraging the circulation of film professionals and talents while fostering foreign partnerships and collaborations. Such activities fit well in the framework of current film market activities but appear at odds with the presentation at festivals such as Cannes and Venice. The target of the project in terms of festival visibility was probably over-ambitious. However, although the actual impact of such works with media and audience rarely goes beyond initial curiosity and festival occasions, the experience of *Taipei Factory II* helped mobilise talent from both countries and circulated images of cross-cultural encounters. It is worth noting that although there is an increasing interest among European film professionals for partnerships that allow an insight into the booming Asian markets, there is very little expertise for such ventures. Regardless of its artistic achievements, a project such as *Taipei Factory II* might resonate positively within the Italian and European networks of film professionals. This is a factor that festivals might take into consideration when programming such films, as this responds to the current festival paradigm of fostering talent and serving the needs of the film industry. This is particularly relevant in support of European film professionals at a time when the European film market and productions are struggling against the giant Hollywood and Asian competitors.[20]

Upon the presentation of *Taipei Factory II* in Venice, both Taiwanese and Italian press releases highlighted the potential for collaboration between the two countries (ASCA 2014), which was one of the aims of the whole project. The three short films ranged from the drama of an Italian businessman who returns to Taipei for the funeral of his former wife in Hsieh Chun-yi's *Luca*, to Cho Li's all-female comedy *Soap Opera*, and Hou Chi-jan's gay vampire story *The Thrill is Gone*. The major limitation of such commissioned works is that they are meant to fulfil too many different sets of interest in a fairly short production timeframe. They should satisfy investors in two countries and have a broad circulation, as well as a life in the film market in order to encourage more international co-productions. Among the three short films, only *The Thrill is Gone* had a successful circulation and was later awarded the top prize at the Taiwan International Queer Festival, held in Taipei, Taichung and Kaohsiung during October and November 2015. How can these works appeal to a major festival where established directors capture the most attention? Even if the presence of the *Taipei Factory* project in Venice and Cannes was widely reported in both the Taiwanese and Chinese news, would such a project be better for promotion than the Best Director award given to Hou Hsiao-hsien's *The Assassin* (*Nie yin niang*) in Cannes in 2015? Whether owing to the difficult balance between financial investments and actual results, or to the structural and political changes that impacted on the role of the Taipei Film Commission in the promotion of Taiwan cinema at international film festivals from 2015, the *Taipei Factory* project was abandoned after the second production in 2014.[21]

Conclusions: the China factor

Wei Te-sheng's brief appearance in Venice and the two attempts of the *Taipei Factory* project point to a significantly changed environment both on the festival circuit and in the Taiwan film industry. The backdrop to this has been the expanding global film business with its complex dynamics. Moreover, the gigantic expansion of the mainland Chinese film market further connects regional and global film practices. The 'China factor' also contributes to defining the Asian region itself, shifting the attention of many international players away from Europe. Even traditional and prestigious events such as Cannes and Venice have to come to terms with the expansion of the Chinese film business. As the two major contenders in the film industry have become Hollywood and China, the role of European productions has been marginalised. Moreover, the traditional role of film festivals in presenting film works which would then circulate in the European arthouse film circuit has shifted to an alternative distribution platform since the collapse of the arthouse market, as testified by the voluntary bankruptcy of the arthouse pioneer Fortissimo Films in August 2016.[22]

Furthermore, with an increasing number of film professionals participating from all Chinese-language territories (mostly from the PRC), Cannes and Venice have started to pay more attention to market activities that target the Chinese-speaking region. These include panel discussions to present features and figures of the Chinese film market, project pitching sessions, and co-production forums such as those that have taken place during Cannes and Venice since 2014, most frequently organised by different film groups and European associations of film producers. Moreover, as the number of Asian film professionals increases, the number of journalists, entertainment lawyers, consultants and many other experts engaged in the film sector is also rising.

Therefore, while the three major European film festivals remain prestigious sites for film premieres, their business activities have expanded beyond film presentation. Cannes, Venice and Berlin can still rely on their prestige to attract world attention, but in addition to showcasing films, they are also essential occasions for networking, film marketing and the wider promotion of film-related activities. Thus the festival serves as a platform for not only cultural exchange, but also commercial activities.

In order to remain attractive to a variety of film professionals, festivals need to maintain their prestige in Asia, particularly in the Chinese region. Since 2013, Cannes has hosted a glamorous China Night as part of the Cannes Film Market. This is the result of an agreement between Chinese investors and the management of the Cannes film market. However, screenings of Chinese-speaking films and the presence of major directors remain the best way to guarantee significant circulation of festival-related news. This is the case for 'brand directors' such as Hou Hsiao-hsien or Tsai Ming-liang. Their presence draws the festival media attention because of their international profile while, at the same time, they confirm the relevance of Taiwan cinema even when the commercial viability of their films remains limited. Tsai Ming-liang's Venice-awarded *Stray Dogs* (2013) and, at Cannes, Hou Hsiao-hsien's award-winning *The Assassin* (2015) testify to the importance of festival screenings. *The Assassin* was conceived as a Taiwan-Hong Kong-China mainstream production, though it corresponded to Hou's authorial cinema.[23]

With the shift of major festivals from being sites for film discoveries, to being platforms for the global film business as well as a circuit for arthouse cinema, the opportunity to present titles that appeal to a more local market has become rare. New directors and directors with a less established European profile such as Wei Te-sheng require significant investment in terms of marketing and promotion to receive the same kind of attention as established directors in competition. However, Wei Te-sheng's popularity draws the interest of Chinese and Taiwanese media which are also valuable for a festival. The presence of *Seediq Bale* served to revitalise interest in the Venice festival in Asia, while at the same time it testified to the relevance of Taiwanese film production in the global film environment.

Notes

1 I wish to thank Michael Warner (Fortissimo Films), Carlo Gentile (RAI Cinema), director Midi Z and producer Vincent Wang for their thoughtful conversations as well as Luca Cao for copyediting the first draft of the chapter.
2 According to archive material, the documentary constitutes of pictures of the eponymous scroll painting while a voice-over explains the story of the artwork which has been preserved as a 1736 reproduction of the original Song dynasty scroll. Diplomat Loh I-cheng of the Republic of China is credited as producer of the documentary.
3 From 1999, I have contributed to the organisation of the Venice Film Festival in different roles, first as a staff member of the programming office and later as a

correspondent for Chinese-language and South Korean films in the years 2004–05 and from 2012 onwards. In the years 2006–11, I was managing director and film researcher of the Venice International Film Critics' Week, one of the independent sections organised within the framework of the festival and devoted to debut films. Starting in the year 2000, I have also regularly attended Cannes and Berlin among many other festivals in Europe and Asia. These different roles have allowed me to gain first-hand information and direct observations, which are here combined with archival research.

4 For a description of certain festival practices in relation to Chinese films during the 1990s, see Pollacchi (2014).

5 Data on the changes in production and distribution in Italy can be retrieved from the yearly reports issued by the Italian Ministry of Culture in collaboration with ANICA (National Association for Cinema, Audiovisual and Media Industries).

6 The structures of Cannes and Venice have become more similar over the years. Nowadays, both festivals have a main competition and another competitive section that is called *Un Certain Regard* in Cannes and *Orizzonti* in Venice. These two sections together with titles out of competition compose the official selection. Moreover, Cannes' *Quinzaine des Réalisateurs/Directors' Fortnight* tends to correspond to Venice's *Giornate degli Autori/Venice Days*, and both festivals have a Film Critics' Week with the only difference being that the Venice one includes only first-time directors while Cannes' Film Critics' Week includes first- and second-time directors. These latter sections are organised independently, as they have separate selection committees and organising staff.

7 Yonfan's *Prince of Tears* (*Lei wangzi*), which was also an entry to the Venice competition in 2009, is a Taiwan-HK-PRC co-production.

8 An 'omnibus film' (or anthology film or portmanteau film) is a feature film consisting of several short films tied together by a premise, a theme, an interlocking event, etc. There is no general rule for the frequency of such screenings at film festivals although the preliminary assumption is that all the short films are equally worthy of attention.

9 For a discussion of the relocation of Hong Kong cinema to mainland China, see Yau (2015).

10 For a general discussion of the development of PRC politics in relation to the use of soft power and international relations, see Lai and Lu (2012).

11 *The Huffington Post* website includes an interview that shed some light on Hollywood-China film business deals in 2014–15. See ScreenCraft (2016).

12 *Cape No.7* was screened at the Asian Film Festival in Vesoul (France) and at the Hawaii Film Festival, which is also a festival with a strong connection to Asian films.

13 A complete collection of the Italian articles that referred to the screenings of *Seediq Bale* on 1 September 2011 is available in the ASAC archives of La Biennale di Venezia. In addition to the archive collection, the ASAC archives have a website which provides some basic information on the various activities of La Biennale di Venezia.

14 For a theoretical description of the festival practices and the stakeholders involved in festivals, see De Valck (2007), Peranson (2009) and Pollacchi (2014).

15 The function, structures and roles of the Taipei Film Commission are strictly connected to domestic political strategies in relation to the film sector and involve both the Ministry of Culture and the Taipei City Government. In 2015, a change of commissioners and policies made the international role of the Taipei Film Commission less prominent at film festivals.

16 'Independent' sections in Cannes and Venice are sections with a different director, programming and managing structure from the ones involved in the organisation of the Official Selection. However, their screenings take place during the Cannes

and Venice festivals and within the framework of these two events. A comparative overview of their regulations and structures is available through their different websites, as exemplified by the Cannes Film Festival Official Selection: www.fes tival-cannes.com/en/selection/competition-1; and Cannes Directors' Fortnight: www.quinzaine-realisateurs.com/en/pro-press/.

17 Further details about the film synopsis and filmmakers' biographies and filmographies can be obtained from a Spotlight Taiwan website: sites.google.com/site/sp otlighttaiwaninedinburgh/taipei-factory (accessed 2 June 2016).

18 My conversation with Midi Z during the 2016 Venice Film Festival (Venice, 6 September 2016).

19 An overview of Chinese-language articles related to the presentation of films in Venice in the years 2012–16 shows that the distinction between films screened as part of the official selection and those screened in the independent sections is much less evident. Chinese articles often report the unique distinction between films in the main competition and all other films without specifying the different sections.

20 The European Audiovisual Observatory provides figures, reports and current trends on the European film market: www.obs.coe.int.

21 In 2015 the promotion of Taiwanese cinema at international film festivals was transferred from the Taipei Film Commission to the Taiwan Film Institute, a new centre for the promotion, restoration and diffusion of Taiwanese cinema which absorbed the structures of the film archive and the Taiwan International Documentary Festival. The news of the restructuring was released in summer 2014. See Frater (2014).

22 For an outline of the reasons that brought Fortissimo CEO Michael Werner to such a drastic decision, see Winfrey (2016).

23 Hou Hsiao-hsien discussed the productive structure and the funding of *The Assassin* at a masterclass at the Cinemathèque Royale de Belgique in Bruxelles on 26 May 2015.

5 Contesting the national, labelling the renaissance

Exhibiting Taiwan cinema at film festivals in Japan since the 1980s[1]

Ran Ma

Introduction

In 2010, delegations from both the People's Republic of China (PRC) and the Republic of China (ROC) disappeared from the green carpet ceremony of the 23rd Tokyo International Film Festival (TIFF). According to the media coverage, the reason seemed straightforward: the head of the PRC's delegation, the vice CEO of the Chinese state-owned film enterprise China Film Group Corporation, required the ROC team to attach 'China' before its official designation of 'Taiwan' (Guo 2010). The delegation from the ROC refused to comply with this request.

Studies have focused on international film festivals as globally interconnected and powerful industrial platforms/mechanisms that not only circulate, exhibit and valorise world cinemas, but also demonstrate transnational financing, (co-)production and trade of film projects (see, e.g. Wong 2011; DeBoer 2014). Nevertheless, while the exhibitionary agendas and industrial mechanisms of contemporary international film festivals have considerably expanded and even rewritten the 'limiting imagination of national cinema' (Higson 2006), the TIFF episode reveals that national cinema returns (often unexpectedly) to centre stage. This reminds us of national cinema's problematic positioning within the contemporary festival configuration.

Therefore, film festivals have figured a discursive terrain in which to interrogate the complexities of programming and exhibiting cinemas from three Chinas – mainland/PRC, Taiwan and Hong Kong – and to explore the discontents and incoherence of the *national* as pertaining to the circulatory politics of the international festival institution. Overall, this study views festival programming as a dynamic, contingent and networked process participated in and negotiated by various actors such as film professionals (including programmers, filmmakers, producers, journalists), cultural authorities, film entities and bodies, and even the audiences. Accordingly, programming (a process of selection and inclusion/exclusion) needs to be situated and examined within specific socio-historical, political and industrial contexts.

Situated at the conjuncture of Chinese film studies and film festival studies, this chapter aims to engage the difficulties and contingencies in locating

Taiwan cinema as a national cinema on the international film festival network. We shall canvass the historical trajectories of circulating and exhibiting Taiwanese films at film festivals in Japan since the 1980s into the new millennium. This periodisation roughly charts out the globally celebrated yet decelerating film movement of Taiwan New Cinema (*Taiwan xin dianying*, TNC) and the rise of a post-New Cinema in the 2000s with emergent filmmakers such as Doze Niu and Wei Te-sheng who are more versed in commercial genres. Significantly, Wei's box office triumph with his 2008 directorial debut *Cape No.7* initiated a 'post-TNC era', but also signalled 'Taiwan cinema's "revival" and "renaissance"' (Lim 2013: 157).

Meanwhile, our case study surveys a broadly defined category of festivals run by Japanese official and/or non-governmental organisation (NGO) bodies, as well as various film exhibitions (co-)organised by the ROC's cultural authorities. Arguably, the dynamics generated by frictions between a persisting national cinema paradigm and the global festival system's networking mechanism have created new exhibitionary space for Taiwan cinema, but at the same time they also problematise and displace this cinema's affiliation with a 'stateless country' that constantly engages in experiments of 'national self-definition' (Davis 2007: 3). Furthermore, Japan is located not merely as the mediating point to investigate the contesting agency and configurations of Chinese cinemas – particularly regarding films from the PRC and the ROC – but also highlights its twisted historical linkages with Taiwan, its former colony.

As Gary D. Rawnsley (2003: 2) noted, Taiwan 'is not considered a legitimate actor in the international system' despite its successful democratisation because it is not a member of the United Nations and has few diplomatic relations of any weight. Although this project does not assume that festival programming reflects directly the diplomatic problems in the relationship between Taiwan, the PRC and Japan, we should not lose sight of the political realities and in particular the friction between the three. This will provide a more nuanced context for understanding Taiwan cinema in Japan.

Framing national cinema in the international film festival system

Investigating the exhibition history of contemporary Taiwan films at three prestigious, so-called first-tier European film festivals (namely Venice, Cannes and Berlin), Song Hwee Lim (2013: 154) observes how Taiwan cinema has achieved a 'small miracle' on the global stage. This is demonstrated by film festival awards won by a 'quartet' of auteurs consisting of Hou Hsiao-hsien, Edward Yang, Ang Lee and Tsai Ming-liang, confirming the power of Taiwan's movie industry.

Lim (2013) has preferred an interpretative framework of national cinema for a politicised reading of Taiwan cinema's global reception on the film festival network (also see Hjort and Petrie 2007), where he also leverages Joseph Nye's notion of cinema as an important 'soft-power resource' (Lim 2013:

154). Here, soft power is understood in terms of the state's ability to attract and co-opt, rather than using 'coercion or payment', to obtain diplomatic goals (Nye 2012). Lim therefore proposes that Taiwan cinema's strength and prestige can be 'measured by awards conferred at international film festivals, since these awards are, in effect, an index of attractiveness decided by panels of judges acting as voting focus groups' (Lim 2013: 154). Lim's observations are not necessarily inaccurate. However, such a point does not differentiate adequately the screenings at film festivals from the spectacles featured at the Olympic Games or even the World Expo. In the latter types of fanfares, ranking and prizes are assigned and awarded to athletes and entities (via the display of artistic creations and/or industrial products) that have respectively 'represented' their countries of origin, wherein a subject often subscribes itself to the nation-state construct in a singular and fixated manner. As such, Lim's discussions may have failed to take into account the layered complexities and negotiations between the national and the transnational engendered through the festival mechanism of circulation and exhibition.

In the first place this chapter will test Lim's claim against a brief review of how the national cinema paradigm has been historically related to the cultural institution of the film festival, an institution that originated in the European continent and has undergone profound metamorphosis since the end of the Second World War. In comprehending the historical trajectories characterising the entanglement between national cinema and the global festival system, we can better understand the paradoxical twist between the rise of Taiwan cinema in international film festival settings as an emerging national cinema (and its renaissance), and the film festival network's de-territorialising dynamics which always displace the nation-state fixation in the global flows of film production, distribution and exhibition. If we turn a blind eye to such paradoxes and problematics underlying Taiwan cinema's global traffic, we might also easily ignore some of the transnational potentialities and components which 'trouble and resist subsumption under the sign of the nation' within Taiwan cinema itself (Lim 2006: 6).

'Initial festivals', namely the Venice (est. 1932) and Cannes (est. 1939) festivals, represented disparate national responses to Fascism and Hollywood before the end of Second World War (Wong 2011: 39). In post-war Europe, newly installed film festivals or those reincarnated from pre-war practices were embedded within specific cultural agendas framed by the nation-state or city. At the same time they also played a role, sometimes unwillingly, in engaging the overarching political leitmotif of the Cold War. Specifically, the national cinema paradigm directly translated into the mechanism of selecting and exhibiting films based on the collaboration between the film festival and national committees of each participating nation, with a national committee selecting and submitting films to the festival. Nevertheless, the selection and exhibition of films at European festivals were not simply an Olympian showcase and celebration of world film art. In the cultural Cold War, film festivals reflected how national cinemas were differentiated and evaluated in terms of their ideological affiliations, as well as the position of their home countries within the polarised world order. Prior to the lifting of martial law in 1987, the Nationalist or Kuomintang (KMT) Taiwan government emphasised the propagandist and pedagogical significance of 'national film' (*guopian*) – films made by the ROC nationals and which used the national language of Mandarin (Lee 2012: 170).[2] Directly supervised and choreographed by the state, the international showcase of national films was never purely artistically driven. For instance, even in 1992, before its official film delegation participated in the Asia-Pacific Film Festival held in Seoul that year, Taiwan reduced the number of delegates in protest against the Korean government's newly established diplomatic ties with the PRC (Yamashita et al. 2014: 111).

The global social movements in 1968 impacted greatly upon the organisational structure of several leading European festivals including Cannes, Berlin and Venice, which re-formed their selection pattern on the authority of national committees. The model of national cinema was less favoured when festivals started to assign programmers and other professionals to scout for and curate films; titles could be obtained through agents or alternative channels without recourse to any national entity (Elsaesser 2005). The end of the Cold War in 1989 further contributed to redefining, if not dissolving, a rigid, ideologically laden national cinema framework. This is most recognisable when a festival selects, evaluates and awards its international film entries in, for instance, its competition section. Festival awards and endorsement are interpreted less as victories of national cinemas than, for example, the triumph of auteurist visions and individual styles. Yet the national cinema model has not become out of date in the post-1968 transformation of the world film festival system.

At the same time, it is worth noting how the framing of transnational cinema might help us reconsider the organisation and the mechanism of the festival institution today. An international film festival in its ideal form, both as an event (therefore a public space) and an establishment, epitomises an interface that, to paraphrase Appadurai (1990), characterises how the global cultural economy intersects and mingles. Specifically, contemporary film festivals have expanded their industrial connections to incorporate and reinforce the marketplace in which to trade finished films and to pitch potential projects. It is common that in collaboration with banks, investment companies and other enterprises, film festivals often establish multiple funds to finance both domestic and foreign film projects that are at different stages of production. As such, even if we could still designate the national identity of a specific film auteur, it is increasingly challenging to identify the country of origin for a film, especially if the work is funded by film festivals or co-produced through such platforms.

Mette Hjort and Duncan Petrie (2007: 11) argued that when elaborating on 'various forms of nationhood' in the cinema of small nations, 'national categories continue to be invoked with reference to sites of production, exhibition, acquiescence, resistance or some form of transformation'. The national cinema model has developed new mechanisms to cope with the transnational dynamics of the film festival apparatus. Although it is not rare for the previously government-affiliated international film festivals to privatise and corporatise themselves following incentives of the free market, it is also under the leitmotif of neoliberalism that the state and various levels of government seek to collaborate with corporate sponsors in supporting a festival, and to frame the festival organisation and development within broader industrial, economic and cultural policies. For instance, the establishment or restructuring of some Asian festivals dovetailed with the accelerated process of urbanisation and has been framed by the regeneration of local/state economies and developing cultural industries, even when it is not directly linked to a robust national film industry. One example is Taiwan's Golden Horse Awards, which was established in 1962 by the Government Information Office (GIO) to promote 'national films' as defined by the KMT. The awards used to play a propagandist role in the post-war Nationalist conservative cultural system, but after democratisation they were finally let go by the government in the late 1980s and have since been highlighted as an important project to invigorate Taiwan's cultural and creative industries. In 1989, the Golden Horse Awards changed its name to the Taipei Golden Horse Film Festival (TGHFF). Currently Taiwan's largest festival, the TGHFF is run by an independent organisation, and is partly funded by the government (Lee 2012: 170–172).[3] The incongruences and overlap between the national and transnational frameworks, while evincing the disjunctive nature of the global cultural landscapes in the post-Cold War world, also underscore the frictions between film festivals as a transnational cultural establishment and the neoliberal milieu in which it is deeply embedded.

Screening Taiwan: a small history

Following the above discussion, we now return to survey Taiwan cinema's circulation and exhibition in the international festival network. Reframing Hou Hsiao-hsien's 'Taiwan trilogy'[4] in relation to the much-debated 'national' that underpins Chinese cinema, Chris Berry (2006: 155) proposes that we should reconsider the old national cinema model that merely emphasises the connections between films 'in relation to the assumed singular culture of a nation-state'. In reinforcing the performativity of the national agency, Berry notes the multiplicity of ways we can connote the 'national' in Chinese cinema, and therefore suggest that any project elaborating on the national should 'engage with the potentially endless project of distinguishing and explaining each of these senses and instances' (Berry 2006: 155). In a similar vein, once Taiwan cinema is included on the international film festival network, festival stakeholders and actors including those from the three Chinas will engage in the multiple projects of 'distinguishing and explaining' the 'different Chinese senses and instances' (ibid., 155). This occurs specifically when a film moves through the disparate yet interconnected festival mechanisms of programming, exhibition, consumption, canonisation (through awards) and trading (via film markets). We shall therefore understand and approach 'screening Taiwan' as multifarious projects, each of which indexes a different assemblage of festival actors and their interconnections, and each of which demonstrates a set of discursive articulations engaging the China connection differently.

The GIO and the Republic of China Film Festival

I will first highlight how the ROC government has been framing and institutionalising 'screening Taiwan' since the 1980s. The GIO performed the crucial role of selecting and supporting domestically produced films to participate in international film festivals (Lee 2012: 173–174). The KMT-led regime lifted martial law in 1987 which connects Taiwan to the post-Cold War order. Meanwhile, it links with the 'neoliberal transition' of Taiwan, a process of state-led marketisation that started in the mid-1980s (Tsai 2001: 359). As Sung-sheng Yvonne Chang (2005: 13) notes, the lifting of martial law 'opened a "Great Divide" in Taiwan's cultural development' and accelerated 'the emergence of a new cultural field already increasingly subject to market forces and the effects of globalization'. I suggest that 1987 marked a turning point for the ROC government to reposition its policy and political framings of the domestic film industry, particularly regarding the GIO's previously dominant national cinema model in selecting films for international festivals and orchestrating film exhibitions overseas.

Signs of cultural liberalisation did occur in 1982 and 1983 when Taiwan New Cinema auteurs made such ground-breaking works as *In Our Time* (*Guangyin de gushi*, dir. Tao De-chen, Edward Yang, Ke Yi-zheng and Zhang Yi, 1982) and *The Sandwich Man* (*Er zi de da wan ou*, dir. Hou Hsiao-hsien, Zeng Zhuang-xiang and Wan Ren, 1983). Both compilations of short films were financed and produced by the state's leading film studio, Central Motion Picture Corporation (CMPC). Nevertheless, as Japanese scholar Saburo Koyama (2014: 5) posits, the TNC emerged at a time when the ROC government still insisted on emphasising ideological indoctrination and propagating anti-communism while supervising local film productions.[5]

Instrumental in and responsive to Taiwan cinema's international festival exhibitions, the GIO's policies reflected the regime's extensive cultural diplomacy programmes. Joseph Nye's conceptualisation of soft power, a term he coined at the beginning of the 1990s, offers a new framework to survey cultural diplomacy in the post-Cold War era (also see Rawnsley 2003). Whereas Lim (2013) argues for film's role in boosting Taiwan's international soft power, I add that it is also necessary to view the ROC government's long-term efforts to promote domestically produced films overseas as part of the multiple 'screening Taiwan' projects since the Cold War.

As early as 1983, the GIO established a standing committee to take charge of scouting for and submitting local films to festivals overseas.[6] In the mid-1980s, second-tier European festivals such as France's Festival des 3 Continents and Switzerland's Locarno International Film Festival started to discover and encourage new works by the TNC such as Hou Hsiao-hsien and Edward Yang.[7] In 1985, with one eye on the TNC's increasing popularity on the global festival circuit, the GIO even directed Taiwan's overseas offices to create Chinese and Foreign Film Trading Information Centres to assist their international circulation. In 1986, not only did the GIO allocate NT $10 million (*c.* US $310,000) to support the participation of domestic films in international festivals, but it also entered Hou's *Dust in the Wind* (*Lianlian fengchen*, 1986) to Berlinale, and Yang's *The Terrorizers* (*Kongbu fenzi*, 1986) to Cannes. In 1987, the ROC government revised its film policies to include financial support for further enhancing Taiwan cinema's participation in international film festivals and granting monetary awards to local filmmakers who won prizes overseas.[8] According to the GIO's statistics, in 1987 there were 37 films from Taiwan entering 43 international film festivals winning eight film awards, the best record so far. 1987 also witnessed the publication of a Taiwan Cinema Manifesto. Boasting 53 signatories 'comprising key TNC filmmakers and luminaries from other artistic fields', this manifesto called for 'another kind of cinema', a claim that in effect signalled the demise of Taiwan New Cinema (Lim 2013: 160).

On 1 January 1984, the GIO lifted its ten-year ban on the import to Taiwan of Japanese films.[9] One of the reasons was that the Motion Picture Producers Association of Japan, a national-level association consisting of four leading Japanese film corporations, agreed to assist Taiwan in launching the ROC Film Festival in Tokyo and Osaka (Huang 2014: 134). Although the first ROC Film Festival, scheduled to take place in October 1984, was postponed due to unclarified 'political issues' (Yamashita et al. 2014: 94), the GIO managed to launch the festival in early 1985 and toured six Taiwanese films in Tokyo and Osaka over two weeks. To accompany the films, Taiwan also sent a delegation consisting of 25 filmmakers, screenwriters, and the leading actors and actresses of the films screened in the festival (Huang 2014: 135). The selection included works such as *Second Spring of Mr. Mo* (*Lao mo de di er ge chuntian*, dir. Li You-ning, 1984) and *Teenage Fugitive* (*Xiao taofan*, dir. Chang Pei-cheng, 1984). Whereas *Mr. Mo* was in the annual 'Top Ten' list for 'Best Mandarin Films' polled by the Taipei-based China Film Critics Association in 1984, *Teenage Fugitive* won four awards at the 29th Asia-Pacific Film Festival held in the same year (Yamashita et al. 2014: 95). Another selected title was Chen Kun-hou's *Growing Up* (*Xiaobi de gushi*, 1983), viewed as one of the pioneering works that 'started the Taiwan New Cinema movement' (Lee 2012: 130).

As Dina Iordanova (2010: 17) points out, 'festivals that are organized with the blessing of governmental and publicly-backed NGOs stand a better chance of visibility and of promoting their causes in the public sphere'. This hard-won film festival in Japan, with the designation of 'ROC' in its title and the appearance of the GIO's deputy director at the opening ceremony in

Japan, was intended to foreground Taiwan as an independent entity, separate from the PRC, in a diplomatic context. According to veteran film critic Huang Ren, Beijing protested that the visit to the festival of a ROC official violated the 1972 Communiqué's agreement between Japan and the PRC which said the latter is the sole legal government of China. Okada Shigeru, the then president of the Motion Picture Producers Association of Japan (i.e. *eiren*, established in 1957), tried to pacify Beijing by offering an opportunity to launch a PRC film festival in Japan (Huang 2008: 293–294).[10] A second GIO-backed ROC Film Festival in Japan did not open until September 1988, and showcased seven films under the title of 'the Second ROC Taiwan Film Festival' in theatres in Osaka, Kobe and Tokyo (ROC Diplomatic Missions 2013: 8–9).[11] However, a third ROC Film Festival never took place.

In the post-authoritarian, post-Cold War era, the ROC government's policies related to the international exhibition of Taiwan cinema have been dually focused. Yvonne Chang (2005: 23) explains how the GIO, impressed by the awards the TNC garnered at international film festivals, 'enlisted film in Taiwan's diplomatic struggle for "international living space"'. On one level, neither the PRC nor the ROC governments has given up the effective format of international film exhibition in implementing cultural diplomacy despite the dissolution of the GIO in 2012.[12] On another level, what matters for the state 'is not so much the ideological content of the film, but whether it will disseminate "Taiwan", to make sure the worldwide audience is able to distinguish' the country (Chen 2006: 143). Despite the implications of the diplomatic competition, these government-supported events no longer simply rely on an explicit ideological contestation, but instead register a discourse of boosting soft power. This occurs in tandem with developing the island's cultural and creative industries, and especially tapping into Taiwan cinema's artistic and commercial potential in the global marketplace.

Cinema on the move: Taiwan cinema as a programming theme

The GIO-backed film festival in Japan has gradually deviated from its hard, ideologically charged mode; 'ROC' was no longer used in the title of such events. In its 'soft' and neoliberal mode, the GIO (and since 2012, the Ministry of Culture) has been able to collaborate with an assemblage of Taiwanese and/or Japanese cultural and industrial entities to develop a 'Taiwan Film Festival' (TFF) into a steady, flexible programming theme that has been launched either as an independent event or a sidebar attached to a Japanese international festival.[13] The shift to the name of 'Taiwan' was not without diplomatic consequences. However, through co-organising and co-sponsoring such events, the ROC cultural authorities have in effect delegated the TFF theme to localised bodies such as a one-off festival executive committee or the festivals themselves. Given that, Taiwan cinema is not only exhibited at international festivals, occasionally Japan's arthouse cinema-oriented, single-screen movie theatre known as the mini-theatre and similar art spaces would also organise and programme a Taiwan cinema-themed *eigasai* (a Japanese term roughly equivalent to that of 'film festival', though with diverse formats), usually a non-competitive, elongated exhibition catering to local audiences. These programmes would be sometimes choreographed as independent of ROC's official assistance or sponsorship.

In recent years, the ROC's overseas representation by the Taipei Economic and Cultural Representative Office (TECRO) in Japan, for instance, and the Taiwan Culture Centre (previously the Taipei Cultural Centre),[14] have collaborated with Japanese festivals and other cultural bodies to install special programmes highlighting new titles and renowned post-New Cinema filmmakers. For instance, a 2015 'Taiwan Film Festival' taking place in the northeastern city of Jōetsu, Niigata, showcased a mixture of six productions made after 2008, including *Kano* (2014), a box office hit directed by Umin Boya and produced by Wei Te-sheng, reminiscing about the first high school baseball team, Kano, from the then colony Taiwan which made it into the final round of the national-level high school baseball championship in 1931. This Jōetsu exhibition orchestrated the participation of the ROC's Ministry of Culture, Taiwan Culture Centre and a Jōetsu-based non-profit organisation for urban regeneration. Though run by an independent festival committee, this event was opened by speeches by the head of the Taiwan Culture Centre, and the mayor of Jōetsu city. This remote but historic city was chosen also because when the Generalissimo Chiang Kai-shek was serving the Imperial Japanese Army in 1908, his division was based at Takada, a region currently merged into Jōetsu.[15]

We also need to take into account the evolving trajectory of Taiwan cinema since the late 1980s and especially its post-New Cinema economic-industrial downturn and recovery. What Lim (2013: 157) designates as the 'quartet' team of Taiwanese film maestros has, in the 1990s, been 'increasingly incorporated into a pantheon of world cinema auteurism'. Probably not unlike their Fifth Generation counterparts on the mainland, maestros like Hou Hsiao-hsien and Tsai Ming-liang also have their films co-produced by multiple international entities so one might have difficulty distinguishing the nationality of their works, while the films may not necessarily address 'a specific local audience' or the 'local history and politics' (Chen 2006: 143–144). On the other hand, between 1996 and 2007, the market share of domestic films merely 'hovered around the 1 to 2 percent mark' (Lim 2013: 157). It was Wei Te-sheng's *Cape No.7* that spearheaded the recovery and boosted the market share to a record high of 12.09 per cent in 2008 (Lim 2013: 158). The renaissance did not grow out of nowhere. Prior to Wei's breakthrough, against the dire situation facing the domestic film industry, acclaimed domestic productions and promising talent emerged occasionally and drew attention. As pointed out by Ming-yeh T. Rawnsley (2009b: 94), the TNC not only continued its creative power after the movement itself was pronounced dead, but also 'gave rise to a generation of film scholars and tutors who have since nurtured new talent in colleges, universities and in the studios'. Meanwhile, we need to note that the ROC government set up the Domestic Film Guidance Fund in 1989 to support financially local film production and has been revising policies sponsoring and awarding Taiwan films' participation at international film festivals. However controversial the system of the Guidance Fund might be, it was not only considered 'a life-saver for the dying Taiwan film industry', but also 'contributed to internationally award-winning Taiwan films' which, without the fund, 'might not have been made' (Lee 2012: 149).

Surveys suggest that since the 1990s, three Japanese international film festivals have taken the lead in programming Taiwanese titles: the TIFF (established in 1985), the Yamagata International Documentary Film Festival (YIDFF, established in 1989), and Focus on Asia Fukuoka International Film Festival (established in 1991, hereafter 'Focus on Asia'). Added to the list since 2000 are the arthouse-centric FILMeX International Film Festival, which later became the sole platform in Japan to premiere Tsai Ming-liang's movies, and also the Osaka Asian Film Festival (OAFF, established in 2006), an international festival in west Japan that has highlighted Chinese-language films.

Here we will take a close look at the presence of post-TNC works at festivals such as Focus on Asia and the TIFF. In the post-Cold War festival economy, even the soft power-driven showcase of Taiwan cinema needs to embed itself within the commercial environment for film exhibition and to appeal to the Japanese cinephile culture.

(i) Focus on Asia Fukuoka International Film Festival

Founded in 1991, Focus on Asia came into being at a transitional juncture when Japanese media and cultural industries started to position and project themselves 'at the center of the Pan Asian cultural sphere' (Tezuka 2012: 147). Stephanie DeBoer (2014: 117) contends that in the early to mid-1990s, Japan became 'popularly conscious of itself as part of the region in the face of the rising significance of its neighbors'. The Focus on Asia festival also constituted one of these 'Asian' projects through which Japan sought to rediscover and reconnect with its neighbours and play the role to conduct and organise the region against the uneven landscape of film and media industries in East and South-East Asia (DeBoer 2014: 116–117). In choreographing a line-up of Asian films for its domestic audiences, the Focus on Asia festival addressed the shared belief in establishing linkages with other film industries and specifically enabling 'many people to see in detail the people and cultures from our neighboring countries of Asia', a quote from the governmental body of the Japan Foundation which co-organises the festival (quoted in DeBoer 2014: 116).

Focus on Asia has been programming the films from Taiwan in connection with other Chinese-language cinemas. This not only illustrates the contrasting trajectories of the increasingly interlinked film industries across Taiwan, Hong Kong and mainland China (with or without the prominent independent filmmaking movement), but also indexes some general programming trends among Japanese festivals in balancing their roles between imparting cinephiliac knowledge on world/Asian cinemas and engaging the audiences' layered, sometimes highly limited understanding of Chinese-language films in relation to other Asian popular culture genres. 'Focus in Asia' showcased Wang Tong's *Banana Paradise* (*Xiangjiao tiantang*, 1989) at its inaugural edition in 1991. The festival started to assemble films from Taiwan with those from Hong Kong and the mainland into special programmes under the title 'Cinemas from Chinese-speaking Regions' in the 1990s. Such a programming strategy partially mirrors how the festival has presented films from the so-called 'Chinese-speaking regions' as cultural products that share certain common ground despite their disparate evolving histories and social contexts. The discourse of 'cinemas from Chinese-language regions' has been widely circulated within the Japanese festival circuit, mini-theatre-themed exhibitions as well as popular cinephilia publications, evincing what Berry has observed as an understanding of 'a supra-state Chinese cultural affiliation' (Berry 2006: 155). Importantly, these seemingly contingent programming gestures coincided with the eventful years (1994, 1995 and 2001) in which the cross-strait film exchanges between the mainland and Taiwan (including Hong Kong) were further boosted through visits by delegations, symposia and film festivals in which filmmakers and film professionals from the three locales participated (Yamashita et al. 2014: 114–116, 124–126).[16] Instead of coalescing three cinemas into an indistinguishable whole, I shall argue that such a programming lens actually helps to pin down the layers and complexities of Chinese-language films by subjecting them to a comparative horizon.

In Japan, the transfer of sovereignty over Hong Kong in 1997 presented an opportunity to redefine 'cinemas from Chinese-language regions'. For instance, in the same year, one of Japan's most prestigious film magazines, *Movie Times* (*Kinema Junpo*), published a supplement of 'the Complete Databook of Chinese Cinemas' (*Chukka denei kanzen databook*), offering comprehensive, dictionary entry-style explanations on films, filmmakers and actors/actresses from Taiwan, Hong Kong and China. Collaborating with the TECRO, Focus on Asia in 1997 launched a special feature of Taiwan cinema showcasing seven titles mostly made by the pre-New Cinema generation masters such as Li Hsing and Wang Tong. Back in Tokyo, in 1997 a festival committee supported by the TECRO, Taipei City Government and Japanese cultural bodies such as the Athénée Français Cultural Centre launched a 'Taiwan Film Festival' (*Taiwan eigasai*) at a local mini-theatre, an unprecedented themed exhibition presenting a line-up of 51 titles from the island. In his essay titled 'Taiwan cinema and Japan', which featured in the festival brochure, renowned film critic and former director of Focus on Asia Tadao Sato emphasised that while Taiwan cinema had been historically connected to both Japanese cinema and Chinese cinema, the emergence of Taiwan New Cinema decisively contributed to building up Taiwan's self-identity (Sato

1997: 18–19). However, throughout the first decade of the 2000s, Taiwanese films had been sparsely selected in Focus on Asia.[17] Since 2010, the festival has initiated a new collaborative pattern in embedding a co-sponsored 'Taiwan Film Festival' into its main programme. Coordinated by an independent festival committee, this Taiwan Film Festival has been continuously supported by TECRO offices in Tokyo, Osaka and the Taiwan Cultural Centre.

(ii) The Tokyo International Film Festival

Currently hosted by the Japan Association for the International Promotion of the Moving Image (UNIJAPAN), a non-profit organisation that has been closely associated with the Japanese film industry and the state cultural authorities, the TIFF is not simply the largest film showcase adding a competitive edge to Tokyo as a world-class media capital, for it has always been a site of intersecting global cultural flows onto which Japan could register itself as a crucial player in regional and even international cultural industries. Although not a state-run festival in the strict sense, the TIFF has been positioned tightly within the state policy framework in developing a national culture and rejuvenating cultural industries.

At international festivals, conventionally the nationality of a film director would decide the country of origin for her or his entry; the national tags prove problematic when a festival has to distinguish films from three Chinas. Referring to the 2010 TIFF episode that starts this chapter, I observe that the Tokyo festival's official affiliations have carried much political weight in terms of its selection and programming of Taiwan cinema and made the event itself an easy target for the ROC and PRC governments to contest over a name.

Taiwan sent its official film delegation to the inaugural TIFF in 1985 without exhibiting any titles (Yamashita et al. 2014: 96). At the second TIFF in 1987, the introduction for the section of 'The Best of Asia-Pacific Films' cautiously mentioned 'young filmmakers from Taiwan', but only titles from mainland China were included. It was not until 1991, the third TIFF, that Edward Yang's *A Brighter Summer Day* (*Gulingjie shaonian sharen shijian*, 1991) was selected as a competition film, though the catalogue merely indicates that this film is a Japan-United States co-production.[18]

Cindy Wong (2011: 215) illustrates how the Hong Kong International Film Festival avoided trouble in differentiating between entries from Taiwan, China and Hong Kong by indicating the languages used in films from these three locales: Mandarin (*Guoyu*, meaning 'national language') for Taiwan, Mandarin (*Putonghua*, meaning 'common language') for China, and Cantonese for Hong Kong. As early as 1994, the TIFF conducted the same experiment in abandoning the labels of origin and simply listed the languages of all film entries. This policy itself was in the first place politically concerned. At the sixth TIFF in 1993, the Fifth Generation Chinese filmmaker Tian Zhuangzhuang's *Blue Kite* (*Lan fengzheng*, 1992) garnered the Grand Prix as a Hong

Kong entry (due to its co-production background between Beijing Film Studio and a Hong Kong company). Partially due to the fact that *Blue Kite* was screened at the Tokyo festival without obtaining the official permit, and also because it is a human drama ruminating the traumatic, dark history of several political campaigns leading up to the Cultural Revolution, the film delegation sent by the Chinese government to Tokyo walked out of the screening in protest. Afterwards, not only was *Blue Kite* banned on the mainland, but also Tian was banned from filmmaking by the then PRC Ministry of Radio, Film and Television.[19] To avoid political controversy, the Tokyo Film Festival changed its orientation from indicating the 'country of production' for entries from the three Chinas.[20] Therefore between 1995 and 2007, the TIFF provided the full production details of a film, instead of simply indicating its country of production. However, critics complained that it was inadequate to indicate only the languages of a film. According to TIFF programmer Ishizuka Kenji, when the Cannes International Film Festival, in tandem with other leading European and American festivals, started to denote the country of production in 2008, the TIFF decided to follow suit and so the three Chinas have become clearly differentiated in festival programmes once again.

Film festivals tend to celebrate and recycle the discourse of Nouvelle Vague of different countries and times. In recent years, festivals have often utilised their extensive programming and funding mechanisms to nurture new wave cinemas by constantly shifting geopolitical and aesthetic emphasis and encouraging emerging filmmakers and works from less explored territories of global cinema. Not unlike some of their European and American counterparts, Japanese festivals have turned their eyes to discovering new voices in Taiwan cinema. In 2005, supported by the GIO, TECRO in Japan and the Taiwan Reference Library, the TIFF's 'Winds of Asia' section presented 11 titles from Taiwan in its sub-section, 'Taiwan: Movies on the Move', claiming that Taiwan cinema 'is making a creative comeback' (Teruoka 2005: 6). Nevertheless, statistics provided in the 2005 festival catalogue show that between 2001 and 2005 the domestic market share and box office performance of the local film industry was hardly optimistic in Taiwan (Teruoka 2005: 12–13). In 2008, the arthouse cinema chain, Cinemart, also joined forces with the festivals to introduce to Japan a younger generation of Taiwanese filmmakers in a special program entitled 'Taiwan Cinema Collection'. This event showcased works by Robin Lee Yun-chan, Chen Huai-en, Su Chao-pin and Doze Niu – names that would later come to define the line-up of most Japanese festivals that programme post-TNC productions.

In 2010, with the support of the ROC's cultural agencies, the TIFF again launched a sub-section called 'Taiwanese Cinema Renaissance 2010: New Breeze of the Rising Generation', underscoring the rhetoric of renaissance signalled by the encouraging performance of post-New Cinema. While it remains unclear to what extent the ROC vs. PRC dispute in 2010 discussed at the beginning of this chapter impacted upon the programming strategies of

Taiwanese titles in the following years, it is noteworthy that since 2011, the TIFF no longer features any special programmes on Taiwan cinema. Nevertheless, the ROC government-backed Taiwan cinema theme has since been launched at the aforementioned Focus on Asia festival and Osaka Asian Film Festival, with the latter retaining the title of 'Movies on the Move'.

As indicated, renewed interest among Japanese film festivals and exhibitors in Taiwan cinema has been related to the box office success of *Cape No.7* and the impressive, continuous growth of the post-New Cinema filmmakers who are 'marked by a more popular mode of filmmaking that aims to appeal to a wider audience' (Lim 2013: 158). While I agree with Lim that post-New Cinema embodies 'people power', the *Cape No.7* miracle is as much about 'shifting the self-image of Taiwan cinema' as about diversifying and multiplying its possibilities (Lim 2013: 158). In effect, popular films by the post-New Cinema directors have been branded by the ROC state and local governments in tandem with films by Hou Hsiao-hsien, Ang Lee and Tsai Ming-liang.[21] It should be emphasised that the current passion for post-New Cinema projects at Japanese festivals also relates to the fact that these events, including the TIFF, are hardly competitive in the hierarchical global festival system. It is quite challenging for them to attract world premieres from established Taiwanese maestros. Japanese programmers' turn to genre productions and a focus on emerging talents prove an effective alternative to carve out new space for another kind of Taiwan cinema and therefore establish connections between Japanese audiences and the changing scenario of Taiwanese film culture. Significantly, the showcase of popular Taiwanese titles at festivals may eventually lead to their theatrical distribution in Japan.

Taiwan cinema: another kind of programming

This investigation of Taiwan cinema in Japan may just be a start to probing the rich discursive tapestries and exhibitionary mechanisms of 'screening Taiwan'. In conclusion, I push the discussion further by highlighting the discursive dimension of festival programming and its inherent politics.

Considering Taiwanese films exhibited at film festivals in Japan – as part of the international festival programme or from the cultural exchange repertoire – I suggest they do not necessarily register a unified, single project of enhancing Taiwan's cultural prowess overseas. Neither do the film texts offer one monolithic imaginary of Taiwan as a small nation. For one thing, the multiplicity derived from narratives and identities cannot be easily integrated into Taiwan's national, cultural and social history. For instance, they may exemplify 'other senses of belonging besides the national' in engaging the lesbian, gay, bisexual and transgender (LGBT) identities and other transgressive sexuality and gender issues (Higson 2006: 17–18), as testified by the Taiwanese entries selected by the Tokyo Gay and Lesbian Film Festivals (ROC Diplomatic Missions 2013). Also, they might deal with the 'contingency or instability of the national' by foregrounding the experiences of the exiled and diasporic communities, as well as displaced subjects (Higson 2006: 17–18). If the Taiwan New Cinema movement directly links to the emergence and recognition of the cinema of a small nation, we have to realise that such a manifestation is also premised on film festivals' multiple framings and contains within itself the dissatisfactions of the national.

Malaysian Chinese filmmaker Tsai Ming-liang, a second wave TNC auteur and an international arthouse darling, contributes to Taiwan cinema less because of the popularity that his works enjoy on the island than because his festival profile is believed to have boosted the cultural profile of Taiwan. Not Taiwanese, Tsai has been passionately promoted by the ROC cultural authorities as Taiwan's auteur. Moreover, while Taipei-based Burmese filmmaker Midi Z (a.k.a. Zhao Deyin) is featured in the brochure on Taiwan cinema distributed for free at major international festivals,[22] we might want to think twice about whether a critical framework of national cinema is adequate for us to engage with his layered diasporic experiences as a Chinese descendent whose family migrated to Burma from south-west China, and as a 'first' Burmese independent filmmaker whose works are obsessed with the impossible homecoming back to Burma. Through these multiple 'screening Taiwan' projects, we could locate Taiwan at the join of these diversified, contesting narratives and identities, and come to see Taiwan in its multiplicity and contesting self-definition.

Notes

1 This work was supported by JSPS KAKENHI Grant Number 15K16665.
2 The KMT government gave Hong Kong-made Mandarin movies the status of 'national film' in order to generate support for the ROC from the Hong Kong film industry (Lee 2012: 170).
3 As declared on its website, the TGHFF strategically positions itself as 'encouraging the development of Chinese-language films'. Opening its stage and awards to films 'made by Chinese internationally' including those from the PRC, the TGHFF triggered many controversies (Lee 2012: 172). For the website of the TGHFF, please see: www.goldenhorse.org.tw/aboutus/about/ (accessed 30 April 2016). For the controversies, please see Bloom (2012).
4 Hou Hsiao-hsien's 'Taiwan trilogy' refers to *A City of Sadness* (*Beiqing chengshi*, 1989), *The Puppetmaster* (*Ximeng rensheng*, 1993) and *Good Men, Good Women* (*Hao nan hao nu*, 1995).
5 In this chapter, all the translations of Japanese and Chinese into English are the author's own unless otherwise indicated.
6 For more on the GIO's film law, see Yeh and Davis (2005: 67). The GIO launched policies in 1983 to provide cash awards to 'excellent' national films. For instance, for the officially selected Taiwanese entries in the 28th Asia-Pacific Film Festival (taking place in Taipei), the GIO promised to offer NT $10.1 million (*c.* US $310,000) if they won the festival prize for Best Film (Yamashita et al. 2014: 91–92).
7 Hou Hsiao-hsien's *The Boys from Fengkuei* (*Fenggui lai de ren*, 1983) won the Grand Prix at Nantes in 1984. Edward Yang's *Taipei Story* (*Qingmei zhuma*, 1985) won an International Federation of Film Critics Award at Locarno in 1985.
8 This revision of policies in 1987 laid the basis for the 'Enforcement Directions Governing the Provision of Incentives and Guidance to the Motion Picture

Industry and Industry Professionals Participating in International Film Festivals', launched in 1992 (Lim 2013: 156). The ROC government divided international film festivals into four categories and offered local filmmakers who wished to attend different levels of financial support and awards depending on the category of festival.

9 The ban was imposed in 1974, two years after Japan and the PRC signed the Joint Communiqué and established a formal diplomatic relationship.

10 According to Li (1992: 63), the PRC and Japan reached an agreement in 1977 that a 'Film Week' for Chinese cinema would be launched in Japan annually and an exhibition of new films from the PRC would be organised every two years.

11 In 1987, Tokyo's Studio 200, a multi-functional space dedicated to contemporary art and run by the Seibu Department Store, launched two sessions of a 'Taiwan New Cinema Young Filmmakers Special'. With a line-up of ten titles, this Special recycled a number of pre-Taiwan New Cinema, award-winning works in addition to two features plus one short film by Hou Hsiao-hsien (ROC Diplomatic Missions 2013: 8).

12 Since the dissolution of the GIO in 2012, some of its functions have been absorbed by the Ministry of Culture (inaugurated in May 2012) and others have been transferred to the Ministry of Foreign Affairs (MOFA), resulting in the creation of two new units within MOFA, i.e. the Department of International Communication and the Coordination Council for Public Diplomacy.

13 This model could be compared with the China Film Week and China-Japan Film Festival which have been routinely run and supported by the PRC's cultural authorities as central to the state's soft power strategies.

14 The Taipei Cultural Centre Tokyo was established in 2010 and was operated by the TECRO. Upon its relocation in 2015 to its new Tokyo office at Toranomon, its title was changed to the Taiwan Cultural Centre.

15 For more information about the Takada-based 2015 Taiwan Film Festival, see taiwan-film-fest-in-takada.appspot.com/ (accessed 25 May 2016, in Japanese).

16 In 1994, the Chinese city of Zhuhai, one of China's designated Special Economic Zones, hosted a film festival to showcase films from the mainland, Hong Kong and Taiwan, the first time in the PRC's history. This occurred even though an official delegation from the PRC had to cancel their visit to Taiwan. In 1995, over 90 filmmakers from the three locales participated in a symposium in Taipei (Yamashita et al. 2014: 114–115).

17 In contrast, the early 2000s witnessed the outburst of '*Hallyu*' (Korean Wave), namely the boom of South Korean popular culture in Japan.

18 Initiated as a biennial festival between 1985 and 1991, the TIFF has been held annually since 1992.

19 According to Zhu and Robinson (2010: 153), Tian's ban was lifted in 1996, but he did not make his next film, *Springtime in a Small Town* (*Xiaocheng zhi chun*), until 2002.

20 My email correspondence with Ishizuka in June 2016.

21 Edward Yang passed away in 2007.

22 See the '2014 Taiwan Cinema' (*Dianying guojishichangzhan shouce*), a publicity brochure produced by the ROC Ministry of Culture and Taipei Film Commission. It is available for download from www.taiwancinema.com/ct_70360_313 (accessed 20 November 2015, in Chinese).

6 Programming Taiwan cinema

A view from the international film festival circuit

Brian Hu

For me, Taiwan cinema was first a film festival concept. Like many viewers based outside Asia, I first encountered Taiwanese films as an organising principle at festivals that played new productions by Hou Hsiao-hsien, Tsai Ming-liang, Edward Yang, Chang Tso-chi, Lin Cheng-sheng, and Cheng Wen-tang. The obsession with nations and discovering national cinemas meant festivals categorised these directors as hailing from Taiwan, an island with an otherwise tenuous relationship with nationhood, and for whom naming had tremendous symbolic significance. Film critics and scholars circling festivals followed suit, proclaiming Taiwan as a new cinematic superpower, searching for thematic and formal coherences along national lines. The 'Taiwan cinema' banner at film festivals flew in contrast to categorisations seen elsewhere. In the US arthouse and academic worlds, such films may have been filed under 'non-Western cinema', 'Third Cinema', 'Asian cinema', or 'Chinese cinema'. In my Taiwanese immigrant home in the 1990s, they would have been called *guopian*, a tricky category that conflated 'national cinema' with 'Mandarin cinema' (which includes Mandarin-dubbed Hong Kong films), without ever having to evoke 'Taiwan' at all (also see Ma in this volume). No, it was at a film festival where Taiwan cinema first sharpened to a focus for me, leading me to more questions about the specificity of such films, as well as inspiring me to think about these films in relation to my own family history. For a Taiwanese American cinephile, film festivals triggered not only a national cinema, but my own cinematic consciousness of nation as it related to my family. It was an exciting opportunity to say the least.

That said, burdensome terms like 'nation' and 'international', a badge of cultural capital at many of these 'international film festivals', made the relationship between festivals and Taiwanese and Chinese-language cinemas a suspicious one. At least as early as 1980, when former Bollywood actress Nargis lodged an attack against international festival darling Satyajit Ray for 'exporting poverty', commentators have been suspicious about the ways film festivals in Europe and America feed into Western ideals of 'Third World' nationhood or cater to Orientalist notions of Asia. Some, like Yingjin Zhang (2002: 31–33), observed the phenomenon of filmmakers consciously or unconsciously producing works that cater to international film festivals and the awards they bestow.[1] This perspective, that Western film festivals selectively produce and encourage skewed notions of national cinemas, as Chan (2011) has argued, pervades beyond academic circles and, in a place like Taiwan, became the dominant way to discuss local films to the point that '*guopian*' and 'Taiwanese film' became synonymous with 'festival film' and 'box-office poison' (also see Mello in this volume). Thus international film festivals and their awards became suspect as agents of Westernisation and cultural imperialism, and threats to Taiwan's own national self-definition and its filmmakers' own artistic freedom.

With the rise of scholarly interest in film festivals within cultural and global studies, as well as the rise of a film festival research subfield in cinema and media studies, came greater notice of the political, economic and cultural roles that international film festivals play within transnational and national contexts. While many excellent studies have emerged discussing the relationship between organising festival and city – or national development, or the new opportunities for subcultural public spheres – studies of film festival programming specifically have so often started with the simplistic idea that programming is cultural gatekeeping.[2] In this formulation, the film festival programmer takes the entirety of cinema (or in our case, national cinema) and filters it for the festival audience. Publicly, this filtering happens under the mantra of cinematic excellence; privately, this filtering reveals embedded ideological agendas rarely in touch with the reality outside the cosmopolitan space of the film festival.[3] As a filter of cinema, film festival programming is, according to this view, above all a subtractive process that at best properly reflects the entirety of cinema (or of a national cinema, if that is our focus), and at worst is a toxic form of self-perpetuating Western ethnocentrism.

With regard to Taiwan, this 'filter' view on programming national cinema is difficult to sustain. While it produces more films than some nations, Taiwan still makes relatively few per year, and with such a small sample size, it is hard to argue that not including one film in a festival slate alters a representative picture of what Taiwan or Taiwanese cinema can be. Moreover, with Taiwan's 'national' character itself subject to debate, it is wrong to expect a film festival programme to reflect it. In this chapter, I propose another strategy to programming Taiwan, one developed from years as a festival attendee, journalist, juror, and now head of programming for the largest regular showcase of Taiwanese cinema of any film festival outside Asia. Following the work of Shih and Liao (2014: 4), I call for an approach to festival programming that is less beholden to the positivist pressures of accurate reflection and representation, and instead engaged creatively with the de-familiarising, re-orienting, even entertaining possibilities of cultural imagination. Under this approach, the curator is not simply a gatekeeper of culture, but an animator of it, bringing to life ideas about culture and preparing it in a way so it can be seen anew. I would add too that the myth of gatekeeping is also one perpetuated by festivals themselves, shrouding programming in an air of power, elitism and privileged access to mystify the selection process and solidify their positions of authority. Instead, I argue that animating culture through festival programming is rarely the work of a single curator – certainly not in the United States, where film festivals cannot rely on state funding – and is necessarily the joint work of a community of supporters and collaborators. These partners too do not simply act as additional sieves in the filter; rather they help set the infrastructure and stage for a collective act of world-building and cultural imagining.

The Taiwan film showcase at the San Diego Asian Film Festival

My experience working with such partners to programme Taiwanese cinema grew in 2012 while I was the artistic director of the San Diego Asian Film Festival (SDAFF). As one of the largest showcases of Asian cinema in North America, SDAFF was already programming films from Taiwan in its regular festival line-up, often with some financial assistance from the Taipei Economic and Cultural Office (TECO) of Los Angeles. Concurrently, University of California San Diego professors Ping-hui Liao and Charles Tu, who represented the University of California, San Diego (UCSD) Taiwan Studies Lecture Series and the UCSD Chuan Lyu Endowed Chair in Taiwan Studies, were hoping to hold a Taiwan Film Festival with TECO support. Instead, the three parties (SDAFF, TECO, UCSD) decided to join forces to ensure curatorial excellence, maximise financial support, provide venue access, produce campus programming and amplify community prominence. The Taiwan Film Festival would thus become the Taiwan Film Showcase, a three-day subsection of the San Diego Asian Film Festival. It would be held at UCSD during the larger film festival, it would have its own opening film and reception, its films would be considered official selections of the San Diego Asian Film Festival, and its screenings would be integrated into all SDAFF marketing materials.

Previously, films from Taiwan at SDAFF would be labelled as from 'Taiwan' and would screen alongside many other films labelled by their home nation. On the other hand, the Taiwan Film Showcase highlighted the act of naming. If this was a time when film festivals like Venice were obscuring the name 'Taiwan' from its festival catalogues to cater to mainland Chinese sensitivity over the idea of Taiwanese nationhood, this joint venture between TECO, UCSD and SDAFF ensured that 'Taiwan' would not only be named the way any other nation would be named on the map of world cinema, but that the discursive act of naming Taiwan would itself be foregrounded as appropriate and normalised nomenclature. In fact, no other national cinemas at SDAFF had their own section in this way. In 2012, TECO's film support operated out of the Press Division of Taiwan's Government Information Office (GIO).[4] Their primary goal was discourse production by the event organisers, by the press, by audience members. The creation of a Taiwan Film Showcase would encourage additional mentions of Taiwan on the festival website, press releases and marketing materials. In addition, as part of the deal, TECO required SDAFF to produce an essay about Taiwan cinema to supplement the film line-up, though I found it less an obligation than a paid opportunity to do what any good curator should: contextualise, frame and give significance to the slate of programming. UCSD's Liao and Tu also required the Showcase to invite filmmaker guests from Taiwan, as well as for the Showcase to be free for UCSD students, faculty and staff. Again, for me, as a festival organiser, their arrangements for more guests and deeper audience outreach was more a blessing than a requirement. The collaboration made a lot of sense from a curatorial perspective. The three days' worth of scheduling slots gave me the liberty to delve more deeply into the diversity of Taiwanese cinema than I perhaps would have been able to. The festival laurels promised by a prominent festival like SDAFF ensured that UCSD could attract the newest and most prestigious films and filmmakers. TECO provided not only financial support, but also tapped into their own regional networks of Chinese-language media.

On the curatorial end, both TECO and UCSD gave me plenty of space to research, select and schedule films independently. That said, their presence did not recede into the background. TECO was mostly concerned with the presentation of the programme – specifically that 'Taiwan' was foregrounded and that the governmental agencies (which later morphed into the Taiwan Academy of Los Angeles and the Taiwan Ministry of Culture) were appropriately acknowledged. In one early instance, TECO also expressed concern that one of the Taiwanese films' North American distributors, which had well-known ties to mainland China, would be listed as a co-sponsor. Meanwhile, the UCSD side presented itself during programming primarily as an opportunity. University support meant that I could programme well beyond the ignorant white festival-goer, a cliché that feeds the idea that international film festivals simply cater to Eurocentric ideals. On a campus that includes a significant international student population, a significant percentage of mainland Chinese, a sizeable Asian American student body, along with some of the most esteemed scholars of Asian cinema anywhere, meant that I could programme to an informed, curious audience of insiders, outsiders and those in between, like myself. As a programmer, it is liberating to be able to count on this audience to 'get it'. In fact, when Taiwanese films at SDAFF were played once at UCSD and again at the main venue of the festival, the audience award numbers at the UCSD screening would regularly tally higher than those for the screening outside the Taiwan Film Showcase proper, where films tended to be valued vis-à-vis longstanding categories of the international film festival circuit like genre and auteur, rather than social, political or industrial contexts. Programming for UCSD, I worried little about pleasing the lowest common denominator of the so-called 'festival audience' because I could expect a diverse set of stakeholders in Taiwan cinema.

Beyond TECO and UCSD, I also had in mind other partners while programming. From the very beginning, Taiwan cinema scholar James Wicks, who teaches at the San Diego-based Point Loma Nazarene University, has

Figure 6.1 Poster for the 2012 Taiwan Film Showcase at the San Diego Asian Film
Festival
(Source: author)

been a tireless partner in introducing films and leading question and answer (Q&A) sessions, and his enthusiasm and expertise also shaped how I could proceed with programming. Just as important was my consideration for the local Taiwanese community, in particular the Taiwanese American Professionals San Diego chapter and the Taiwanese American Community Center of San Diego, who have regularly supported SDAFF's Taiwanese programming as community partners and audience members. Their presence reminded me that the value of the Taiwan Film Showcase was also to validate a minority culture and language. All of these supporters contributed to a combined imagination of Taiwanese cinema that was necessarily local, regional, transnational and comparative.

Animating an argument

As those possibilities for imagination fell into place, I had a framework for identifying some thematic threads and putting together a programming slate that was meaningful and inspiring to all parties and to myself. During the work of programming, the limitations of simply seeing programming as a 'filter' become most clear, for that perspective discounts the many other tools of curation: juxtaposition, sequencing, de-familiarisation, (re)contextualisation. These tools construct an argument, which media curator and scholar Laura U. Marks (2004) holds as curation's defining goal. For Marks, creating an argument through selection and sequencing not only gives the slate significance and meaning, but is an ethical gesture of respect to artists because it demystifies the selection process. I would add that curating to an argument also provides an essential layer of justification. In the case of programming Taiwanese cinema, an argument helps to answer the central question: 'Why Taiwanese cinema?' Beyond the financial underwriting and the aforementioned opportunities inherent in collaborating on a Taiwan Film Showcase, the film programme begs explanation for naming 'Taiwanese cinema', an explanation that no doubt dovetails with the larger question: 'Why Taiwan?' How do such films legitimise Taiwan – if not as a nation, then as discourse? While no film programme alone can do justice to such weighty questions, collectively they chip away at doubt, inspire other questions and draft a blueprint for further inquiry.

Because TECO used to require festivals to produce essays for the Taiwan showcases they supported, there exists documentation attempting to justify 'Taiwan' at film festivals. For instance, in the 2012 programme booklet for the New York Asian Film Festival (NYAFF), programmers called their slate 'a story about how Taiwanese filmmaking changed for good' (NYAFF 2012: 49), and then introduced to their audience the well-known tale of how Taiwan cinema went from near-obsolescence to new-found glory with the box office success of *Cape No. 7*. That year's essay in the Los Angeles Asian Pacific Film Festival catalogue introduces its Taiwan line-up in much the same way, describing the populist splendour of post-*Cape No. 7* Taiwanese films, including the ones in their festival line-up that year (Wang 2012b).[5] These essays made a case for 'Why Taiwanese cinema now?' and their film programmes breathed life into their answer.

For the San Diego Asian Film Festival's Taiwan Film Showcase, I have space to probe a bit deeper because of our resources to show more films. In 2012 for instance, I paired the 30th anniversary restoration of *In Our Time* (*Guangyin de gushi*, dir. Tao De-chen, Edward Yang, Ke Yi-zheng and Zheng Yi, 1982) with the 2011 omnibus film *10+10* – 20 short films by 20 different Taiwan directors – to show how 'taking stock of the times' has changed across two critical moments of Taiwanese (film) history. The juxtaposition also drew attention to issues of thematic and formalistic diversity, the art of the short film in Taiwan, and the different phenomenological experiences of 'time' itself in Taiwanese cinema.

For the three-day Taiwan Film Showcase in 2015, I dedicated an entire day to making an argument about the growing disaffection of youth in Taiwan, with a consideration for different cinematic approaches to this problem: Jim Wang's comedy *We Are Family* (*Wo men quan jia bu tai shou*, 2015) (about the disposability of children) was followed by Sunny Yu's social realist *The Kids* (*Xiao hai*, 2015) (about cultural mores that alienate teenagers), which was followed by Chang Tso-chi's dreamy *Thanatos, Drunk* (*Zui sheng meng si*, 2015) (about the abjection of young adults). The following day, I changed register and honed in on Taiwan cinema's transnational claims and routes, with an emphasis on transnationality as spectacle. I began with an experimental short film programme that included Taiwan-based, Sinophone Burmese Midi Z's *The Palace on the Sea* (*Hai shang huang gong*, 2014), which tracks the hallucinatory wanderings of South-East Asian woman labourers in Taiwan. That short was followed by Taiwan-based, Sinophone Malaysian Tsai Ming-liang's *No No Sleep* (*Wu wu mian*, 2015), which shadows Lee Kang-sheng's red-robed monk (from Tsai's *Walker* series) as he treks in searing long-takes into an other-worldly Tokyo bathhouse. Those shorts were followed by *Flowers of Taipei: Taiwan New Cinema* (*Guangyin de gushi: Taiwan xin dianying*, dir. Hsieh Chinglin, 2014), a documentary about the Taiwan New Cinema movement that practically ignores the Taiwan context altogether, focusing instead on how its films and filmmakers created ripples in Thailand, Japan, Italy, Argentina, China and elsewhere in a succession of talking-head cameos and international travels. The day ended with a screening of Hou Hsiao-hsien's *The Assassin* (*Nie yin niang*, 2015), Taiwan's Cannes-honoured Academy Award submission that enlivened historical China with a sublime vibrancy never before experienced in cinema. These films were sequenced in Shih and Liao's (2014) spirit of 'comparatising Taiwan', considering Taiwan and its cinema across multiple, crisscrossing lines of global labour, financing, storytelling, appropriation and distribution. The day of films supplemented the Taiwanese language with Burmese, Vietnamese, Thai, Indonesian, Japanese, Italian, Spanish and Tang dynasty Mandarin – as well as the cosmopolitan gesture of silence. However, beyond just stockpiling languages, the programme allowed audiences to consider the ways they bumped into each other (or not) within films and between films. Why Taiwanese cinema? Here, it is because Taiwanese cinema exists in the world, tracing the routes, whether geographic, cultural, economic or emotional, that give meaning to what we mean by the global.

Aside from juxtaposition and sequencing, the Taiwan Film Showcase also allowed us to give one film a special platform with the opening night slot, which typically bestows the film greater visibility and access. Between 2013 and 2015, we programmed opening night films that are frequently considered by both local and foreign observers as being too 'Taiwanese' for the international film festival circuit as a way of de-familiarising Taiwan cinema internationally, as well as a way to give a nod to San Diego's Taiwanese immigrant audience who might prefer such films. In 2013, we opened with *Forever Love* (*A ma de meng zhong qing ren*, dir. Aozaru Shiao and Toyoharu Kitamura, 2013), a comedic homage to Taiwanese-language cinema in the 1960s, and in 2015 we opened with *The Wonderful Wedding* (*Da xi lin men*, dir. Huang Chao-liang, 2015), a pun-heavy, star-studded comedy about cross-straits relations that, due to its incessant Taiwanese jokes, no Chinese audience is meant to appreciate fully.

With their crass localism, these are films that Ma (2015b: 64) would call 'unglobalizable'. Both films have had a difficult time finding audiences outside Taiwan. Our screening of *The Wonderful Wedding* was the film's North American premiere even though it had already had a hugely successful theatrical run in Taiwan and was already available on DVD. After the screening of *Forever Love*, the film's co-director, the Taiwan-based Toyoharu Kitamura, began the Q&A by asking the audience if they even understood the film. His incredulity speaks to Taiwanese cinema's continued dilemma with the international film festival circuit: nobody in Taiwan wants more 'festival films', yet nobody seems to know of any other path to international recognition except through film festivals.[6] Kitamura's question to the audience alluded to that dilemma and then implicated the audience in it: can you understand Taiwan on Taiwan's terms? The answer need not be as simple as yes or no, but if we set up the screening and its opening night slot correctly, it could potentially re-frame what a Taiwanese festival film could be. Here, the films and the Q&As with filmmakers answer the question 'Why Taiwanese cinema?' by proposing that we consider the gaps in what international audiences know about Taiwan to begin with.

In 2014, we opened the Taiwan Film Showcase with a film Taiwanese consider excessively 'local' in its evocation of history, language and sensibility: *Kano*.[7] Yet, the film has 'globalizable' elements that give it some international legibility. It is a baseball film as well as a sports film about underdogs, oppression and teamwork. So we played *Kano* twice at the festival that year, once as the opening film of the Taiwan Film Showcase, and a second time at the main venue of the festival next to films from all countries. Both screenings yielded very high audience award ballot scores. In fact,

Figure 6.2 Poster for the 2016 Taiwan Film Showcase at the San Diego Asian Film Festival
(Source: author)

between the two screenings, *Kano* had the highest average audience score of any narrative film in our entire film festival that year. Significantly, though, the two screenings were framed differently. In the Taiwan Film Showcase, *Kano* was hailed as a quintessentially local Taiwanese film. Director Umin Boya's post-screening Q&A focused almost exclusively on the ways in which the film was rooted in Taiwan's history. At one point he even dug into the ground to mime what he meant by Taiwan's roots. The conversation and the screening celebrated a non-Sinitic, multilingual approach to Taiwan historiography that, in Boya's estimation, spelled something authentically Taiwan, translatable or otherwise. On the other hand, the screening of *Kano* outside the Taiwan Film Showcase was pitched to audiences in a number of other ways. It was of course still called a 'Taiwan' film, but it was also sold as a Japanese-language film, as a cross-cultural baseball movie (alongside another baseball film about overseas Japanese, *The Vancouver Asahi*), and even as an epic alongside other 3+-hour films like Ann Hui's *The Golden Era* (*Huang jin shi dai*, 2014) and Lav Diaz's *From What is Before* (2014). If the first screening contextualised the film as a story of Taiwan's colonial history, the second screening could also contextualise *Kano* as a story about Japan's colonial exploits. The film's alternative framing in the festival opened up other lines of comparison and inquiry.

However, the screening in the Taiwan Film Showcase assured that 'Taiwan' would necessarily be a node in at least one of those lines. As a joint venture between stakeholders in naming 'Taiwan', the Showcase initiated a collaborative conversation about Taiwan on an international film festival circuit notorious for making distorted claims about Taiwan and Taiwanese cinema. While our screening of *Kano* ultimately only represented one imagining of Taiwan, the Showcase more broadly brought multiple imaginings of Taiwan together in a way that does not claim to fully represent all of Taiwanese cinema, but, it is hoped, brings it to life in a spirited, thought-provoking way. Through UCSD's and TECO's resources for filmmaker travel, through UCSD's venue, and through the Taiwanese American audience's presence and questions, the San Diego Asian Film Festival was given a precious space for programming that could open up Taiwan to unfamiliar paths of consideration on the international film festival circuit.

The continued success of the Taiwan Film Showcase speaks to the continued interest in imaginings of Taiwan, based perhaps in audiences' passing curiosity or personal investment in seeing a peculiar nation's 'phantom images' as it struggles with disappearance (Ma 2015b: 6). For this audience, a film festival for Taiwanese films cannot simply be a 'cultural gatekeeper' because Taiwanese culture is necessarily an ongoing work of the imagination. Similarly, the film festival cannot simply be a subtractive 'filter' because it is understood that 'Taiwan' is never a stable, whole and positivist entity to begin with, and so a film programme cannot be taken for granted in the same way Taiwan itself cannot. Given these stakes, film festivals should continue to be essential sites for Taiwanese cinema to be named and framed. The idea that

Taiwanese cinema is a film festival concept is a lot less scary a proposition when festival slates are seen as proposals of an idea rather than representations of a larger corpus. As spaces of comparison and imagination, film festivals can strive to be dynamic spaces for thinking through nation, society, community and the intricacies of global cinema.

Notes

1 For observations on the Taiwan situation, see Wu (2007).
2 Examples are numerous. See for instance Bosma (2015: 8), who writes that 'the core function of the film curator could be described as being a "gatekeeper" or a "cultural intermediary"'.
3 For a more nuanced version of this take on programming, see Rastegar (2012).
4 The GIO was dissolved in 2012 and some of its functions were transferred to the Ministry of Culture (inaugurated in May 2012).
5 My own essay that year was a bit more hesitant to proclaim any cinematic 'renaissance' as the other festival essays did. I introduced the SDAFF line-up by talking instead about the diversity and adaptability of film productions in Taiwan. See Hu (2012).
6 For a discussion of the 'festival film' and its implications, see Wong (2011).
7 Christa Chen of ARS Film Production (Wei Te-sheng's production company) explained to me the difficulties the film faced in terms of international sales and festival play: the film's foreign-sounding English title, its long running time, its lack of stars, its unfamiliar history of Taiwan, and its difficult-to-classify cultural character.

7 Interventions on cultural margins

The case of the Chinese Film Forum UK and the presence of Taiwan cinema in the UK

Felicia Chan and Andy Willis

Whilst movies from Taiwan, particularly the work of auteurs such as Edward Yang, Hou Hsiao-hsien, Tsai Ming-liang and Ang Lee, were once highly prominent at UK film festivals and in independent arthouse or specialised cinemas, today very few Taiwanese films are released in the UK. Indeed, the contemporary films that make up Chinese cinemas in the broadest sense are now worryingly under-released onto the UK specialised cinema circuit, particularly outside London. This has resulted in Taiwan cinema becoming a marginal rather than central component of the British film culture's engagement with East Asian cinema. Since its formal launch in 2009, the Chinese Film Forum UK (CFFUK), a Manchester-based research network comprising the University of Manchester, the University of Salford, Manchester Metropolitan University, the Confucius Institute at Manchester, the Centre for Chinese Contemporary Art (CFCCA, formerly the Chinese Arts Centre) and HOME (formerly Cornerhouse, an arts venue with a three-screen cinema), has sought to make a modest but significant intervention by screening a number of contemporary films from Taiwan that have otherwise not been picked up for UK distribution. The network also contributes to audience development and literacies for these films by organising a number of public-facing events around them. Screenings have included *Cape No.7* (dir. Wei Te-sheng, 2008), *Hotel Black Cat* (*Hei mao da lü she*, dir. Hsu Li-wen, 2010), *You Are the Apple of My Eye* (*Na xie nian, wo men yi qi zhui de nü hai*, dir. Giddens Ko, 2011), and *Salute! Sun Yat-sen* (*Xingdong daihao: Sun Zhongshan*, dir. Yee Chih-yen, 2014). All of these films were received with great enthusiasm by the Manchester audiences that saw them, suggesting that spectators could be cultivated with the appropriate support from institutions whose remit is to develop audiences for specialised cinemas.

Following a reflection on the distribution and exhibition of Taiwanese cinema within the UK and Asian cinema more generally, this chapter will suggest, through a consideration of the work of the CFFUK, a potential model for how academics and programmers working on Taiwanese cinema can, through the development of strategic partnerships, begin to make small but significant interventions in building a broader understanding of Chinese cinemas more generally and of Taiwanese cinema in particular. In the case of the CFFUK this has also meant rethinking the role of film scholars and their activities beyond the confines of their academic institutions, which involves working with filmmakers, venues and international distribution companies and sales agents, not only to bring recent work to wider international audiences, but also to expand the boundaries of academic discourse in the field.

Taiwan cinema in the UK

Song Hwee Lim (2013: 157) describes the present state of Taiwan cinema as a 'bifurcation between Taiwan cinema's international profile and its domestic self-image', between the new wave arthouse cinema that emerged in the late 1980s following the end of martial law in Taiwan in 1987 and the more popular (populist?) cinema spearheaded by *Cape No.7* in 2008. The cultural legacy of Taiwan New Cinema (*Taiwan xin dianying*, TNC) has been long and fairly consistent in the past decades. Lim (2013: 155) points out its continued visibility at international festivals and the number of awards it has won collectively, noting 'just over one award every two years from 1989 to … [early 2012]'. These international awards include those from the three most prestigious international festivals, Berlin, Cannes and Venice (Lim 2013: 154). This form of international recognition has ensured 'the effect of building an auteur status over time' (Lim 2013: 155), and has cemented the reputations of Hou, Tsai and Yang as auteurs of a cinema from Taiwan. These films have been argued to speak to Taiwan's internal and external struggles and reflect its national 'ethos of sadness' (Wu 2005: 76). TNC thus can be said to have often successfully married elements that appeal to an international arthouse market – that is filmmaking driven by an auteurist sensibility and films that can be potentially read as national allegories. According to James Udden, the Taiwanese state supported this move to the detriment of its own domestic industry, arguing that 'decades of government policy eventually produced a cinema now almost entirely predicated on art and culture at the expense of any industry whatsoever' (Udden, quoted in Lim 2013: 155). Lim, however, argues for this move as a shrewd exercise in soft power, cinema being 'its most effective diplomatic tool' by a relatively 'small' nation-state like Taiwan (ibid., 155), where even a seat at the United Nations remains out of reach as long as the People's Republic of China (PRC) maintains its diplomatic ties with Western powers.

This festival presence, however, is belied by the relative obscurity of their films in both domestic and international mainstream markets. Taiwanese cinema struggles to find theatrical release domestically, even after having won international film awards and much critical accolade. Ang Lee's *Crouching Tiger, Hidden Dragon* (*Wo hu cang long*, 2000), which saw widespread global success, was an exception. However, Ang Lee cannot technically be said to be a TNC auteur, even though his early trilogy, *Pushing Hands* (*Tui shou*, 1992), *The Wedding Banquet* (*Xi yan*, 1993) and *Eat Drink Man Woman* (*Yin shi nan nü*, 1994), was made with state funding from Taiwan. However, Lim notes that beyond these films, 'Ang Lee has virtually no relation to Taiwan's film industry' (Lim 2013: 156). This argument is based on the fact that although born in Taiwan, Lee has spent most of his adult life and career in the United States working out of New York and Hollywood, the result of this being that, aesthetically and politically, his work cannot be said to share the same concerns as other Taiwanese auteurs, nor can his latter films be naturally considered to be products from 'Taiwan'.

In the UK, despite numerous festival awards, Taiwan cinema remains relatively unknown and unfamiliar compared to the Chinese cinemas from mainland China and Hong Kong (and one might argue that recently even these are not particularly well known). In her report on the CFFUK's 2012 symposium on 'The Distribution and Exhibition of Chinese and Asian Cinema', Ming-yeh T. Rawnsley sums up what she calls a 'curious' scenario. She notes that the 'apparent global popularity of East Asian films does not correspond with the daily experiences of viewers in the UK', even though 'we know that Chinese and Asian films are proliferating and many Asian governments and film companies have established a variety of mechanisms to help their films reach audiences worldwide'. Yet 'the greater visibility of Asian cinema in the international arena does not necessarily translate into improved accessibility to Chinese and Asian films in UK cinemas' (Rawnsley 2013: 535). Part of the problem is that such films hardly get a sustained theatrical release in the UK and most are not easily available on DVD or other home media formats or platforms either. This lack of visibility and thus awareness of these films for UK audiences, even among the 'specialised cinema'[1] market, in turn contributes to a lack of demand for them and thus fuels the reluctance of distributors and exhibitors to take greater risks in releasing and programming them.

Table 7.1 broadly indicates the films from Taiwan that have seen a theatrical release in the UK since 1987.[2] This list is not comprehensive and is based on information gathered from *Monthly Film Bulletin* and *Sight & Sound* magazines published between 1987 and 2015.[3] It also does not cover festival releases, re-releases or retrospectives, although it does include co-productions where Taiwan is cited even though the film may not conventionally be identified as a 'Taiwan film'. In addition, the data gathered do not indicate where in the UK they were released, although it is reasonable to assume that a large number of them would have been released primarily in London venues, notably the Institute of Contemporary Art (ICA), with sporadic screenings in venues such as regional film theatres and independent arthouse cinemas in other cities in the UK. Nonetheless, even when it comes to familiar directors, the relative paucity of the selection should be noted: eight of Hou's 21 films, three of Yang's eight, and five of Tsai's 11. In September 2015, the British Film Institute (BFI) hosted an international touring retrospective (it had played in Madrid prior to landing in London) at their South Bank complex of all of Hou's works, including those that have not seen a subtitled DVD release into UK markets, partly in anticipation of his new martial arts film, *The Assassin* (*Nie yin niang*, 2015, Taiwan/China/Hong Kong/France), for

Table 7.1 Taiwan films released in the UK from the mid-1980s (compiled by Fraser Elliott)

Films	Year of theatrical release in the UK	Available on UK DVD
A Summer at Grandpa's (*Dongdong de jiaqi*, 1984, dir. Hou Hsiao-hsien, Taiwan)	1987	No
A Time to Live and a Time to Die (*Tongnian wangshi*, 1985, dir. Hou Hsiao-hsien, Taiwan)	1988	No
The Terrorizers (*Kongbu fenzi*, 1986, dir. Edward Yang, Taiwan)	1989	No
Daughters of the Nile (*Niluohe nü er*, 1987, dir. Hou Hsiao-hsien, Taiwan)	1989	No
A City of Sadness (*Beiqing chengshi*, 1989, dir. Hou Hsiao-hsien, Taiwan)	1990	Out of production. VHS by Artificial Eye; no DVD release
Dust in the Wind (*Lianlian fengchen*, 1986, dir. Hou Hsiao-hsien, Taiwan)	1990	No
A Brighter Summer Day (*Gulingjie shaonian sharen shijian*, 1991, dir. Edward Yang, Taiwan)	1993	No
The Wedding Banquet (*Xi yan*, 1993, dir. Ang Lee, Taiwan/USA)	1993	No until 2015*
Eat Drink Man Woman (*Yin shi nan nü*, 1994, dir. Ang Lee, Taiwan)	1995	No until 2015*
The River (*He liu*, 1997, dir. Tsai Ming-liang, Taiwan)	1998	No
A One and a Two (*Yi yi*, 2000, dir. Edward Yang, Taiwan/Japan)	2000	Yes (ICA)
Crouching Tiger, Hidden Dragon (*Wo hu cang long*, 2000, dir. Ang Lee, Taiwan/Hong Kong/USA/China)	2001	Yes
What Time is it There? (*Ni nei bian ji dian?* 2001, dir. Tsai Ming-liang, Taiwan)	2001	No
Millennium Mambo (*Qianxi manbo*, 2001, dir. Hou Hsiao-hsien, Taiwan)	2001	Yes
Beijing Bicycle (*Shiqisui de danche*, 2001, dir. Wang Xiaoshuai, France/Taiwan/China)	2002	Yes
Blue Gate Crossing (*Lan se da men*, 2002, dir. Yee Chih-yen, Taiwan)	2004	Yes
Three Times (*Zuihao de shiguang*, 2005, dir. Hou Hsiao-hsien, Taiwan)	2006	Yes
I Don't Want to Sleep Alone (*Hei yan quan*, 2006, dir. Tsai Ming-liang, Malaysia/Taiwan)	2007	Yes

Films	Year of theatrical release in the UK	Available on UK DVD
The Wayward Cloud (*Tian bian yi duo yun*, 2005, dir. Tsai Ming-liang, Taiwan)	2007	Yes
Flight of the Red Balloon (*Le voyage du ballon rouge*, 2007, dir. Hou Hsiao-hsien, France)	2008	Yes
Lust, Caution (*Se jie*, 2007, dir. Ang Lee, USA/China/Taiwan)	2008	Yes
Red Cliff (*Chi bi*, 2008, dir. John Woo, China/Hong Kong/Japan/Taiwan/South Korea)	2009	Yes
Reign of Assassins (*Jian yu*, 2010, dir. Su Chao-pin and John Woo, China/Hong Kong/Taiwan)	2013	Yes
Stray Dogs (*Jiao you*, 2013, dir. Tsai Ming-liang, Taiwan/France)	2015	Yes
Exit (*Hui guang zou ming qu*, 2015, dir. Chienn Hsiang, Taiwan)	2015	Yes
Our Times (*Wo de shao nü shi dai*, 2015, dir. Frankie Chen, Taiwan)	2015	(on theatrical release, November 2015)

Note: *Released as part of an Ang Lee Trilogy box set by Altitude Film Distribution together with Pushing Hands (Taiwan 1992).

which Hou took the Best Director award at Cannes. Valentina Vitali has noted the disparity between the (lack of) availability of Hou Hsiao-hsien's films on European cinema screens and the elevation of their cultural capital in European exhibition cultures underpinned by festival reviews and cinema journals (Vitali 2008; also see Vitali in this volume), and her findings may be easily extrapolated and applied to the other TNC auteurs as well. For those attuned to film festival news and world cinema releases, these names and titles may be 'known' but how often and how widely are they 'seen'?

If the auteurist cinema from Taiwan struggles for visibility in UK markets, its popular cinema is all but unknown. The global success of *Crouching Tiger, Hidden Dragon* may be read as an exception, especially as it was an international co-production and backed by the marketing machinery of Sony Columbia Pictures. However, in reality, while having received some Taiwanese investment, *Crouching Tiger* is rarely thought of as a 'Taiwanese' film, apart from when the birth nationality of its director is factored in. As noted in a number of chapters in this volume, and as the year's top-grossing film at the domestic box office, Wei Te-sheng's *Cape No.7* is credited with resuscitating the waning confidence of Taiwan's film industry. According to Lim, '*Cape No.7* has done for Taiwan cinema within its domestic market what *Crouching Tiger, Hidden Dragon* did for transnational Chinese cinemas on a global scale: both smashed box office records and injected a new confidence in their products in their respective markets and audiences' (Lim 2013: 157). It was, as Lim puts it, 'a domestic miracle' (ibid., 157). This domestic success, while it did little to raise the profile of Taiwan films in the West, 'led the way in shifting the self-image of Taiwan cinema from the auteur-centered, film-festival participating, domestic-audience-alienating TNC period of the 1980s and 1990s, to a post-TNC period in the new millennium marked by a more popular mode of filmmaking that aims to appeal to a wider audience' (Lim 2013: 158). For the CFFUK, of which the authors are founding members, the timing of the release of *Cape No.7* coincided happily with the formal launch of our research network in the spring of 2009.

The Chinese Film Forum UK

The formation of the CFFUK emerged out of sporadic and informal conversations between a number of Film Studies academics based at the different Manchester universities and film programmers based at Cornerhouse, Manchester's leading multi-arts venue at the time. When it became apparent that our interests in Chinese cinemas were intersecting, we established a network to address a number of issues we saw facing the distribution and exhibition of East Asian cinemas more generally, and Chinese cinemas in particular, within the UK. Central to the CFFUK's operations was a desire to raise not just the profile of these cinemas with audiences, but also to contribute to and expand the debate around both independent and popular filmmaking in Chinese-language cinema, as well as exploring Chinese cinemas from the wider diaspora.

This work was supported by a research networking grant from the Arts and Humanities Research Council (AHRC) and, crucially, close collaboration with other cultural partners with whom a number of strategic relationships have been developed. As noted above, the core network comprises representatives from the three universities across Greater Manchester (the University of Manchester, Manchester Metropolitan University and University of Salford), alongside those from the Confucius Institute at Manchester, the Centre for Chinese Contemporary Art (formerly Chinese Arts Centre) and HOME (formerly Cornerhouse), which critically for the work of the CFFUK now includes five independently programmed cinema screens. Over the years, further collaborations have taken place with a number of festivals and events within Manchester and beyond, such as the Abandon Normal Devices (AND) festival, where an independent Chinese animated feature *Piercing 1* (*Ci tong wo*, dir. Liu Jian, 2010) was screened in the presence of the director; the Asia Triennial Manchester; the Manchester Literature Festival; the Pan-Asia Film Festival in London; and Manchester University's Sexuality Summer School. Beyond these, working relationships have been established with the Hong Kong Economic and Trade Office, and the Taipei Representative Office in the UK, as well as the regional representatives of UK Trade & Investment (UKTI). These partners have offered support by way of funding for film premieres, acquisitions and shipping, as well as hospitality for visiting speakers and filmmakers, whose availability for question and answer (Q&A) sessions and master classes accompanying screenings have been central to the CFFUK's efforts to cultivate audiences' knowledge and understanding of Chinese cinemas in the broadest sense. Other support for such public-facing events has been offered in kind, in the form of one-hour talks and pre-screening introductions setting out the contexts for understanding the films which may be unfamiliar to audiences, and the organisation of Q&A sessions with visiting directors and producers.

These activities now form the core practice of the CFFUK, but it is worth noting that when *Cape No.7* was first screened for Manchester audiences in 2009, its programming was still wholly an experiment. The CFFUK was formalised in April 2009, and was looking for a suitable film for its first formal screening in May the same year. At the time, *Cape No.7* had been reported in the UK film industry press and East Asian newspapers to have broken box office records in Taiwan and parts of East Asia, as well as winning a number of prestigious Golden Horse awards (*Jin ma jiang*). As a popular Taiwan film, it was also unexpectedly given the 'green light' for a release in mainland China (Yu 2009), and was to be distributed by the state-owned China Film Group (Kuipers 2008).

Aesthetically and thematically, the film was well placed to facilitate what the CFFUK was setting out to do in Manchester, for whose audiences the cinema and cultural politics of Taiwan were relatively unknown. First, as a popular, even populist film, *Cape No.7* sets itself apart from the aesthetics and style of the TNC, whose films at any rate would have likely been known only to a niche audience. Where the TNC films were frequently slow-moving, meditative and set in the urban malaise of Taipei, *Cape No.7* was fast-paced, filled with colourful characters and concluded with the feel-good triumph of a community concert in the coastal town of Hengchun. Cultural knowledge was not crucial to engaging with the film: the historical romance, especially of the lost letters, was poignant, and the comic band of misfits attempting to form a rock group is a familiar trope in mainstream Western cinema, such as *The Commitments* (dir. Alan Parker, 1991) and *School of Rock* (dir. Richard Linklater, 2003). Yet, there was sufficient socio-political content in *Cape No.7* that it could speak to audiences of 'world cinema' within the UK. A blogger on Chinese cultural affairs for the West, Peter Zarrow, refers to *Cape No.7* as 'an energetic bon-bon of a film': 'Light romantic comedy with an edge of tragic love lost. And above all, let's all rock together – Hoklo, aborigines, young and old, Japanese – even an energetic Hakka! – invited into the mix' (Zarrow 2009). 'Hoklo' (also known as 'Min' or 'Hokkien') refers to the Chinese dialect spoken by many native Taiwanese, a language sometimes invoked consciously as a marker of identity distinguishing itself from Mandarin as the official national language of both Taiwan and the PRC. However, as the specifics of local linguistics and cultural politics in Taiwan may not have been evident to Manchester audiences, the screening was accompanied by a set of film notes written for (then) Cornerhouse by Ming-yeh T.

Rawnsley. The notes, which remain available for download on the HOME website, outlined a brief history of Taiwan, its former colonial relationship to Japan and its multilingual communities, alongside a brief introduction to the characters in the film, their ethnic origins and the actors who play them (Rawnsley 2009a). All this background information is useful and enables audiences to take in the wider contexts of the film beyond its baseline story and be introduced to Taiwanese popular culture and its intersections with East Asian popular culture more broadly. For instance, it is unlikely that Manchester audiences would have recognised Van Fan, the actor who plays the lead role of Aga, as a well-known pop singer in East Asia who had a hit with the theme song 'I Believe', for the Korean romantic comedy *My Sassy Girl* (dir. Kwak Jae-young, 2001). *My Sassy Girl* was a major hit in most East Asian markets of South Korea, Japan, Hong Kong and Taiwan as well as in South-East Asia, and has spawned a number of remakes and sequels. Nor would it have been evident to Manchester audiences that Van Fan is also descended from one of the 16 officially recognised aboriginal tribes in Taiwan, whose casting in the leading role conspicuously foregrounds the multiplicities of Taiwanese identities beyond Taiwan's historical confrontation with mainland China. Maggie Lee of *The Hollywood Reporter* writes that 'the film gives too much screen time to each minor character, which makes the narrative very spread out, [but] its guileless charm makes one overlook its flaws' (Lee 2008). However, these minor characters testify to the range of local identities all too frequently subsumed by the broad national narrative sweeps of Taiwan's historical hostilities with the PRC. Lee herself notes that '[t]he characters, though caricatured for comic effect, are pulled straight out of Taiwan provincial life, including a Chinese banjo player in his 80s and an aboriginal who keeps breaking into indigenous folksong' (Lee 2008). Significantly, in the film it is Fan's character, Aga, who symbolically re-establishes relations with Japan through his return of the love letters, his relationship with Tomoko (Tanaka Chie's character), and his duet with the Japanese pop star (Kousuke Atari as himself), but only after having rejected the draw of Taipei, returned to Hengchun and formed a fraternity with other locals, including another aboriginal character, Lao-ma (played by Min-hsiung), and the comic 'Mala-sun' (played by Ma Nien-hsien), from the Hakka community (constituting about 20 per cent of the population in Taiwan). To a degree, it is not necessary for UK audiences to be able to read all the cultural nuances within the film to access the story, but providing knowledge of it enhances the experience of the film, something that has remained a key component of the cultural interventions proposed by the CFFUK. Thus the choice of *Cape No.7* as the inaugural film for the CFFUK was significant, as the CFFUK was particularly looking to launch the idea that it was interested in working with a wider selection of Chinese films beyond simply those older, established auteur directors with already established international profiles.

The success of *Cape No.7* with Manchester audiences indicated that there was an appetite for Chinese-language and more popular Taiwanese films that could be built upon. The fact that *Cape No.7* did not at the time have UK distribution – the CFFUK had to apply directly to the international sales agent and pay for the screening rights and for a 35 mm print to be sent to the UK – also indicated that relying on prints already available to cinemas within the UK would not be enough for the Forum to achieve its aims. With this situation repeated for films from other parts of East Asia, it was clear the CFFUK would have to be more interventionist in its search for titles that were outside even regular specialised film circulation in order to fulfil its aims of reaching audiences with a wide range of examples of Chinese cinemas. Ultimately, this would mean dealing directly with international sales agents, as the Forum did with Good Films Workshop for *Cape No.7*, in order to bring in prints of films not bought for UK-wide distribution, to screen in Manchester. This more flexible and interventionist approach to securing prints increasingly became central to the programming strategies adopted by the CFFUK.

After *Cape No.7*

Many English-language reviews are aware of the box office success of *Cape No.7* in East Asian markets, but note that it would likely struggle to translate into Western ones. *Variety*, the magazine chronicling developments in the film industry in the United States, cheered on the film's regional success and its 'remake potential', but nonetheless predicted that 'chances of a big bust-out in Western markets look slim' (Kuipers 2008). The success of *Cape No.7* in Manchester in 2009 proved to the CFFUK that popular Chinese films, especially Chinese romances and comedies normally seen to be untranslatable to Western audiences, could be well accepted by Manchester audiences when accompanied by sufficient context and a public engagement programme.

The annual Chinese New Year is one such context. Initially established within Hong Kong cinema when it saw its peak in the 1980s, many of these 'Chinese New Year films' (*he sui pian*) tend to be madcap comedies, satirising (and celebrating) not only aspects of Hong Kong's hyper-modern culture but also its film culture by casting some of its biggest stars in slapstick roles. As commercial film production in mainland China expanded in the 1990s, its most successful director of the period, Feng Xiaogang, established the Chinese New Year film tradition in mainland China with three films: *The Dream Factory* (*Jia fang yi fang*, 1997), *Be There or Be Square* (*Bu jian bu san*, 1998), and *Sorry, Baby* (*Mei wan mei liao*, 1999). By the 2000s, Feng was unrivalled as a box office draw in mainland markets, and in 2010, the CFFUK marked the Chinese New Year in Manchester with the UK premiere of the Chinese mainland box office hit, *If You Are the One* (*Fei cheng wu rao*, dir. Feng Xiaogang, 2008). A contemporary romantic comedy, *If You Are the One* proved something of an eye-opener for some in the audience who were more used to Chinese films that were martial arts extravaganzas, rural melodramas or historical epics. Albeit a celebration of popular, commercial cinema, the strategic programming of these films as a specific cultural intervention into the Chinese film diet of UK film audiences built on the CFFUK's commitment to challenge audiences' expectations by screening as wide a variety of film styles as possible and offering up many facets of Chinese cinemas for viewing.

In the Chinese New Year season of 2013 the CFFUK hosted the UK premiere of one of the most popular Taiwanese films of all time, Giddens Ko's *You Are the Apple of My Eye* (2011), at Cornerhouse. As now was becoming the norm, the screening was accompanied by a public talk on 'Popular Taiwan Cinema beyond the Arthouse' by Felicia Chan. The contextualisation of the film for Manchester audiences in terms of narrative concerns, characterisation and genre, was necessary to frame their viewing experience in an exhibition culture that offered little by way of explanation for character motivations and behaviour. Michael Lyons, Cornerhouse's own staff reviewer at the time, admitted attending the talk to clarify for himself his ambivalent responses to the film. The Chinese 'high school story' bears very little resemblance to its US or UK counterparts, and the 'grating melodrama, complete with a break-up in the rain and syrupy Asian pop music' (Lyons 2013) that he complains about are central to the genre and form of East Asian high school romantic comedies. In the case of *You Are the Apple of My Eye*, the protagonists' nostalgia for their school days and teenage years, rendered in flashback, accentuated memory's capacity for fantasy and reinvention.

The success of the screening of *You Are the Apple of My Eye* at Cornerhouse, albeit a one-off event, reaffirmed the work of the CFFUK in bringing in Chinese films that had not received formal UK distribution to UK audiences. The CFFUK has also extended the reach of its audiences through collaborations with other partners. In 2011, the CFFUK organised special screenings of several Chinese-language films with the Asia Triennial Manchester (ATM) as part of its official film programme. Alongside the UK premiere of Hong Kong action director Dante Lam's *The Stool Pigeon* (*Xian ren*, 2011), and a visit to Manchester by director Derek Kwok to discuss his Hong Kong award-winning local hit *Gallants* (*Da lei tai*, dir. Derek Kwok and Clement Cheng, 2010), the ATM film programme included the off-beat Taiwanese comedy of 2010, *Hotel Black Cat*. The film was Hsu Li-wen's debut and its UK premiere was supported by the Taipei Representative Office in the UK. Hsu's presence at the Q&A that accompanied the screening of the film allowed audiences a rare chance to engage directly not only with a young filmmaker from Taiwan, but also one who was willing to discuss openly the issue of being a female director within the Taiwan film industry. The positive responses to the collaboration with the ATM led to further contributions to the 2014 event. This in turn has resulted in some initial planning and discussions for the film programme for the next ATM to have a focus on twenty-first-century Taiwanese cinema.

The CFFUK will seek, as it has done since its screening of *Cape No. 7* in 2009, to showcase up-and-coming directors and not simply those who are more established internationally on the film festival circuit. The programming of popular cinema – the latest of which was Yee Chih-yen's *Salute! Sun Yat-sen* (2014), a high school heist story set in Taipei – has enabled the CFFUK's programme to be in dialogue with the established, major festival-friendly versions of Taiwanese cinema that are in circulation, albeit through the limited releases of auteur-directed films. For example, *Stray Dogs* (*Jiao you*, dir. Tsai Ming-liang, 2013), theatrically released in the UK in 2015, and Hou Hsiao-hsien's award-winning martial arts production of 2015, *The Assassin*, released theatrically in the UK in early 2016. In an already over-saturated exhibition marketplace, the limited releases of this pair of specialised titles, regardless of how impressive they both are, reveals the continued link between established auteur directors and UK releases. There are small indications of possible changes on the horizon as yet another high school teen romance of 2015 from Taiwan, Frankie Chen's *Our Times* (*Wo de shao nü shi dai*) – noted to have outstripped *Cape No.7* and *You Are the Apple of My Eye* at the Taiwanese and East Asian box offices due to repeated viewings (Ng 2015) – at the time of writing was still enjoying a run at the Odeon and Vue cinemas in the UK over a number of weeks across November and December 2015.

Cultural interventions, critical reflections

Beyond public-facing events, it should be noted that film programming and public engagement activities of the CFFUK are built on academic research into the varieties of Chinese cinemas across different markets, and as part of the terms of the AHRC research networking grant have also organised two symposia and an international conference fostering dialogue between academics, postgraduate students and industry personnel. After all, the Forum itself was originally constituted as a research network among academics and cultural practitioners. Reflecting on his collaboration with Cornerhouse on the *Visible Secrets* programme, showcasing Hong Kong women filmmakers, prior to the formation of the CFFUK, Andy Willis makes the case for 'the curation of film seasons and retrospectives as professional practice and the ways in which this might relate to an academic's research output' (Willis 2010: 161). This approach takes academic public engagement activities beyond classification as merely 'impact pathways' and into 'action research' as cultural intervention with critical outcomes. Mark Haslam (2004: 49) makes a polemic claim for curation and programming as 'tools' that can help shape 'ideas in counterpoint to the increasingly dominant ideologies of the mainstream media juggernauts', asking:

> How do each of us as programmers and curators contribute to the media environments we live in, and what future media environments do we want to play a part in creating? It is tempting for us to sit back and claim that we have no control over what is made, that we are simply at the mercy of the submissions we receive. But we do make choices – of what to screen,

of whom and what to bestow awards on, of what to programme in prime-time slots, of how to frame the works we've selected. Each decision has potentially far-reaching consequences. We should not hide behind an aesthetic veil and deny our responsibilities as members of our society.

(Haslam 2004: 59)

It is the research into the genres, styles and historiographies of Taiwanese cinema that has enabled the CFFUK to enrich its programme, blending both popular films and more traditional art cinema fare. This research also emerges as a direct result of a number of years that the CFFUK has worked with Chinese filmmakers and producers as well as visited film festivals that have showcased their work to get a fuller picture of the current trends and developments. Without this extensive research and its application within the programming, the work of the CFFUK would not offer the depth and variety of new work that has marked its offerings. These small, but vital, cultural interventions made by the CFFUK create a space – crucially – outside the formal distribution and exhibition channels within the UK. The smallness of its size and the manageability of its operations have ensured flexible decision making and rapid response times which have enabled such rarely seen Chinese films, and Taiwanese films in particular, to be seen by UK audiences who would not otherwise have had the opportunity to see them.

Notes

1 This is the term used within the film distribution and exhibition industries to categorise foreign-language and independent films that do not usually find exhibition in mainstream cinemas within the UK market.
2 The authors wish to thank Fraser Elliott for assisting with the table of Taiwan film releases in the UK.
3 *Monthly Film Bulletin* and *Sight & Sound* were published separately until the former was merged with the latter in 1991. Since that date the information is taken from *Sight & Sound.*

Part II

Taiwan cinema and social change

8   Becoming a nation

The shaping of Taiwan's native consciousness in Wei Te-sheng's post-millennium films

Chialan Sharon Wang

Ushering in the renaissance of Taiwan cinema, Wei Te-sheng's films have attracted history-making box office sales. Explanations for Wei's success identify marketing strategies and government funding systems, but discussions also consider political and economic contexts of *Cape No.7*'s release in 2008. Most important are the ambivalent and complex sentiments Taiwanese audiences have about Taiwan's colonial past, namely the 'modernist vs. nativist' literary debate during the 1960s and the 1970s which highlighted divided notions of what constitutes Taiwan's native culture.[1] Capturing viewers with dramatic effects, Wei's two directorial pieces, *Cape No.7* and *Warriors of the Rainbow: Seediq Bale* (2011), as well as *Kano* (2014), which he produced and invited Umin Boya (a.k.a. Ma Zhi-xiang) to direct, reconfigure the colonial past in a way that presents Taiwan's collective memory as a process of reflection on the present.

In these films, historical materials are reinterpreted rather than faithfully represented, and they imagine possibilities of engaging with the past beyond simply invoking sentiments of nostalgia and trauma. This chapter focuses on Wei's two directorial productions, *Cape No.7* and *Seediq Bale* and discusses how the notion of 'return' operates as a trope of immanence and contemplation. As the millennial Taiwan continues to see the development of nativisation (*bentuhua*), the problematic of what is native or national generates ongoing debates. Since the 1990s, many institutional efforts have been made to re-characterise Taiwan's nationhood, including curricular reform to offer courses in Taiwanese vernaculars, revision of historiography to emphasise the centrality of the island, recognition of sovereignty of indigenous groups, and redefinition of Taiwanese literature (Hsiau 2012: 4–19). *Cape No.7* and *Seediq Bale* emerged as products of this particular cultural habitus, to borrow Pierre Bourdieu's concept. Partaking of the localist trend, Wei's films invoke a sense of return. The term 'return' thus connotes several meanings: a temporal movement to the past in order to rediscover the forgotten or the repressed; re-visitation of monuments that document the cultural or social experience of the island; an act of restoring the sovereignty to a community that claims singular cultural practices and historical experience; a tendency or desire to search for a cultural, national or even ethnographic origin. All the implications, in Wei's cinematic narratives, inevitably involve a process of imagination and reinvention of national narrative. Thinking about the inter-linked meanings of 'return', I argue that as *Cape No.7* and *Seediq Bale* con-jure up Taiwan's colonial past, both films dislodge Taiwan's colonial history from a binary opposition between the coloniser and the colonised. In explor-ing an empathetic interpretation of Taiwan's nationhood, the two films generate palimpsest meta-narratives which defer a unified nationhood.

Wei's post-New Cinema: imaging of the past

Having worked closely with Edward Yang[2] and Chen Guo-fu,[3] Wei takes up the materials of Taiwan's local history and develops them with the aesthetic sensibility of commercial films. With elements of mass culture, underdog story-lines and epic sequences, Wei appeals to the local audience through familiar Hollywood formats and melodramatic performances, while attempting an alternative understanding of Taiwan's colonial past.

Underscoring the continuity between Wei's works and those of his pre-decessors, Song-yong Sing (2010) delves into the formal and aesthetic impli-cations of the term 'renaissance' used to refer to the rising ticket sales of domestic films since 2008. Sing points out that instead of indicating a break from film production prior to 2008, the notion of renaissance connotes post-New Cinema's interconnection with and development of Taiwan New Cinema (*Taiwan xin dianying*) of the 1980s. As Sing notes, the relationship between the New Cinema and post-New Cinema is 'continuous, enigmatic, and paradoxical' (Sing 2010: 141). Sing's reading of post-New Cinema films such as *Winds of September* (*Jiu jiang feng*, dir. Lin Shu-yu, 2008), *Orz Boyz!* (*Jiong nanhai*, dir. Yang Ya-zhe, 2008), and *Cape No.7* describes their treat-ment of Taiwan's collective past as an act of transforming the heaviness of history into an enigmatic levity. Taking its cue from Derrida's notion of tele-pathy, his reading discerns the polyphonic and spectral transmission of his-torical memories of these films and underscores post-New Cinema's fluid and multivalent re-presentation of Taiwan's history (Sing 2010: 154–155).

Wei stands alongside his contemporaries and predecessors who draw on the island's local culture and address the experience of lower classes or minority groups. Besides the widely discerned relationship between Wei's works and Taiwan New Cinema, Ivy I-chu Chang also notes an apparent thematic affi-nity between *Cape No.7* and the works of healthy realism (Chang 2015: 247). In the 1960s, healthy realism (*jiankang xieshi*) emerged as a state-sponsored movement. Promoted by the newly appointed director, Gong Hong, of the then state-run Central Motion Picture Corporation (CMPC) as national cinema, healthy realist films adopted the style of Italian neo-realism. How-ever, while directors such as Vittorio De Sica and Roberto Rossellini used on-location shooting and non-professional actors to expose the harsh living conditions of the poor and the lower class in post-war Italy, healthy realist films tapped into the rural and agrarian culture or the working class in an urban milieu in order to present an uplifting and idealised prototype of the hard-working, optimistic and virtuous everyman/woman in Taiwan. Representative works of healthy realism include *Oyster Girl* (*Ke nü*, dir. Li Hsing, 1964), *Beautiful Duckling* (*Yangya renjia*, dir. Li Hsing, 1964), and *Lonely Seventeen* (*Jimo de shiqisui*, dir. Bai Jing-rui, 1967). As opposed to crude and bombarding propagandist films, the melodramatic and approachable genre of healthy realism offered a more palatable national ideology.

Scholars have noticed the thematic parallels between Wei's works and those of his predecessors. Whether dictated by state ideology or motivated by filmmakers' declared resistance against global hegemonic forces, healthy realism of the 1960s and Taiwan New Cinema of the 1980s turned to Taiwan's locality. Nonetheless, the temporal and spatial return to the past in search, whether successfully or in vain, for an idyllic sense of national belonging characterises these two moments of Taiwanese cinema in drastically different ways. For instance, both Guo-juin Hong (2013) and James Tweedie (2013) discuss the intricate relationships and discrepancies between the two trends. They see the New Cinema and healthy realism as two prominent moments when local consciousness emerged as products of and reactions to historical circumstances. As films of healthy realism inadvertently moved away from narratives of a mythical, historical China and tapped into Taiwan's local scenery and culture, Guo-juin Hong points out that a sense of stasis invoked by such a utopian vision of Taiwan's agrarian past ironically ends up playing down, or even repressing, the presence of the state apparatus (Hong 2013: locations 1627–1631).[4] Although healthy realist films, because of their melodramatic nature and commercial appeals, eventually veered away from the nationalist ideology, they nonetheless lacked a critical edge in both film aesthetics and political interventions. As Hong (2013: locations 1295–1297) notes, 'Healthy Realism was a unique cinematized stasis of change, a peculiar condition for a modernizing nation in which the notion of change – progress, movement – is caught in a perpetual state of stagnation wherein film aesthetics is trapped by nationalist ideology'. In his insightful analysis, Hong sees a revitalised effort at contesting the stylistic and thematic paradigm of healthy realism and intervening in Taiwan's social and cultural conditions in the New Cinema. Challenging the style and themes of commercial films, Taiwan New Cinema presents a detached and observational point of view to look at Taiwan's present and past with its long shots and long takes, posing 'questions about Taiwan's history and its cinematic representation' (Hong 2013: locations 1924–1925).

Having learned their trade as apprentices of healthy realism, senior filmmakers such as Li Hsing and Bai Jing-rui, as well as New Cinema auteurs such as Ke Yi-zheng, Edward Yang and Hou Hsiao-hsien, all turned their attention to the past when the island faced dramatic economic and political transitions. Tweedie (2013: locations 3272–3733) notes that the distinctive difference between Taiwan New Cinema and healthy realism lies precisely in their treatment of the past. While healthy realism presents Taiwan's rurality as a pastoral utopia that wards off the rapid, sometimes destructive urbanisation of the island and its gradually isolated international status, Taiwan New Cinema zooms in on the possible grim consequences of such a return. According to Tweedie, the return to the past in the New Cinema, particularly in Hou Hsiao-hsien's early pieces – for example, *The Boys from Fengkuei* (*Fenggui lai de ren*, 1983), *A Time to Live and a Time to Die* (*Tongnian wangshi*, 1985), and *Dust in the Wind* (*Lianlian fengchen*, 1986) – only underscores the vanishing of such a past in Taiwan's vertiginous economic development, globalisation and industrialisation.

In Wei's films, the desire to return operates differently in Taiwan New Cinema and healthy realism. It can be argued that the act of invoking the past (even if it is a stylised and artificial past) and addressing the life of the underclass as a way to make sense of, articulate, as well as construct the present has been a recurrent narrative mode for both individual and collective experiences in the history of Taiwanese cinema. However, while Wei's films weigh in on the shaping of Taiwan's historiography and, as is the case of *Cape No.7* and *Kano*, hold out a sanguine, nearly utopian vision of local community, incongruity and ambivalence inform his works in a way that sets them apart from healthy realist films, whose form and content eventually serve an unambiguous nationalist ideology. In addition, Wei's determination to bring Taiwan's film industry on a par with the scale of Hollywood production and attract domestic audiences back to the theatre for locally made films also distinguishes him from Taiwan New Cinema auteurs.

The revisit of Taiwan's collective memory in Wei's works not only foregrounds the undetermined nature of Taiwan's national status, but more significantly it triggers different public discourses. The native consciousness invoked in Wei's films prompts different readings of what it means to be a Taiwanese who inherits, relates to and appropriates the island's long and tortuous colonial history. In these films, the past is presented as sorrowful, traumatic, and loaded with conflicts and violence, while the portrayal of historical figures, the interaction between fictional characters and history, as well as the anachronistic representation of historical events seem to be geared toward rethinking the present with more tolerance and empathy. In other words, there are moments in Wei's films in which reified representation of ethnic cultures and facile humanism are implied, but a spatial and temporal distance between the present and the past persists, and with such a distance a discursive indeterminacy emerges. I argue that instead of foreclosing the national narrative, such an indeterminacy is an invitation to what Alison Landsberg (2015: locations 347–350) terms an 'affective engagement' activated by historical films.

In her book, *Engaging the Past: Mass Culture and the Production of Historical Knowledge*, Landsberg (2015) compellingly argues for the affective power of mass media in contributing to historical consciousness. Widely drawing on insights of historians as well as thinkers in cultural studies, Landsberg investigates the way in which affect theory[5] could serve as a useful framework to understand the formation of historical knowledge through what Raymond Williams refers to as 'structure of feelings' (Williams and Orrom 1954: 22). Arguing that media of popular culture present another form of engaging with history compared to traditional academic historical studies, Landsberg considers the affect transmitted through historical films as 'a catalyst to a new thought or to action, pressing the individual to process a particular experience intellectually, to grapple with that which has previously been unthought' (Landsberg 2015: location 387). Significantly, Landsberg distinguishes her research from theories based on the notion of identification. She proposes the analytical mode of affective engagement to discern the subjectivity of the viewer in both receiving and processing the affects conveyed through film. Instead of being completely absorbed into the psyche or ideology of characters, the viewer, being touched or moved by cinematic affects, nonetheless recognises a 'personal stake in knowledge about the past [which] can in turn catalyse one's desire to engage in politics, to work against injustices in the present' (Landsberg 2015: location 411).

In light of Landsberg's thoughts on mass media, the emotional effect for the audiences produced by both *Cape No.7* and *Seediq Bale* go beyond the diegetic realm. The emotional intensities in Wei's films saw well-disposed responses in their box office sales. It is precisely such affective responses provoked in the viewer by Wei's films that make impossible the return to a homogenous collective memory, ethnographic origin and national identity. Bringing the domestic audience back to the theatre sparks meta-narratives around these two films and opens up the authorship of Taiwan's colonial history to debates, personal testimonies, cross-generational memory, and revisions of official archives. Moreover, almost as if anticipating the contentious and heterogeneous meta-narratives, formal and diegetic ruptures in the cinematic texts of *Cape No.7* and *Seediq Bale* fracture and deflect the ostensible return both titles seem to promise.

Cape No.7: a line of escape from the orphan complex

In response to Wei's emphasis on the cordial relationship between Japan and Taiwan in *Cape No.7*, critics sometimes discredit Wei's cinematic treatment of Taiwan's history as suppressing the reality of Japan's systematic subjugation of Taiwanese to colonial violence and thus eliding Taiwan's traumatic memory. Debates over such issues began immediately after the film rose to the top of the box office charts and have been addressed by scholarly publications.

Notably, a few years after the release of Wei's *Cape No.7*, Sheng-mei Ma (2015b) provided a fascinating reading of its phenomenon. Ma views the film as a manifestation of an extended 'orphan' psychic state illustrated in Wu Zhuo-liu's 1945 novel, *Orphan of Asia* (*Yaxiya de guer*). Ma interprets Wei's favourable portrayal of the Japan-Taiwan colonial relationship as a wish fulfilment of an abandoned orphan looking for comfort from the imaginary return of his/her parents. According to Ma (2015b: locations 463–467):

Figure 8.1 Cast of *Cape No.7*

What Wei accomplishes is tantamount to an abuse victim whose defence mechanism erases memory of the abuse itself, or to cultural amnesia that forgets past wrongs in favour of present infatuation. Personal unrequited love in Wei comes to compensate for the history of trauma in Wu and fellow authors, as the contemporary Taiwan wishes away bad memories and orphan complex.

Ma's discerning analysis teases out Taiwan's current anxiety over its political and diplomatic isolation predominantly owing to the constant threat from the Beijing government, and implies that the film offers escapism. The levity in Wei's film, as Ma implies, glosses over the identity crisis of the island and plays down, even silences, the colonial trauma with superficial reconciliation in the form of melodrama. The running theme of underdog success in Wei's films apparently captures the island's keen awareness of its dwarfed international and national status.[6] It is also plausible that the wild popularity of *Cape No.7* does reflect the vexed question of how to interpret Taiwan's colonial legacy as well as its troublesome political situation. Nonetheless, to characterise the sanguine presentation of Taiwan's local community as solely an act of amnesia or consolation might perpetuate a totalising discourse which relegates postcolonial cinematic renditions of history to a compulsive perpetuation of victimhood narrative, and overlooks the dynamics of de-territorialisation invoked by *Cape No.7*. Certainly, *Cape No.7* and the other locally made

Taiwanese films that have come out since the late 2000s did not pronounce a manifesto against the neo-colonial power of Hollywood and film production made for mass consumption as did the filmmakers of Taiwan New Cinema, but it is precisely Wei's adoption and re-appropriation of both arthouse and commercial approaches that brings the local audience back to the theatre and generates bottom-up discussions around the meaning of Taiwan's colonial legacy.

Delving into the complex relationship among Taiwan's colonial experience, Japanese popular culture and globalisation, scholarship on Wei's works also proposes more productive readings. While such readings display different degrees of ambivalence about *Cape No.7*, they also discern innovative visions in the film. For example, according to Min-xu Zhan (2010: 176), while the relationships among the band members in the film suggest the tensions among the indigenous, Hakka, Hoklo (also known as 'Min' or 'Hokkien'), and foreign (Japanese) communities, *Cape No.7* also envisions the possibility of a tolerant coexistence of differences. Citing Appadurai, Zhan underlines the political force behind the representation of grassroots and popular culture. He points to the film's subversive potential in enforcing the 'critical act of optical reversal' (Zhan 2010: 175), where local elements in the film contest the hegemonic power of globalisation. In a similar vein, Ivy I-chu Chang (2010: 108) also notes:

> The encounter between the residual colonial reminiscence and the emerging ethnicities in the film *Cape* and its meta-narrative (including the social impact and the heated discussions of the film) disrupt the national allegory told in a unitary nationalist – be it Chinese nationalist or Taiwanese nationalist – narrative, suggesting an alternative way of imagining 'nation'.

Building upon these readings of *Cape No.7*, I want to nuance the temporal and spatial trajectories of the film. Revising the nostalgic sentiments and the lingering sadness about the colonial past, *Cape No.7* at once revisits the colonial legacy and departs from it.

With the motif of undelivered letters, the film unfolds an open-ended trajectory. It begins with two scenes of departure: the Japanese teacher's deportation back to Japan at the Keelung port with his own voice-over reading out his confessional love letters to Kojima Tomoko; and Aga's full-blown frustration with Taipei, which prompted him to get on his motorcycle to return to his hometown, Hengchun. Serving as a lead-in to the narrative, the connection between Aga and the Japanese teacher thus epitomises the recurrent motif of personal encounters with history. Both narratives launch a journey of homecoming, but neither of them arrives at a destination, and the narratives finally converge as Aga opens the letters. Even though Aga does not understand Japanese, the teacher's voice-over comes up almost as Aga's memory in several montages and juxtaposed frames of Aga and the Japanese teacher. In other words, the undocumented past whose existence is only evidenced in the private epistolary confession no longer finds its address in public historical records. It is only re-enunciated through its serendipitous encounter with another individual.

The encounter between the past and the present envisions a community held together with empathy, and along with it various personal appropriations of Taiwan's colonial legacy. As the opening of the film takes the audience back to the end of the Japanese colonisation, rather than performing an exorcism of colonial memory, the development of the narrative underscores the agency of those who either lived through colonisation or inherited the experience. Such agency is performed through characters relating to the legacy under their individual circumstances. Their relationship to history is also inextricably intertwined with a collective embroilment in the global economy. In the film, the influence of globalisation always looms large. The commercial dictates of American and Japanese popular culture as global soft powers inform both the relationship among the characters, and their musical creation and performances. Geographical, racial and national hierarchies as a result of neo-colonialism are ubiquitous in the film: between the northern and southern parts of Taiwan; between the Asian and Western bodies (as seen in the foreign models during the photo shoot); between the Japanese popular cultural agents (Tomoko and the pop star played by Kousuke Atari) and the local Taiwanese; and more importantly, between the invisible conglomerate capitalists behind the build-operate-transfer project and various exploited forms of labour, not least Tomoko herself. As contemporary global hegemony complicates the relationship between Taiwan and its past, the narrative focuses on the way the cultural and capital imports are received and appropriated as a community of difference takes shape.

Two salient examples are the characters Uncle Mao and Lin Ming-chu, Kojima Tomoko's granddaughter as well as Dada's mother. Their critical roles in facilitating understanding between the modern Tomoko and other band members also enable re-articulation of the colonial trauma and revision of the past's meaning. It is Uncle Mao's invitation to Tomoko in Japanese to a wedding banquet that allows Tomoko to participate in the carnivalesque gathering in which cultural and colonial hierarchy breaks down. The banquet provides an opportunity for all the individuals involved in the music performance to reveal their personal stories. Their camaraderie forms after they recognise each other's secret past, and it is Ming-chu's willingness to listen to Tomoko divulging her affection for Aga in Japanese that prompts Ming-chu to mellow out and give away the real address of her grandmother, thus eventually expediting the confrontation of history.

It is crucial that such a confrontation does not offer a closure to Taiwan's past. Although Aga's journey back to Hengchun leads to self-discovery accomplished by his reintegration into society, his reconciliation and love affair with Tomoko nonetheless point toward a possibility of yet another departure. Aga's declaration of love, 'either you stay, or I'll go with you' is at once a validation of such a new-found community built upon the recognition and tolerance of the other, and a refusal to be bound by its geographical confines. In other words, the willingness to travel again is ironically motivated by Aga's new affiliation with the island's past. On the other hand, the Japanese teacher's longing to return to his lover remains unassuaged until his death. Even if the letters are delivered in the end by Aga to the aged Kojima Tomoko, the silence of the latter does not exactly promise a reciprocated nostalgia. Making no attempt at assigning a definitive meaning to the colonial history, the film's presentation of such a re-encounter generates multiple emotions which take the imagination of nationhood onto an uncharted and uncertain path.

If Kojima Tomoko is addressed by both the Japanese teacher and Aga, that is, she is the 'destination' of their homecoming, then her silence is the ultimate break between the present and the past. The historical 'facts' will never be retrieved, but the underlined distance between the past and the present alerts the viewer to the conundrum of Taiwan's nationhood. During the finale of the film, the band's performance of the German tune 'Heidenröslein' brings the narrative to a climax with the montage of the aged Tomoko discovering the letters delivered to her and the young Tomoko searching for the face of the Japanese teacher at the port. Amidst the celebratory chorus of the Taiwanese band, Kousuke Atari, and the children singing, the viewer is actually prevented from accessing Kojima Tomoko's reactions. In this way, the film disavows both a destination in its homecoming trajectory and a unified articulation of the past. The camaraderie established towards the end of the film promises a potential community whose inclusiveness only gestures toward differentiation among individuals, rather than the stabilisation of national identity.

Seediq Bale: indigenous sovereignty and national myth

The temporal and spatial return in Wei's 2011 production *Seediq Bale*, a project started long before the production of *Cape No.7*, complicates the notion of nationhood by centring the historical experience of the marginalised communities in Taiwan. Certainly, *Seediq Bale* is not the first film about the aborigines in Taiwan; neither is it the first film that represents the Wushe Incident of the 1930s[7] on the island. Since the 1980s, a rich amount of literature, print media, films and music have been produced, along with demands for political and social reforms that aim to return sovereignty to the aboriginal groups.[8] Scholarships, documentaries, manuscripts and testimonies of the survivors of the Wushe Incident have also made up a significant corpus of aboriginal studies in both Taiwan and Japan (Zhou 2010). However, Wei's *Seediq Bale* is the first mega-production of an epic about the island's indigenous groups which forays into international film festivals. The levity deployed in *Cape No.7*'s treatment of history is absent in *Seediq Bale*, in which history is presented as a sensational spectacle, particularly through the film's graphic depiction of violence. The act of return is manifested in *Seediq*

Bale in two senses: it is at once a return of sovereignty to the Seediq indigenous group, and a return to a presumed essence of humanity.

A cinematic text that generates multiple readings of history, *Seediq Bale* is also a catalyst of a series of publications that have in their titles the term '*bale*', which means 'real' or 'true' in the Seediq language, and a chain of museum displays of the 'true' Seediq culture. Adapted from Chiu Ruo-long's (1990) comic book and based on Deng Xiang-yang's (1998) non-fiction book as historical reference for the Incident, Wei Te-sheng's *Seediq Bale* represents an attempt to restore the subjectivity of a marginalised group. Working closely with Dakis Pawan (a.k.a. Guo Ming-zheng) as film consultant, Wei demanded his actors deliver lines in both the Seediq language and Japanese to represent historical authenticity. In 2014, a documentary, *Pusu Qhuni* (*Yu sheng: Sai de ke ba lai*, dir. Tang Shiang-chu), a term that refers to the Seediq tribe's location of origin, was released as the third part to the feature *Seediq Bale*. Directed by Tang Shiang-chu and produced by Wei's ARS Film, the documentary consists of interviews with survivors of the Wushe Incident who were relocated by the colonial Japanese government to Chuanzhong Island (now renamed Qingliu) after the event and have been there ever since. In a way, supplementary cultural products and literature generated around the film join the local government's effort in the anthropological taxonomising and appropriating of cultural knowledge (also see Lee in this volume). Quite a few museum exhibitions of the Seediq culture were organised following the release of Wei's film. For example, an exhibition entitled 'Memory of the Seediq' was held in 2011 in Shihsanhang Museum of Archaeology. In the same year, the National Museum of Natural Sciences held a special exhibition of 'Seediq Bale'. Similarly, the National Taiwan Museum held a two-month exhibition entitled 'The Hero Returns: The Seediq Bale Exhibition' in September and October 2011. The National Museum of Natural Sciences newsletter explains that since 'the four-hour film narrative has its limitations', the exhibition aimed to 'present a comprehensive picture of history in the hope that after walking out of the movie theatre, viewers [of *Seediq Bale*] will be able to acquire further understanding of the story [of the Wushe Incident] and its cultural significance' (National Museum of Natural Sciences 2012).[9] Ironically, in the discursive reproductions of 'realness' and emotional impact, what unravels is a multiplication of 'authenticity'. In this sense, an investigation is required into the driving force behind the search for an original truth.

Violence and return to the essence

In the feature film *Seediq Bale*, the tradition of headhunting has been presented graphically to a degree deemed by some critics (including the film consultant to Wei's *Seediq Bale*, Dakis Pawan) as excessive. Yet reviews in favour of the film emphasise the fact that its ambitious yet empathetic vision prompts Taiwanese viewers to rethink the island's national sovereignty. These reviews consider the gruelling scenes of violence to be a faithful representation of history that allows audiences to understand and sympathise with the motives for killing. For example, in an article entitled 'Choosing the way to die: *Seediq Bale* and Taiwan's new memory', En-chieh Chao (2013) praises the commercial film for moving beyond moral dichotomies and taking to task the definition of civilisation, the racist underpinnings of colonial discourses and the operation of cultural hegemony. As Chao (2013) points out, *Seediq Bale* is 'not a story about a "different" culture'; the aim of the film is to 'redefine [what it means to be] and identify with Taiwan, centring the aboriginal communities that were about to be forgotten in the signifying system of the new Taiwanese consciousness'.[10] As the viewer identifies with the anti-colonial struggles of the Seediq warriors, the indigenous history finds its way into Taiwan's mainstream culture as yet another contentious voice. Yet the attempt at ethnographising the Seediq culture itself calls to mind the question posed by Gayatri Spivak (1988): 'Can the subaltern speak?'. The question becomes even thornier when the indigenous groups have repeatedly been misrepresented in the history of Taiwan cinema in support of the Han-centric state ideology.

In *Seediq Bale*, the term 'savage' has been placed in its trailer tagline to combat the inhumane weaponry and discriminatory administration of the 'civilised' imperialist Japanese. In the film, not only is Mona Rudo portrayed as an epic hero, but also his struggle to defend his personal dignity is coterminous with the collective will of the Seediq group to protect its national culture. Delving into the history of indigenous groups as a way to project a country's nationhood has indeed been a common practice in Hollywood films. In her study of Western fascination with primitive cultures, Marianna Torgovnick (2013) defines primitivism as a trope that connotes a modern desire for a utopian return. Such a fantasy for a utopia, she claims, is often mapped onto the North American indigenous communities. As Torgovnick (2013: location 81) notes:

> Primitivism inhabits thinking about origins and pure states; it informs desires for known beginnings and by extension, for predictable ends. Primitivism is the utopian desire to go back and recover irreducible features of the psyche, body, land and community – to reinhabit core experiences.

Such a penchant for seeking an origin untainted by modernity implies an object of fantasy contained and manipulated by knowledge constructed around it from the outside.

In the fantasy of a perennial, exotic other, the primitive origin thus ties human beings back to a cosmic relationship with nature, calling attention to the spirituality of human existence. Torgovnick's insights into a conflation, or inseparability between the organic essence and indigenous cultures in the modern psyche, help illuminate our reading of the driving force behind the Seediq tribe rebellion in Wei's film, the ancestral spirit (or *utux* in the Seediq language). It also sheds light on the extent to which the Seediq tradition of returning to the ancestors might serve a new myth that informs the reinvented Taiwanese-ness.

For the warriors in *Seediq Bale*, the only way to fulfil the essence of the Seediq culture is through embodying the sacredness of death. The violence that brings forth the sublimating death therefore serves as a significant ritualistic, almost festive affect which celebrates its sanctity. Re-joining the ancestral spirit is the *raison d'être* of the whole community. In the film, the principle of *gaya*, a call for the 'return to the ancestors' as an ultimate purpose of life that governs and motivates the characters' actions, is thus presented as an organic way of being. The rebellion itself in particular coincides with young Seediq boys becoming 'true men' through their participation in the uprising, where they carry out their first killing before they cross the legendary bridge of the rainbow (*hako utux*, literally, the bridge to the ancestors) in their return to the ancestors. Observation of *gaya* will eventually lead the Seediq people to live up to their group identity as 'Seediq Bale', which means 'the "true" human being'. Thus the infringement of *gaya* by foreign invasion not only perpetrates a crime against national sovereignty, but also violates the sacred bond between human and nature.

In this sense, the atrocity in the film seems to be more than simply an act of resistance of the colonised. It thus implies cleansing and rebirth. In analysing the nearly senseless violence in the film, Chao-yang Liao (2013) responds to the critical reviews of the film that judge the violence excessive and self-indulgent, as well as to the scholarship that reads the violence as purely aesthetic expression. Liao reads the seemingly anarchic and indiscriminate violence in the mass killing of the Seediq revolt as a way in which, through the total destruction of the political life form imposed by imperialism, the violence achieves de-territorialisation and sublimity. Such extremity, according to Liao (2013), constitutes a complete break from the reification of law and state. In other words, since the spectacle presents the tragic experience of a community confronted with an identity crisis, the affect invoked by the movie is tantamount to a powerful reaction and expression of the uncertainty and existentialist angst of the collective psyche.

A fractured and foiled return

Such readings transform the histories of indigenous groups into an allegory of modern violence of civilisation versus primordial retaliation of nature. In this sense, whether the film successfully allows for the voice of victims or survivors of the Wushe Incident to be heard calls for more perusal and contemplation, and rightfully scholars and critics have expressed their misgivings and rectifications. However, rather than seeking to justify the graphic violence, I would like to focus on a particular moment in the film as a self-foiled attempt in narrating and constructing a national narrative. In the epic myth about Mona Rudo, the arc of the heroic tragedy following a cause-and-effect logic is disrupted near the end of the film. Nevertheless, I interpret the moment of rupture as a juncture where the film is released from linear narratological sequences and becomes a series of uncategorised potentialities.

In the Taiwanese cut of *Seediq Bale*, the narrative thread is somehow broken after the encounter on a rope plank bridge between the Seediq warriors led by Mona Rudo and the Japanese army led by Kamada Yahiko. Up against the Japanese artillery, the bare-footed Seediq warriors armed with mainly machetes charge forward in a suicidal attack. After a few shot-reverse-shots, the camera zooms out to show the warriors running ahead as the bridge is blown up simultaneously. In the international cuts, the scene of the blown-up bridge wraps up the account of the incident before the film ends with a Seediq warrior, contemplating, on top of a mountain years later.

However, in the Taiwanese version, the explosion scene cuts to a montage of scenes that defy the logical progression of past, present and future. After the scene in which the explosion occurs, the take cuts to close-range combat among two Seediq clans. We are presented with a series of scenes from the chief of the Toda clan, Temu Wallis's hallucination, to a group of Seediq women and children on the run, and to the point of view of Mona Rudo and other warriors standing in the midst of the woods unscathed. In this confusing moment when it is unclear how these Seediq warriors survived the explosion, Mona Rudo dances and sings and bids farewell to the rest of his clan. The next scene presents Mona Rudo dressed up in the Seediq traditional costume, shooting his wife and demanding the rest of the group commit suicide as a sacrifice to complete the Seediq men's souls. After he burns the dead bodies of the women and children, Mona Rudo walks into the thick of the woods and disappears. The denouement of the film depicts a young Seediq man hunting in the woods years later. He stumbles upon Mona Rudo's bones and has a vision of the martyred Seediq warriors singing and walking across the rainbow bridge in the sky, a questionable green-screen shot done in unconvincing computer-generated images.

In the series of scenes described above, one sees fragmented and disjointed sequences. Viewers and critics have also referred to them as the film's irremediable failing (also see Rawnsley 2016b). Not only do these scenes not make logical diegetic sense, but they also turn the realistic attempt at restaging the past into a dream-like fantasy. Nonetheless, and perhaps inadvertently, these jolting sequences present aberrant movements that are 'purely optical and sound images' much as what Deleuze (2005) calls time images. In the collage of these images, the viewer is 'no longer in any indiscernible distinction between the real and the imaginary', where 'the true and the false now become undecidable or inextricable' (Deleuze 2005: 272–274). The collapse of the real and the imaginary at the end of the film, no longer offering a narrative, becomes a pure enunciation, a signifier with no assigned meaning. That is, in what seems to be Wei's attempt at compiling as much historical information as he could to inform the Taiwanese viewers, the narrative inconsistency disrupts the illusion of reality and creates affective intensities. In these irrational moments the film surrenders its authorial credibility as if it is impossible to present a holistic picture of history. As incomprehensible and unverifiable as Mona Rudo's cold-blooded extermination of his tribes-people, his sudden renunciation of the war betrays the purpose of representing a unified history. If violent death is central in immortalising the warriors in the film, the presentation of life after death in the affected final scene undermines the monumentalised sacredness of national trauma. The walk on the rainbow bridge, stripped of its representative authority, becomes the immanent present, an almost carnivalesque intention to subvert the authority of history, and thus transforms such immortality into a conviviality of a community in the making.

Conclusion

In a journal article, Emily Yueh-yu Yeh (1999) concludes her discussion of the relationship between localism, globalisation and Taiwan New Cinema with a shrewd observation:

> Both in the past and the present, Taiwan New Cinema has been associated with the practice of localism in various ways. It [the tendency] will not change much in the globalised future. As [Stuart] Hall notes, the monstrosity of globalisation comes with its oppositional undercurrent, which reinforces localism and nationhood, giving rise to the dialectics of articulations of identity, culture, and art. For the New Cinema and Taiwan's future films, Taiwaneseness is the best access to crossing [national] boundaries.
> (Yeh 1999: 61–62)[11]

Seeing that the only possible way for Taiwanese films to flourish as a form of regional renegotiation with the hegemony of globalisation is through actively involving Taiwanese viewers (in her words, whether it is through their 'invectives, support, or investigation'), Yeh's statement seems to presage Wei's films and those of his post-New Cinema peers. Operating as an intervening force within globalisation, the localism introduced by *Cape No.7* and *Seediq Bale* exemplify the effects of what Alison Landsberg (2004) calls the 'prosthetic memory' – that is, collective memory rendered infinitely malleable and multidirectional. Besides witnessing and relating history, individuals populate public forums and participate in writing history. According to Landsberg (2004), with the circulation of image and narratives precipitated by the emergence of the commodified mass culture, historical and cultural memory is not only appropriated by individuals. The dissemination of prosthetic memory enabled by technologies such as film sutures an individual into history. Wei's films have done just that. Vying for visibility on the international cinematic scene, the melodramatic, mass cultural appeal in these history-invoking works also competes for the attention of their domestic audience. With their popular legibility and ambivalent treatment of historical memories, *Seediq Bale* and *Cape No.7* not only mediate history; they put the spectator in the middle and trigger singular interactions between the individual and history.

Notes

1 For further details about this important literary debate in Taiwan, see, for example, Wang and Rojas (2007).

2 As one of the most prominent Taiwan New Cinema filmmakers, Edward Yang directed important works such as *Taipei Story* (*Qingmei zhuma*, 1985), *The Terrorizers* (*Kongbu fenzi*, 1986), and *A Brighter Summer Day* (*Gulingjie shaonian sharen shijian*, 1991). Wei Te-sheng began working with Yang in the 1990s and was promoted to the position of assistant director on Yang's film, *Mahjong* (*Ma jiang*, 1996). Yang continued to provide Wei with inspiration and mentorship while Wei was working on the five-minute demonstration film of *Seediq Bale* in 2005. Yang passed away when Wei was shooting *Cape No.7* in 2007 (Wang 2015: 255–256).

3 A critic-turned-director, Chen Guo-fu began directing films in the 1990s and is often considered one of Taiwan's Second New Wave, or post-New Cinema, directors from 1987 to the present. Chen became the head of the Columbia Pictures Film Production Asia in 2000, and directed a joint US-Taiwan production, *Double Vision* (*Shuang tong*), in 2002. The thriller boasted of the highest production cost in Taiwan's film history at the time. Wei Te-sheng was the assistant director on the film. *Double Vision* also launched Wei's collaborative relationship with producer Huang Zhi-ming, who later produced *Cape No.7*, *Seediq Bale* and *Kano*. Rather than viewing Hollywood as a force of cultural imperialism, Chen's attitude is ambivalent. As noted by Hsiu-chuang Deppman (2009: 439), Chen Guo-fu 'hesitates to make Hollywood the victimizer and Taiwan Cinema the victim'. He 'works diligently within the capitalist system to ensure the marketing competitiveness of his films after production'. Wei often accredits his vision of the Hollywood production model to his working experience with Chen.

4 According to Hong (2013: locations 1607–1659), it was not until the 1970s, when Taiwan faced a dire situation of diplomatic isolation, that national crisis figured in healthy realist films as formal and diegetic incongruence.

5 The affect theory, in the fields of humanities and social sciences, has been developing for the past 20 years. The critical thought focuses on emotion, sensation and visceral forces, and delves into the notion of 'potentiality'. See, for example, Tomkins (1962) and Ekman (1999).

6 Tzuhsiu Beryl Chiu (2010) compellingly unpacks the various levels of political statements made by Wei's underdog success story in *Cape No.7*. In Chiu's analysis, the coming together of disaffected characters in the southern town of Taiwan indicates a rebellious effort. Such an effort, while showing a recent tendency of nativisation in Taiwan, constitutes what Arjun Appadurai (2001: 15) terms 'globalisation from below', a strategic intervention from a Third World country 'from the south' to combat the Euro-American imperialist globalisation. Not only are the character Aga's journey to the southern town, Hengchun, and his involvement in organising a local band a reinvention of Taiwan's national/native identity and a gesture of resistance against the northern capital, Taipei, a metropolis that assimilates the neo-colonial force of capitalism and Western cultural superiority. More important, the climactic concert at the end of the narrative envisions a composite manifestation of what Chiu (2010) describes as 'spatial localism', 'historical nationalism' and 'social transnationalism'.

7 The Wushe Incident (or 'Musha Incident' in Japanese) is an anti-Japanese uprising initiated by the Seediq tribe in Taiwan. The attack on the Japanese took place on 27 October 1930. The killing of the Japanese culminated when the attack was launched during a sports meet at Musyaji Elementary School. The uprising was suppressed within a few months, followed by a retaliative attack on the Seediq tribe by other indigenous groups working with the Japanese administration in 1931. The 1931 attack is usually referred to as the Second Wushe/Musha Incident.

8 Among the cultural productions of the Wushe Incident are Chiu Ruo-long's comic book (1990), *The Wushe Incident* (*Wushe shijian*) and his documentary (1998), *Gaya: The 1930 Seediq Tribe and Wushe Incident* (*Gaya: 1930 saidekezu yu wushe shijian*); Deng Xiang-yang's creative non-fiction book (1998), *The Wushe Incident* (*Wushe shijian*) and his novel (2000), *Red Cherry Blossoms in the Wind* (*Fengzhong feiying*); Director Wan Jen's TV drama series (2004), *Dana Sakura* (*Fengzhong feiying*) based on Deng's novel; and a music album (2005) entitled *Seediq Bale* (*Saideke balai*) by the Taiwanese band, ChthoniC.

9 My own English translation.

10 My own English translation.

11 My own English translation.

9 Imagine there's no China

Wei Te-sheng and Taiwan's 'Japan complex'

Chris Berry

Introduction

After years of steady decline in both production output and box office success for Taiwan's feature film industry, Wei Te-sheng's *Cape No.7* (2008), *Warriors of the Rainbow: Seediq Bale* (2011), and *Kano* (2014), which he produced but did not direct, have broken the drought. *Cape No.7* smashed box office records for domestic features in Taiwan, topping the annual overall box office in 2008, and earning more than half as much again as its nearest Hollywood rival (Box Office Mojo 2015a). *Warriors of the Rainbow: Seediq Bale* (hereafter *Seediq Bale*), was the only Taiwanese film to make it into the top ten in 2011 (Box Office Mojo 2015b), and *Kano* was also the top performing domestic film in 2014, taking almost a third of the total box office for the 33 domestic releases that year (K. Ma 2015a).

However, although *Cape No.7* got some attention in East Asia, in general Wei's films have had less success at international festivals or at the box office outside Taiwan. Nor have they started a new golden era for Taiwan commercial cinema which, despite the efforts of many young directors, continues to languish at the domestic box office. Kevin Ma (2015b) notes that 2014 saw a drop in the numbers of features produced from 44 in 2013 to 33 in 2014, with a total market share of only 10.2 per cent. By comparison, South Korean and Chinese domestic films often take over 50 per cent of annual box office share in their domestic markets.

The Taiwanese situation follows the pattern for cinemas of small nations under conditions of globalisation. Open markets as required by World Trade Organization membership and so on not only leave local film industries unprotected in competition against more highly capitalised behemoths like Hollywood, but they also have to compete for local attention in a domestic system dominated by distributors and exhibitors closely affiliated with or owned by global corporations. In a case study on Singapore cinema written together with Mary Farquhar, we noted three patterns in domestic feature film production under such circumstances: low-budget films aimed at international festivals and with no domestic market; crossover films that attempt to make it out from international festivals into the global exhibition marketplace; and popular films whose heavy reliance on local culture and issues to attract domestic audiences impedes export. Since we undertook that research, the decline of the arthouse and independent exhibition circuit has made the second type rarer than ever. In Singapore, the films of Jack Neo (i.e. Liang Zhiqiang) are the local box office champions that have not travelled well (Berry and Farquhar 2006: 213–222). It seems that in Taiwan, Wei Te-sheng's films may have a similar status as local commercial films that have touched a strong local nerve but do not find a welcome elsewhere.

Wei's films are not the only Taiwanese films in recent years to emphasise local culture and commercial film techniques in pursuit of the box office, but they are by far the most successful. So how can we account for the extra-ordinary domestic appeal of his films? What are the local issues and local culture that Taiwan audiences find so compelling?

A full answer would require extensive audience research, extending the work done by Hong-chi Shiau (2009) about the reception of *Cape No.7*, and would cover many different factors. Ivy I-chu Chang (2010) has attempted such a complex multi-factored analysis for *Cape No.7*, for example. However, this chapter focuses on a particular factor that runs through all three of Wei's films so far and is not found so consistently in other commercial films full of local content – the Japanese colonial era. This common element has raised the issue of Taiwan's alleged 'Japan complex' again; in other words, Taiwan's alleged love for its former coloniser (also see Liao in this volume).

In the second section of this chapter, I explore how Wei's particular mode of engagement with the 'Japan complex' places Wei's films in a long lineage of works that imagine Taiwan in an infantile relationship to a larger father-figure country, or as an orphan-like, abandoned country. Yet, few people are alive today who have direct memory of Japanese colonialism. In such cir-cumstances, the significance of Japanophilia may vary historically according to contemporary issues. In the final section, I follow this logic to argue that perhaps Wei's 'Japan complex' can only be understood in relation to something else that is conspicuously absent in all three films: China.

The 'Japan complex' in Wei's films

As well as being slickly made commercial films that share what Ming-yeh T. Rawnsley (2012: 139) calls a 'feel-good' factor in her analysis of *Cape No.7*, each film in Wei's trilogy engages with the 1895–1945 half-century during which Taiwan was a Japanese colony. Both *Kano* and *Seediq Bale* are entirely set during the colonial era, and each is based on real events. *Cape No.7* oscillates between a contemporary love story about a Taiwanese man and a Japanese woman, and a historical romance about a Japanese male teacher and the Taiwanese girl student and lover he left behind when he was repatriated to Japan at the end of the war.

The basic narrative of each film can also be seen as a corrective one, recti-fying the unbalanced colonial relationship. In *Cape No.7*, the contemporary love story continues when the Japanese Tomoko decides to stay together with Taiwanese man, Aga, thus correcting the abandonment of the Taiwanese Tomoko by her Japanese lover at the end of the war. The narrative can also seem corrective from a patriarchal perspective, with a male Taiwan and a female Japan in the contemporary narrative replacing the colonial male power and feminised Taiwan of the frame narrative.

Seediq Bale corrects the Japanese stories of aboriginal Taiwanese as eager supporters of their empire. In the film world, these are exemplified by the most famous film shot on Taiwan during the Japanese colonial era, when there was no local production industry. *Sayon's Bell* (*Sayon no Kane*) was directed in 1943 by Shimizu Hiroshi and stars Li Xianglan, also known as Yamaguchi Yoshiko, in the title role of the aboriginal girl, Sayon. Based on real events that occurred in 1938 (Lin 2012: 145), the film tells the story of a young aboriginal woman so devoted to the Japanese empire that she sacrifices her life while leading recruits to the imperial army down the mountainside in a storm. As Stephanie DeBoer (2004: 25) points out, *Sayon's Bell* is the idealised Japanese version of the Japanese policy of assimilating aboriginals to Japanese culture, and specifically in its *kominka* form that emphasised preparation for war. Not only are the aboriginal young men in the film eager to join the army, but the whole village is shown tending the soil and raising livestock in productive and bucolic scenes, pausing only to bow towards the Japanese flag when it is raised up the village flagpole in the morning.

Seediq Bale corrects this kind of image of aboriginals under Japanese rule. Chia-rong Wu (2014: 26) argues that the film reveals the destructive cultural impact of the Japanese policy of assimilation, for example blocking the passage to manhood by banning the headhunting that was a rite of passage for young men. From an eco-critical perspective, Chin-ching Lee (2013) argues that the film corrects the Japanese vision of Taiwan as a landscape to be exploited by revealing it as place of belonging for the Seediq. However, although corrective in these ways, it must also be acknowledged that, as Che-ming Yan (2012) details, Wei's film also diverges from the historical record in its efforts to create an effective narrative. In both *Sayon's Bell* and *Seediq Bale*, aboriginal Taiwanese symbolise the island, but in *Seediq Bale* they are not colonial mascots but national heroes. As in *Cape No.7*, *Seediq Bale* also exhibits strong gender dimensions, masculinising the island, in contrast to the way *Sayon's Bell* metaphorically represents the island as a young woman.

Finally, in *Kano*, a multicultural baseball team from the south of the island counters low expectations of Taiwanese from the perspective of Japanese colonial culture to successfully get into the 1931 Japanese high school championships, held at the famous Koshien Stadium in Nishinomiya in Japan itself. Instead of being always defeated, they not only overcome their island rivals, but even triumph over some Japanese teams. Again, there is a strong masculinist gender dimension, because this is a male team.

However, the films' focus on the Japanese colonial era has inevitably brought up the issue of Taiwan's 'Japan complex' again, with, as Li-hsin Kuo

(2009: 55) points out in his analysis of *Cape No.7*, some critics making accusations of regret for the end of colonisation. As discussed in essays by Ivy I-chu Chang (2010: 88–89) and Yu-wen Fu (2014: 239), the sociologist I-chung Chen made a splash in the newspaper, *China Daily* (2008), accusing the film of exhibiting a desire to be colonised. Chiaoning Su (2009: 177) notes that the Chinese government was uncomfortable with its apparent romanticising of Japanese colonisation, and that this caused a delay of the film's release in the People's Republic of China (PRC), and Yu-wen Fu (2014: 239–240) notes this position was echoed by Chinese scholars and bloggers.

Kuo, Chang, Su, Fu and many other analysts, including Chialan Sharon Wang (2009a, 2012a; also see Wang in this volume), all argue that there is more to *Cape No.7*'s appeal than the simple love of the coloniser of which its critics accuse it, with Chang in particular revealing the complex array of factors nurturing enduring Japanophilia in Taiwan. Yet, it is also true that all three films are not simply patriotic and patriarchal correctives to the colonial narrative. This is not only because in the end the Japanese do suppress the aboriginal rebellion in *Seediq Bale* and the Taiwanese baseball team in *Kano* is defeated by a Japanese team and does not win the championship. Upon more careful examination, in each narrative a pattern emerges where the repeated goal is not pushing away the coloniser, but rather receiving recognition from the coloniser.

This search for Japanese approval is most evident in *Kano*, where the very ambition to enter the Japanese championship presumes acknowledgment of the supreme importance of the Japanese baseball system. Also, their coach and manager is a former Japanese baseball hero, and all their efforts are to please him. Furthermore, on their first appearance at the Koshien Stadium, a Japanese reporter is heard speaking in a racist and dismissive manner, but after a few matches, he is full of support and approval as are many of the spectators. The team may not have won the championship, but they have won Japanese respect. The film further underlines this theme by using a frame narrative, as *Cape No.7* did. In the case of *Kano*, the film opens with a Japanese soldier travelling across Taiwan on his way to the front in the Philippines in 1944 and taking a side trip to 'Kagi', as he pronounces Jiayi, home of the Taiwanese baseball team. It turns out that he was one of the opponents who learnt to take them seriously as opponents, and at the close of the film, we see him at the baseball field where the team trained, paying his respects.

Amongst the three films Wei has made so far, *Seediq Bale* is the one that seems least admiring of the Japanese colonisers, who appear both racist towards the aboriginal Taiwanese and merciless in their suppression of the rebellion. Yet, after the Japanese have restored their order and the heroic tribal leader Mona Rudo has disappeared into the mists, the Japanese commander Kamada Yahiko appears framed against cherry blossoms and extols his defeated opponents. Not only does he note that a small number of aboriginal fighters was able to hold their own against many more and better-equipped

Japanese soldiers, but also he attributes to them the *bushido* spirit of the Japanese warrior, long lost in Japan itself. This scene is entirely extraneous to narrative progression, and therefore can only be seen as confirming the significance of winning Japanese respect for the film and filmmakers.

Finally, it is *Cape No.7* that supplies the most melodramatic and elaborate scenes of Japanese approval. The present-day Tomoko is responsible for the local organisation of a concert by Japanese star Atari Kousuke. She gets Aga to lead a local band as a warm-up act for Atari. The concert becomes Aga's last-ditch opportunity to profess his love for Tomoko, begging her to stay as he sings on stage. Tomoko is standing in the wings, and as Aga turns to look at her, the TV cameraman follows his gaze and then Tomoko's image appears on the huge screen above the stage, much to the excitement of the crowd. For the film audience, a shot and reverse-shot pattern between Aga and Tomoko also encourages us to feel the full excitement and suspense shared by Aga and the crowd.

When Tomoko accepts the aboriginal necklace offered by one of the band members as a sign of love, the narrative appears to be complete, with delivery of a 'happy ever after' ending. However, it continues. Atari appears in the wings, alongside Tomoko, waiting to go on stage. The crowd demands an encore from Aga and his band. They perform a local folk song which Atari then claims to know, too. He joins Aga on stage to sing 'The Wild Rose' together with him in what is signified to be an anthem of shared Taiwanese and Japanese culture. (In fact, the song is Robert Schubert's 'Heidenröslein', but that further level of hybridity is beyond the scope of this chapter.)

How should we understand this second ending? Although Aga gets his girl, it seems that in the logic of the film narrative, getting approval and recognition from the Japanese male star is equally important. In this way, the scene echoes fatherly Japanese acknowledgement of Taiwanese male achievement in *Kano* and *Seediq Bale*. However, the film audience will recognise Atari not only as the star who makes an appearance at the concert that ends *Cape No.7*, but also as the actor who plays the role of the colonial-era teacher who abandons the Taiwanese Tomoko at the beginning of the film. This casting decision opens up a whole queer dimension of unstable gender and sexuality. If Atari is, in a sense, the teacher returning, then who is his contemporary Tomoko? He is friendly towards the Japanese Tomoko, but it is Aga with whom he is placed into a shot and reverse-shot structure, culminating in an all-male duet. Furthermore, insofar as patriarchal culture usually associates women with place and men with movement (De Lauretis 1984: 109), as in the Japanese teacher leaving Taiwanese Tomoko on the island, in the contemporary era there is a gender reversal, because it is the male Aga who risks being left behind in Taiwan by the Japanese Tomoko. To add to the gender instability, as Sheng-mei Ma (2015b: 25) points out, Atari, who sings in falsetto and appears as a nurturing and gentle person, is more of a mother (*Okasan*) than father figure.

Orphans and father figures, nostalgia and cultural memory

In his analysis of *Cape No.7*, Sheng-mei Ma (2015b: 15) also points out that the film engages with the long-established characterisation of Taiwan as an orphan – in this case, abandoned by Japan. Ma notes that all seven members of the local band put together to open for Atari are, in a sense, orphans, hyperbolically underlining the metaphor. The use of the orphan metaphor fits well with the pattern of searching for recognition and respect that I have noted runs through Wei's films; imagining the search for recognition as a search for a lost father helps to explain why the Japanese figures that bestow respect upon their Taiwanese counterparts in Wei's films are usually older men. However, also, in spite of the corrective elements in Wei's films, it does indicate the persistence or, at minimum, an echo of a colonial dependence mentality where one longs for approval from a big Other.

The most famous example of the longer lineage of variations on this orphan and father pattern is Wu Zhuo-liu's novel, *Orphan of Asia* (2006), which was written in Japanese during the colonial era. Precisely because, as Sheng-mei Ma (2015b: 10) points out, the forlorn protagonist is not an actual orphan, the title's metaphorical reference to Taiwan's inability to find a home in Asia with either China or Japan is underlined, as the protagonist travels around in vain and finds himself alienated and excluded, eventually even in Taiwan itself.

The Japanese village officer in *Sayon's Bell* is also depicted by the film as a father figure to the aboriginals, guiding them, assisting them and, where necessary, disciplining them. He is shown acting as a doctor, bringing modern health and hygiene practices to the village, issuing directions on the building of a bridge, and offering advice to resolve tensions amongst the villagers. Sayon's parents are noticeably absent, making her another metaphorical orphan, and she looks up to the officer in all things. In turn, the large numbers of children in the village look up to her as their elder sister.

This parental metaphor gets taken up in the earliest surviving Taiwanese feature film, Bai Ke's *Descendants of the Yellow Emperor* (*Huangdi de zisun*). It was made in 1956, after the Chinese Nationalist (i.e. Kuomintang or KMT) rule had been securely established on the island and reinforced by martial law and what is now known as the 'White Terror'. Just as *Sayon's Bell* opens with aboriginals bowing to the Japanese flag, *Descendants of the Yellow Emperor* opens with the Republic of China (ROC) flag flying in a schoolyard, in which the portrait of Chiang Kai-shek is also prominently displayed. The children sing about being descendants of the Yellow Emperor, legendary founder of China and the Han Chinese ethnic group. However, when the teacher asks one little boy whose descendant he is, he replies that he is his grandfather's descendant. The rest of the film works to ensure that the Taiwanese audience, infantilised by this comparison with small schoolchildren as surely as the aboriginals are in *Sayon's Bell*, do not make a similar mistake and fail to understand their national paternal lineage. For the regime, presumably, this was a national educational project, but perhaps for those islanders who saw the KMT Nationalists as new rulers from overseas, the pedagogical attempt to replace blood paternity with political paternity might have been strikingly similar to the familiar orphan and adoptive father model.

Although Wei's films also fit into this lineage of Taiwanese narratives of orphans seeking out fathers and father figures, as mentioned in the introduction, they are also fundamentally different. *Orphan of Asia, Sayon's Bell*, and *Descendants of the Yellow Emperor* were all produced and circulated either in the era depicted or in close living memory of it. In contrast, neither Wei Te-sheng nor his audiences are old enough to have any direct memory of the Japanese colonial era.

Insofar as Wei's films inspire nostalgia for the Japanese colonial era, this is what is sometimes called 'false nostalgia', or nostalgia for something the sufferer never experienced. Regular nostalgia is based on personal memory and can be something private and not shared, but nostalgia for something never experienced has to be induced by others. In this sense, it is part of the larger phenomenon of cultural memory (Assmann 2011) or collective memory (Halbwachs 1992). However, to understand such a phenomenon fully, precisely because it is not part of its producer's or audience's personal memory, it is necessary to ask what present circumstances are motivating its mobilisation.

In the lineage of works that imagine Taiwan in terms of orphans and fathers and also invoke the Japanese colonial era, at least one other group beyond personal memory appeared before Wei's. These are the films of Taiwan New Cinema, which emerged in the 1980s and is associated with directors like Edward Yang and Hou Hsiao-hsien. Not only is this new generation of filmmakers too young to have any direct memory of the Japanese occupation, but also many of them, including Yang and Hou, came from mainlander (*waishengren*) families, who came to Taiwan with the KMT retreat from China. Personal nostalgia appears in these films through memories of childhood, but that childhood is often permeated by the legacy of the colonialism.

Probably the clearest and most elaborated example linking fathers, orphans and the Japanese colonial era is Wu Nien-jen's 1994 autobiographical debut film, *A Borrowed Life (Duo sang)*. The protagonist's father is a miner. In his magisterial essay analysing the film as a postcolonial work, Darrell W. Davis quotes a British officer writing in 1946, that 'the conditions of labour in the mines is Formosa's prime example of Japanese exploitation' (Davis 2005: 241). In the film, it is portrayed as not only gruelling but also dangerous and, in the long term, fatal because of the lung diseases the miners develop. Yet, to his dying day the father believes Japanese products are superior, and his greatest wish is to visit Japan. The film exposes an undeserved nostalgia and communicates a certain undertone of anger towards the father, both for being blind to Japanese responsibility for his illness and for dying prematurely, leaving the protagonist an orphan. However, it is also the case that the film is about learning at least to understand the father, if not share his feelings.

Also ambivalent about the Japanese colonial era is Hou Hsiao-hsien's 1985 autobiographical film, *A Time to Live and a Time to Die* (*Tongnian wangshi*), for which he also co-wrote the screenplay. It follows the growing up narrative that is typical of the *bildungsroman* or coming-of-age story, but instead of a Euro-American oedipal tale in which the father is overcome, in this case the father simply sickens and dies, as do the mother and grandmother, leaving the children as orphans sad about their departure. 'The father ... never leaves the dark confines of the Japanese-style house (a remnant of the Japanese Occupation)' (Yip 2004: 79). If understood metaphorically, Taiwan is figured as an orphan left with a 'Japanese remnant'.

The personal nostalgic dimensions of both films are evident in their focus on the filmmakers' own childhoods and their relationships to their fathers, but Hou's 1989 family epic, *A City of Sadness* (*Beiqing chengshi*) moves into cultural memory while still engaging with the metaphors of fatherhood and colonialism. The film opens with the voice of the Japanese emperor on the radio announcing surrender as the mistress of one of the four brother protagonists is giving birth: the question of political succession is mapped onto that of personal succession. Furthermore, when we see scenes of sad farewells between Taiwanese characters and their Japanese friends and teachers who are being repatriated – like the teacher at the beginning of *Cape No.7* – we are encouraged to see benign elements in Japanese colonialism. As Ming-yeh T. Rawnsley points out, 'we learn that while countless Chinese and Taiwanese are victimized by Japanese aggression, there are ordinary Japanese settlers in Taiwan who are victims too' (Rawnsley 2011: 205). On the other hand, the deaths of the four brothers suggest that no new father figure emerges for Taiwan, the orphan island.

A City of Sadness also reveals the contemporary triggers for these Taiwan New Cinema films to engage with the island's Japanese colonial legacy. As is well known, the core event that never appears directly on screen in the film but structures the entire narrative is the 2/28 or February 28 Incident in 1947, when an uprising of islanders against the recently arrived KMT administration was put down brutally. After this event martial law was declared, and the Incident was taboo until it was repealed 40 years later. *A City of Sadness* rewrites the history and cultural memory of Taiwan to include this repressed event.

In so doing, *A City of Sadness* participates in a larger rewriting that challenges the KMT assertion found in *Descendants of the Yellow Emperor* that Taiwan was a part of China like any other. The Nativist movement in literature (Chang 1993), along with the Taiwan New Cinema, inscribed all the elements that marked the locally specific and which the KMT wished to overlook, from the diversity of spoken language to all the remnants of the Japanese colonial era – such as use of Japanese nicknames in *A City of Sadness*, the father's nostalgia for Japan in *A Borrowed Life*, and the Japanese house in *A Time to Live and a Time to Die*. In this way, we see that the 'Japan complex' as found in Taiwan New Cinema is less to do with Japanophilia than it is to do with repudiation of the KMT and its legacy.

Imagine there's no China

The Taiwan New Cinema examples of films that represent the Japanese colonial era and its legacies given in the last section share with Wei Te-sheng's films both an interest in the Japanese colonial era and the deployment of the orphan metaphor. They are also outside the scope of personal nostalgia and must be understood to be motivated by contemporary factors. However, they also differ significantly. There is no search in these films for approval from a father figure or, metaphorically, a larger power. In these circumstances, we must ask why it is pleasurable for Taiwanese audiences today to imagine Japanese colonial and postcolonial father figures as benign figures bestowing approval on Taiwan when very few people alive have any direct memories of the Japanese colonial era.

To understand this specific character of Wei's engagement with Taiwan's Japan complex, I suggest we need to consider the specificity of Taiwan's situation today and correlate it to the characteristics of the films. As well as imagining Japan as a benign paternal figure who bestows recognition on Taiwan, Wei's films are also marked by a notable absence: China. In her analysis of *Cape No.7*, Ying-bei Wang (2009b: 269) notes that 'it is interesting to see the Taiwanese culture represented in *Cape No.7* turns out to be one in which the Japanese influence is everywhere and the Chinese influence is reduced'. Indeed, China is absent from all the films, and I would go further than Wang: Chinese culture is not just reduced, but any connection to the China on the continent is thoroughly erased.

At first, this absence of China may seem natural in *Kano* and *Seediq Bale* given that they are set in the colonial era. However, as the narrator's sojourn in Shanghai and the surrounding area in Wu Zhuo-liu's *Orphan of Asia* reminds us, there was plenty of travel and communication between China and Taiwan in the 1930s, before the outbreak of war, when these two films are set. As Shi-chi Mike Lan (2014: 100) observes, although the population of Taiwanese in China during this period only numbered in the thousands, they 'consisted of people of all walks of life, and … were found all over China in the period from 1931 to 1945'.

The absence of China in Wei's films is even more marked when one considers *Cape No.7*. Just about every other ethnic group including Western tourists is represented in the film, but not Chinese, although it is difficult to imagine a tourist spot like Hengchun without any mainland Chinese tourists today. The absence of any reference to China stretches the realist conventions that otherwise shape Wei's films, suggesting that it is more than chance. Perhaps we can consider it as a structuring absence. As Richard Dyer (1993: 105) points out in his essay on the British film *Victim*, a structuring absence 'does not mean things which are simply not in the text, or which the critic thinks ought to be in the text'. Instead, it is something that a text 'skirts around, or otherwise avoids, thus creating the biggest "holes" in the text …' (Dyer 1993: 105). In other words, the absence of China is not like the absence of, for example, Finland in Wei's films; it is not something beyond the text, but a space of erasure produced within it.

I-chung Chen (2008) also understands this absence as in relation to the way Japan appears in Wei's films: he accuses Wei of making Chinese absent in *Cape No.7* because they would get in the way of what he believes is the film's fantasy of being re-colonised. However, this is to ignore the corrective elements that I have argued are also common to all of Wei's films, and which work against the unbalanced, exploitative colonial relationship. The memory of colonialism is replaced with the fantasy of a benign big Other.

When we think about Taiwan's relationship to China today, perhaps it is not difficult to see the appeal of such a figure. A stark contrast emerges with the early 1980s when Taiwan New Cinema emerged. Then, Taiwan was completely cut off from the PRC. The threats of mutual invasion between the ROC's Chiang Kai-shek and the PRC's Mao Zedong had faded into a stand-off. There was no trade, young Taiwanese had never been to China and, given Taiwan's economic take-off and China's poverty and isolation, there was little prospect that they ever would. China was nowhere near as important an issue as the internal politics of the island itself. Even the role of the United States was diminished after it had recognised the PRC. In other words, there was no big Other state pressing strongly on people's consciousness.

In the new century, all that has changed. The internal political system of Taiwan, transformed into a multi-party democracy, is relatively stable and well-accepted. However, in contrast with the recent past, close economic and social links with China have been established. Between 1.5 and 2 million Taiwanese, or 10 per cent of the adult population of the island, live inside the PRC (Chiu et al. 2014: 1), often drawn by economic opportunities associated with China's economic boom. According to Taiwan.gov.tw (2013), the official government website, 39 per cent of Taiwan's export trade was with China in 2012, almost four times as much as with the United States in second place, making China by far the island's most important trading partner. Approximately 40 per cent of the island's tourists also came from China in 2014, according to the Tourism Bureau (2015).

At the same time as Taiwan's prosperity has become hugely dependent on China, there has been no political rapprochement. The PRC continues to regard Taiwan as an integral part of China, as consistently demonstrated on Chinese maps that picture the island as part of the territory of the People's Republic (Tharoor 2014). As China presses its claims, fewer and fewer Taiwanese identify with China. An annual survey carried out by the Election Study Centre, National Chengchi University (2014), shows only 17.6 per cent of respondents identifying as Taiwanese in 1991, whereas 25.5 per cent identified as Chinese, and 46.4 per cent as both. By 2014, 32.5 per cent identified as both, only a tiny 3.5 per cent identified as Chinese, and the majority 60.6 per cent identified as Taiwanese.

In other words, in the new century, Taiwan is presented with a big Other with which it cannot establish a satisfactory relationship. In these circumstances, perhaps the appeal of an imaginary construction of colonial Japan as benign is easier to understand. This benign good father for the orphan island in Wei's films functions as a displacement, substituting a comforting image for the anxiety-producing image of China. To adapt a phrase from John Lennon, for a couple of hours, viewers can relax and 'imagine there's no China'.

10 *Kano* and Taiwanese baseball

Playing with transregionality and postcoloniality

Ping-hui Liao

Introduction

In many respects, films directed or produced by Wei Te-sheng mark distinct steps away from narrating the nation orientation of Taiwan New Cinema. They highlight transregional factors and call attention to the vibrant (even though unsettling) cultural dynamics of a postcolonial era. Unlike Hou Hsiao-hsien, Edward Yang and Tsai Ming-liang, who help promote a contemporary national art cinema by incorporating 'elements of indigenous Taiwanese life, especially visible in language, literary adaptations, and rural subjects' (Yeh and Davis 2005: 56), often making films for young professionals or college students, Wei tends to involve talents in Japan-Taiwan collaboration, to provide a multilingual platform, and to offer more revealing visual accounts of the ways in which peoples from different communities and temporalities struggle to rewrite Taiwan's postcolonial histories on top of grappling with the glocal neoliberal market economy.

This is most evident if we compare Hou's *Dust in the Wind* (*Lianlian fengchen*, 1986), a film about the passage from adolescence to adulthood from a male perspective, with Wei's *Cape No.7* (2008) in which colonial and postcolonial romances cross-cut each other. In *Dust in the Wind*, Hou uses Hokkien (also known as 'Min' or 'Hoklo') throughout his film, suggesting the native language spoken by the majority on the island is coming back after a long period of political suppression under the Chinese Nationalist (i.e. Kuomintang or KMT) regime which imposed martial law between 1947 and 1987. In the film, the character Grandpa (a patriarch played by Li Tian-lu, Hou's favourite actor in his 'Taiwan trilogy'[1]) symbolises the resilience of the Taiwanese in developing counter-memories. The film ends with Grandpa's words of wisdom: 'We need to start over after a typhoon.' A typhoon is a metaphor for unexpected disruptions in the national allegory, but it is also a sexist reference to the grandson Ah-ching's unfortunate experience with his former girlfriend who marries someone else.

In contrast, *Cape No.7* has no official language claiming sole authority as a cultural medium of decolonisation: in it, Chinese, Hokkien, Hakka, Austronesian and Japanese are spoken. In the film, intergenerational differences and transregional competitions are brought to light. In fact, the music band eventually teaming up in the film is an ensemble in celebration of diversity – in terms of age, gender, class, ethnicity, and indeed everything else. Hou largely draws on film scripts by writers like Zhu Tian-wen and Wu Nien-jen, but Wei bases his films on large and small events in Taiwan's colonial and postcolonial histories – the Wushe Incident in *Seediq Bale* (2011), for example. Hence, a major change in style, theme and audience by Wei is of historical epics in transnational scale, of giving voices to the subaltern and of general (albeit commercial) appeal to practically all movie watchers.

It is therefore not totally out of place to say that Wei seems to defy the received idea or image of confessional fictions or lyric dramas that develop well-made plots around private lives and are often associated with Taiwan New Cinema or the national cinema in terms of the quest for a local cultural identity. His work continues to frame transregional, postcolonial and intergenerational subjects in portraying the island's entangled history and ethnicity. This is evident in *Cape No.7, Seediq Bale* and particularly *Kano* (dir. Umin Boya/written and produced by Wei Te-sheng, 2014). Nevertheless, Wei has frequently been criticised for throwing too much positive light on the Japanese period, failing to contribute to the national cinema or to reach global audiences, only bringing in Japanese components in the co-production projects, or reinforcing the exclusivist, marginalising and commodified southern Taiwanese identity politics. Guo-juin Hong (2011: 187), for instance, concludes his succinct (albeit introductory) interpretive accounts of Taiwan cinema with these words: 'the film [*Seediq Bale*] returned home without any acknowledgement many in Taiwan had so passionately desired; vindication once again denied to Taiwan's national cinema in playing a stellar role in the global cinema'. Sheng-mei Ma (2015b) is another critic who is even more blunt in mourning the 'unglobalizable' figuration of the 'last isle' in contemporary Taiwanese popular culture. Ma (2015b: 25) alerts us to the fact that films such as *Cape No.7* have been flops outside Taiwan mostly due to their 'local beliefs' and 'theatrical practices': 'Wei Te-sheng opts for wish-fulfilling melodrama. Judging from its domestic box office success, *Cape No.7* has allayed, temporarily, Taiwan's orphan symptoms through the loving kindness of an uncanny Japanese Okasan.' These symptomatic readings are certainly valuable to some extent. However, they appear to be unjustly dismissive of transregional successes of these films and to be neglectful of the gradual spread of Asian popular culture in different parts of the world. This is a global trend that has been meticulously documented by a number of books like *East Asian Pop Culture*, co-edited by Huat and Iwabuchi (2008).

On 7 November 2014, when *Kano* opened the University of California, San Diego (UCSD) Taiwan Film Showcase (its premiere in the United States), in conjunction with San Diego's Asian Film Festival, up to 300 people turned up. Within a week, it was shown twice at the festival to large audiences. It was warmly received, and director Umin Boya (a.k.a. Ma Zhi-xiang) told me afterwards that he was pleasantly surprised to find so many enthusiastic fans

Figure 10.1 A poster for the film *Kano*
(Source: Central Motion Picture)

in the audience at the question and answer (Q&A) session.[2] Asked if the film
Kano was about nostalgic memory of Taiwan under Japanese colonial rule,
Boya replied that it was based on a historical episode in which a Taiwanese
high school baseball team joined the 1931 national tournament and won
recognition even though the Kano team ('Kano' is the shortened Japanese
pronunciation of the Jiayi High School of Agriculture in southern Taiwan)
was defeated after several rounds. Questions were raised around the principle
of selection and significance: 'Why baseball? How to retell truthfully the
tournament in 1931? What was the impact of the tournament on Taiwan's
sports history?'

    Boya went on to point out that he and the production team had gone
through Japanese newspaper sports columns of the time and footage of the
games to represent the subaltern voices. The cast remained faithful to historical situations and was evenly distributed in ethnic origins: two Han Chinese,
three Japanese and four aborigines. In many ways, the film was motivated by
a desire to reveal the historical trajectories of Taiwan's youth league baseball
and its challenging road to international fame. Its main concern is how baseball developed on the island as a national sport and eventually became part
of Taiwanese identity. However, in retelling the story Umin Boya actually
considered the ethnic representation of team players and cultural politics of
baseball as the sport took shape in acquiring many of its modern components –
physical and mental strength through self-discipline, game rules, management

skills, teamwork, virile (and largely masculine) nationalism, international competiveness, and postcolonial spectatorships vested with conflicting interests and ideologies. In this regard, it may not be appropriate to consider *Kano* simply in light of its local or national constituencies. Here I propose that we examine this recent film, written and produced by Wei, along the direction of its transregional, transcultural, postcolonial and intergenerational dynamics.

Transregional competing modernities and transnational predicaments

Like cricket for Indians and football for Brazilians, baseball has been a national sport marked by local Taiwanese athletes' attempts to renegotiate and even overcome the colonial past. Arjun Appadurai (1996) has observed that sports present illuminating cases of indigenisation and decolonisation. He uses cricket in India to suggest that the sport is 'a product of collective and spectacular experiments with modernity' (Appadurai 1996: 90). He singles out many dimensions in the indigenisation of a sport like cricket: 'it has something to do with the way the sport is managed, patronized, and publicized' (Appadurai 1996: 90). For on top of class structure and elite values, 'it has something to do with the dialectic between team spirit and national sentiment, which is inherent in the sport and is implicitly corrosive of the bonds of empire [...] it has something to do with the construction of a postcolonial male spectatorship that can charge cricket with the power of bodily competition and virile nationalism' (Appadurai 1996: 91). Appadurai nevertheless teases out warring forces within such self-conceptions of identity and nationhood, that in spite of its art, etiquette, conduct and publicity cricket in fact reinforces 'recolonization by forces of international capital' (Appadurai 1996: 106). He finds the 'aggressive, spectacular' ways in which audiences thirst for national victory to be very much commercialised and 'out for the buck' (Appadurai 1996: 107). While true in many aspects, a national sport like baseball as celebrated in *Kano* and Taiwan's youth leagues does not easily fall into Japanese colonial code or become 'subordinated to the transnational flow of talent, celebrity, and money' (Appadurai 1996:108). As Andrew D. Morris (2004) points out, Taiwan's baseball has its local, national and global dimensions; it affects people as a minor art of daily life and helps shape Taiwanese identity, especially on the eve of the youth league in the tournament being number one in the world. As a result, the film *Kano* is not just about boys – Japanese, Taiwanese and aboriginal – who are recruited to the baseball team that eventually wins recognition (though not victory) in a major tournament in Japan, but also is about the Japanese coach Hyotaro Kondo (played by Masatoshi Nagase), who has left for Taiwan as a high school teacher after suffering humiliation back in Japan.

At first, Kondo does not want to be known in the colony as having any experience with baseball, not to mention expertise as a famous player, promoter and even coach. The reawakening scene only occurs when one day a baseball is randomly thrown by the high school boys in the playground and almost knocks him down. Teacher Kondo slowly reclaims his former identity and starts to coach the boys, who are apparently amateurish and in need of discipline. By reasserting his identity as a coach, Kondo succeeds in leading the Kano team to become domestic champions and ultimately to be invited to represent Taiwan in the 1931 Japanese High School Baseball Championship. This is an interesting case of colonialism and modernity having to do with transregional experiences that involve public/private resources, personal/transnational predicaments, and colonial/postcolonial situations.

In many ways Kondo's exile, self-disavowal and then reaffirmation can be considered parallel to what Tanaka Tyozaburo (1885–1976), Ishikawa Kinichiro (1871–1945)[3] and many others went through during their stay in Taiwan while the island was under Japanese colonial rule (Liao and Wang 2006). For it was common for Japanese intellectuals and politicians on the margins – Kansai, Kyushu, Hokkaido, etc. – to migrate to Taiwan as colonisers and teachers in search of better job opportunities and, for that matter, more productive diaspora or exotic experiences. These individuals often find themselves to be part of competing modernities in the colonies after they have encountered obstacles in the metropolis, unable to put forth urban or science projects as intended. It is not without irony that they should enjoy freedom to bring about new experiments in the colony and thereby realise their human capabilities – or in the words of Giorgio Agamben (2016), 'potentials' in their political and social existence – to the full while away from home. Like the engineer Yoichi Hatta (played by Takao Osawa) in the film who manages to finish the first canal in Taiwan, Jianan, which helps turn local farmers into the best rice-growers in the empire, Coach Kondo manages to put the Kano baseball team through many games and win, a remarkable deed he has never been able to accomplish back home. Without the teams and their efforts in the colony, these Japanese colonisers may not be able to fulfil their dreams or fully develop their potential. Here personal/transnational predicaments play important roles in the ambivalent formation of fortune and even destiny, especially in conjunction with the new historical situations or environment available at the time.

International and transregional tensions were on the rise with the Great Depression in 1929, after many years of implementing the colonial policy of localisation and incorporation, especially under the leadership of administrators like Den Kenjiro, the first civilian governor-general in Taiwan between 1919 and 1923, and Goto Shimpei, an important figure promoting public health and infrastructure building. At this time Japan began to tighten its control over Taiwan in response to the disastrous Musha uprising (i.e. Wushe Incident)[4] in 1930, vividly captured in Wei Te-sheng's *Warriors of the Rainbow: Seediq Bale*. Japan was also aiming to take over China and Manchuria, while suppressing Korea and engaging Russia at the same time. As the Sino–Japanese and Pacific Wars were launched, Taiwan's Association for Culture (founded by the local elites and professionals like Lin Hsien-tang and several physicians in 1915) was forced to go underground. However, Coach Kondo might bear witness to the hard times as also good times, with a number of intellectuals at the time cultivating the opportunities of transcultural cross-pollination across the region: Liu Na'ou (1905–40), a Taiwanese native, working in Shanghai between 1926 and 1940 to establish a series of *Women's Pictorial* (*Furen huabao*) on top of producing new films; Tanaka Tyozaburo, a Japanese professor in the agricultural division of Taipei Imperial University (the forerunner of the National Taiwan University, set up in 1928), becoming the first university librarian between 1929 and 1934, charged with the task of building special collections; and many artists studying in Japan and travelling back and forth to push forward, in the words of Karen Thornber (2009), 'the empire of texts in motion' to make transculturation a transregional daily practice.

Professor and librarian Tanaka would be an interesting case here to illustrate how transregional competing modernities become entangled with personal and transnational destinies. An eminent Japanese orchard horticulturalist, Tanaka came from a very wealthy family. In 1930 his father, founder of Kobe Bank, left him an inheritance of US $100,000, just the right amount and at the right time for the horticulturalist to purchase the rare early European books and periodicals owned by Otto Penzig, several of which were printed between 1480 and 1499. Tanaka put these treasured 3,326 volumes in the university library and went on to build more special collections, using his personal and public revenues, making himself a notable agronomist in the field. However, when the Japanese emperor acknowledged defeat and gave up sovereignty over Taiwan in 1945, Tanaka left his collection and manuscripts behind as the KMT government declared them the property of National Taiwan University (Liao 2006: 78–82). Tanaka returned to Japan empty handed.

In contrast to Tanaka, Coach Kondo is much luckier. He has both his family and the Kano team to help reclaim his place and honour. In the film, Kondo tries to modernise his baseball team, not only feeding them using his own stipends and drawing on public funds, but also building his training programmes in response to the strengths and limits of the team members, including the Japanese, Taiwanese and aborigine. He teaches different techniques to sustain and to complement the need of each player, drawing on situated local and global knowledge of the body and mind. He coaches them to compete and collaborate in the constitution of an ideal community. The training procedure is juxtaposed with the canal construction project as the engineer Hatta attempts to coordinate all sorts of human resources and materials available to help provide irrigation for local farmers. Coach Kondo's encounter with his competitor (Coach Sato, a former teacher, played by Togo Igawa) back home reveals his traumatic journey to the colony and his ethical reawakening on top of his confidence in his team.

Kondo is shown to be caught in the root/route dilemma, struggling over the old affiliations (national origin) and a new affiliation (Kano), as he leads his

Taiwanese team back to Japan, wishing to defeat his own countrymen, including a team coached by his master and mentor. He originally intends to develop a new, amnesic identity and to be solely on a civilising and colonial mission in Taiwan, yet his life in diaspora experiences the return of the repressed, to open up opportunities for new life, redemption and legacy. Ultimately, Coach Kondo pushes the team to become first-rate baseball players, in not just appropriating the competence and efficacy known only to the Japanese champions, but also in overtaking them, or at least striking back. While Kondo fails to accomplish that in Japan, in the colony he is finally able to create an indigenous team and the tools to compete with the modern masters back home.

In the film, decolonisation takes the form of winning communal support from the farmers and relatives, and above all showing the spirit of perseverance. The Taiwanese pitcher (played by Tsao Yu-ning) wins over his rivals even though worn out and defeated in the last game. In the film's concluding scene, the Japanese pitcher Josha Hiromi (played by Ken Aoki) from Hokkaido visits the Kano playground and envisions what the Taiwanese team must have endured under such primitive and harsh circumstances to become so impressive and awesome. Hiromi is on his way to the Pacific War and later probably dies in battle. The imagery of his honouring the rivals evokes the lingering message of if the empire should be the winner of the game – especially when it is caught in a transregional war and competition.

Playing with postcoloniality: transcultural gaming and intergenerational reconciliation

In paying tribute to the Kano team, Hiromi sums up a number of large and small, immediate and remote transregional tensions. First, he is constantly reminded of (if not tormented by) the very scene of his own defeat at the hand of an exhausted and wounded pitcher from Taiwan, who appears to have impressed the Japanese audiences more than anyone from the metropolis and because of his perseverance wins a standing ovation. Hiromi does not seem able to get over the trauma and memory of humiliation, especially experience of loss in the game to players of a supposedly inferior race, a colonised subject from the countryside on a distant island. Second, when Hiromi is drafted to join the Pacific War, he says to himself that he wants to visit Taiwan, the only island immediately ringing a bell geographically and psychologically. He needs to see the place in which his rival has been raised and trained as a better pitcher. In visiting Taiwan, Hiromi puts himself in the position of colonial encounter, of 'south advance' (taking over the Pacific),[5] except it is in the mode of reverse hallucination: the coloniser suddenly catches his own mirror image as a loser in the baseball game and in the transregional contest – including the battle in the Philippines and South China Sea. Third, by honouring the past glory that belongs to someone else, Hiromi also recognises the international game rules and sees himself as part of sport spectatorship. He sees the results of Japanese colonial modernity on the island, especially in the background Japanese Baroque buildings and fashionable girls. They look familiar while at the same time uncannily strange as constructs of competing modernity in the colony. Suddenly, Hiromi examines things around him through the lens of an outsider. He should be proud of his home country's contributions to Taiwan, a colony, but he is surrounded by images and sounds that he cannot comprehend. Somehow he still manages to grasp the street names and language as they are mostly in Japanese. After all, he is placed in the midst of colonial modernity and education. However, he does not appear to be appreciative. Instead, he sees alternative modernity developing at the Kano playground: local boys playing their games in their own ways, setting out to win honours in Japan. A sense of ambivalent, discrepant cosmopolitanism, of being at home in a strange place, of arriving but soon departing, preoccupies his mind. Last but not least, Hiromi will be on a journey to another Pacific island where transregional war is being fought and where Japan will be losing the game.

It is interesting that in the film the training process takes up more than half of the playing time. The Kano baseball team is seen running on the streets, in the fields, the rice paddies, and along the canal. Through their eyes we witness the construction of the grand canal Jianan, the changing landscape, and the communal participation in the sport as part of modernisation and glocalisation processes. Coach Kondo is strict in bodybuilding and team management, but he is most meticulous in developing nuanced baseball techniques properly suited to the players in light of their physical and ethnic construction, especially in ways to bring the different races together as a syncopated and synthesised organism.

In answering questions from the audience, director Umin Boya said that he chose the players from hundreds of high school teams and devoted several months to recruiting them, including coaching them in Japanese. In other words, the players are real players and they are all very knowledgeable of the historical trajectory in which the Taiwanese teams have outdone the Japanese. In making the film, not only are the director and producers reconstructing the historical incident around Kano, but also the actors are reliving past glories, playing with postcolonial memories of how the colonised have overtaken the colonisers. It is apparent that the Taiwanese have dedicated themselves to baseball as a national sport, particularly with strong emotions and symbolic capital invested in the youth league. In many ways, it is very much like what Arjun Appadurai (1996) advocates about Indian cricket. However, as Taiwan is often labelled as a state without nationhood since the loss of its United Nations membership in 1971, the international sponsorship and spectatorship that Appadurai associates with Victorian commodification and British re-colonisation are not applicable. Rather than displaying 'erotics of nationhood' by beating former masters (Appadurai 1996: 91), Taiwanese baseball highlights the virtue of perseverance, but not power or money. In the film, it is the transcultural or translational aspects that Coach Kondo emphasises in adopting and readjusting Japanese sportsmanship, so that the local team can find a new articulation positionality. This is most evident in the way Kondo talks to his former mentor Sato, in suggesting that he has developed a new stance in response to his past experiences as a coach in the metropolis.

Another aspect that films by Wei Te-sheng often touch upon is inter-generational communication. For example, the magnificent seven in *Cape No.7* consist of musicians not only from different ethnic backgrounds, but also across ages and generations. The old and new romantic relations that unfold around love letters and rock concerts are intergenerational. In *Kano*, the intergenerational competition and communication occur when Coach Kondo discusses with Coach Sato about ways to win the game. In returning to Japan from the colony, Kondo assumes a new identity of a rival and iro-nically represents the subaltern, on top of the colonised, marginal and Third World countryside. Kondo's conversation with his former mentor is not just to renew friendship, but to gather information and to discover a new vantage point so that his Taiwanese team can succeed in the major tournament. The episode parallels that of Hiromi's stopover in Taiwan, and reveals an inter-esting twist of postcolonial mimicry and intergenerational memory. Kondo learns the secret of his master's success and then goes on to beat him in the game, pushing his team to imagine ways to decolonise and to play with postcoloniality. Though a Japanese citizen and coloniser, Kondo has a new role to play in defence of his name, his wronged past and his invested interest in the Kano team from the colony. It is not without irony that even in the 1930 documentary *Happy Farmers* (*Xingfu de nongmin*), made by the Taiwan Education Society under the colonial government on the opening of the Jianan grand canal, one third of the shots were dedicated to a local wedding ritual and procedure. Though on a mission to celebrate and self-congratulate, in glorifying Japanese colonial modernity the documentary production team was more fascinated by the local traditional customs and lifestyles, finding them unique and worthy of preservation (Taiwan Education Society 2008).

The film *Kano* ends with views of the island as the Kano team is returning on the cruise ship. Even though they did not win the game, the team and the coach show hope and confidence. They will be greeted back home as victors. Travelling across the Pacific Ocean, the players see the beautiful island emerging on the horizon and have faith in its future because of its people's perseverance that is deeply ingrained in their bodies.

In 1920, a writer by the name of Sato Haruo (1892–1964) must have entertained such hopes when he was put on the cruise ship returning to Japan after a three-month stay in the colony. Writer Sato (different from Coach Sato) produced a series of stories over the span of 20 years between 1921 and 1943 on his travels in the colony; he reissued several of them in a collection titled *Musha* (1936). A distinguished writer in post-Meiji Japan, Sato visited Taiwan for three months in 1920 on an invitation of a high school classmate; he compared the customs and discursive practices between the Japanese and the Taiwanese, in addition to being fascinated by the aborigine's tall tales.

Sato showed interest in meeting the poet in Taiwan whom he heard was capable of doing all sorts of experiments with classical Chinese. After pressing Mr A (his Taiwanese guide) a few times, he eventually managed to acquire the four volumes of poetry. While this might in part be triggered by curiosity or a desire to show off his knowledge of classical Chinese, Sato's eagerness to appreciate the local expressive culture appears to be sincere and persistent. He even went on to transcribe a poem that seemed both archaic and relevant, though he found most of the poems very difficult to read, with some on aboriginal deer-hunting, the new middle class's collection of phonographs, earthquakes in Jiayi, and some even lamenting the national treasures stolen during the Opium War. Sato writes, 'I was immediately taken by the extraordinarily novel and place-based lyric subjects' (Sato 1936: 293). 'I try to make sense of the poetic lines even though my Chinese vocabulary is quite limited. As I read on I cannot help becoming more intrigued by a rich diversity of unusually lively expressions. The reading process is hardly smooth; I get frustrated all the time; however, the more so to get me totally fascinated by the verbal magic'. Sato (1936: 294) quotes the section of a regulated verse on the unsuccessful attempt to quit smoking opium, as follows:

> Half of my life devoted to alchemy,
> Only to realise my body rotten and decaying,
> I flee and escape into practising Zen Buddhism.
>
> As ancient hermits drown their sorrows in wine,
> So I indulge in eating opium,
> To summon what is left and to blow out the smoke,
> The pipe contains and relieves my youth and ambition,
> As if I were lord of the rosy castle,
> Or master poet of the famous hall,
> With no exit or outlet in view,
> Puffing air that fills the cosmos,
> Lying on a small bed, surrounded by hundreds of books,
>
> With a pillow as my sole companion in a tiny urn.[6]

Sato associates the poem with Baudelaire's *Fleurs du mal*, suggesting that the Taiwanese writer Hung Qi-sheng (1867–1929) deploys the Chinese language in such innovative fashion that it sounds very French and modern. Sato (1936: 295) considers this episode a climactic moment charged with 'inexhaustible poetic thrills – even though accompanied by excruciating pains of extreme indigestion'. The way Sato praises the poet in terms of literary modernism and nativism, highlighting aesthetic values of strangeness and obscurity while savouring the humour and cynical reason embedded in the poem, sets him totally apart from many of his Japanese colleagues who tend to be condescending and even in denial. Because of such a Sinophone reading encounter, Sato developed sympathetic affinity with local cultural dynamics to such an extent that he found Taiwan's tropical heat and humidity very refreshing. He even concludes his travels to the colony by predicting that the Taiwanese would endure and may eventually outdo the Japanese with their diligence and capacity to survive harsh weather.

As Kondo is returning to Taiwan, refreshed after touching base with his mentor and ethically reawakened in the baseball tournament, he must feel writer Sato's prediction to be very relevant and revealing. In the training process, he actually tries every way to deploy strategic devices in response to the local climate, especially the heat and humidity, to make the Kano team more able to cope with difficult and challenging situations. He pushes them to go beyond limits, but also nurtures them to cultivate superhuman strength and to be more persevering. The baseball field proves to be an arena for the development of human capacity not only for the team members but also for the coach, as Kondo finds himself constantly marvelling at what the team can do with such scant resources. Writer Sato and Coach Kondo would agree that moral luck may be subject to change in due time. Writer Sato suggests that in 50 or 100 years Taiwanese may be more advanced than Japanese, but Kondo seems to say that on the baseball field it only takes a few years.

To return to Wei's critics, we should say that *Kano* might have answered several questions regarding the future of Taiwan film. As we have shown, the film is more about transregional predicaments and intergenerational communication in its reconstruction of a historical event. In many ways, the film can be seen also as a critical response to the Japanese national broadcaster Nippon Hoso Kyokai's (NHK) first episode of the series *Japan in the World* (2011), which uses Taiwan to amplify the Japanese colonial legacy on the island in a derogatory representation of Taiwanese veterans, and in particular aborigines as if they were animals in the World Expo's Human Zoo. As the NHK film opens, a number of Taiwanese veterans of the Second World War sing the Japanese national anthem and traditional songs to salute the emperor, their former ruler. Then the documentary takes us to many wonderful achievements of the Japanese empire in Taiwan: the railway, education, industrialisation, and indeed all sorts of infrastructure construction. Even the 'primitive' and 'barbaric' aborigines were domesticated and modernised; a number of them were on display in the Expo as a showcase of how Japan overtook European colonisers in efficacy and technological innovations. What the NHK documentary series neglects to mention is that those aboriginal representatives exhibited later committed suicide when they returned to Taiwan.

The NHK documentary brought harsh criticism within Japan, not to mention in Taiwan. It might have been in the background when the film *Kano* was made. It is therefore revealing that the Kano team and Coach Kondo demonstrate that the colonised can beat their master at the game. There is certainly a subversive subtext if we take into consideration the fact that *Kano* is directed by Umin Boya, an aboriginal actor and filmmaker, who deliberately highlights the team to be multiracial and representing the subaltern. Rather than retelling a postcolonial story from the father's pro-Japan perspective, as in Wu Nien-jen's film, *A Borrowed Life* (*Duo sang*, 1994), *Kano* zooms in on baseball and colonial modernity which mediate so many people's lives, to tease out conflicting, competing and collaborative forces in the making of a specific moment in baseball's and indeed the island's colonial or even postcolonial histories.

Notes

1 Hou Hsiao-hsien's 'Taiwan trilogy' refers to *A City of Sadness* (*Beiqing chengshi*, 1989), *The Puppetmaster* (*Ximeng rensheng*, 1993) and *Good Men, Good Women* (*Hao nan hao nu*, 1995).
2 Highlights of the Q&A with Umin Boya are available at taiwancultureucsd.wordpress.com (accessed 27 September 2016).
3 Tanaka Tyozaburo was the first librarian of Taipei Imperial University; he used a large sum of the inheritance from his father to purchase the Penzig Collection – 3,326 rare volumes from Renaissance Europe, with four of them printed between 1480 and 1499. He went on to build several precious collections like Ino, Huart, Ueta, Monoki and so forth. The irony is that he had to leave all the valuable collections behind when Japan was defeated in 1945, and as a result, they were declared to be National Taiwan University's property. For details, please consult Liao (2006). Ishikawa Kinichiro was art teacher in Taipei Normal School between 1923 and 1931; he was instrumental in introducing modern landscape painting and in founding the Taiwan Watercolour Society. See Yen (2006).
4 'Musha' is the Japanese pronunciation of 'Wushe'.
5 'South Advance' was Japan's colonial policy in using Taiwan as a bastion to dominate the Pacific.
6 The English rendition is mine; here I use the original Chinese poem cited in Chiu's (2002) translation of Sato's work in 1936.

11 *Seediq Bale* as history

Robert A. Rosenstone

For several decades now I have been concerned with the contributions to our understanding of the past provided by history films. My own fields are Modern European and American history, and I have focused on works in those areas because one can only make a serious evaluation of particular historical works if one knows the discourse out of which they arise and to which they refer. In this chapter, an updated and much rewritten version of a piece I wrote some time ago (Rosenstone 1995b: 45–79), I make a general argument about the contribution of history film and include reflections on how this could be applied to Taiwanese filmmaker Wei Te-sheng's *Seediq Bale* (2011).

History is always fought on contested terrain. It is not just that there are differing ways of interpreting past events, but that what counts as evidence for that past and the manner in which that evidence is enfolded into a presentation for an audience, scholarly or popular, is also always at issue. Think of it: the two great fathers of history in the Western tradition used approaches that would be completely out of bounds for scholars today, and yet we still know them as historians: Herodotus recorded random oral tales he gathered from various 'experts' and 'witnesses' in a variety of lands; and Thucydides had historical characters deliver lengthy political speeches which he invented. Later generations of historians have often used other modes of creating history that can seem outlandish to a modern, secular consciousness: some utilised God as an explanatory factor for human events; others called on race or religion as a way of accounting for the rise and/or fall of civilisations.

The medium in which the past is delivered, its attempts to represent events and people long gone, has its own problematics. The tradition of writing history has for more than two millennia in the West been one of creating stories that fix our sense of the past on the page and allow us to contemplate it in a way that was largely impossible for the preceding oral tradition. In the twentieth century, new technologies for representing the world, the visual and, more recently, the electronic media have arisen to challenge the written word as a way of describing realities, past and present. Yet these media have only been taken seriously as conveyers of history by any – and actually just a few – academically trained historians since the early 1990s.

The earliest of these new technologies, film, is now more than a century old, yet the issues it poses for historical telling may be taken as a kind of test case for these new media for rendering history. There is little doubt that visions of the past on film trouble and disturb academic historians – have indeed troubled and disturbed them for a long time. Listen to Louis Gottschalk of the University of Chicago, writing in 1935 to the president of Metro-Goldwyn-Mayer: 'If the cinema art is going to draw its subjects so generously from history, it owes it to its patrons and its own higher ideals to achieve greater accuracy. No picture of a historical nature ought to be offered to the public until a reputable historian has had a chance to criticize and revise it' (quoted in Rosenstone 1995b: 46).

How can we think of this letter today? As touching? Naive? A window onto a simpler age that could conceive of Hollywood as having 'higher ideals'? If the attitude can seem dated, however, the sentiments are not. Today professional historians still distrust historical films, and do so for reasons that are both overt and covert. The former includes notions that such films are always inaccurate; they distort the past; they fictionalise, trivialise and romanticise people, events and movements. The covert reasons include the fear that film is out of the control of historians; that the visual media create a historical world with which books cannot compete for popularity; that movies are a disturbing symbol of an increasingly post-literate world (in which people can read but don't).

This chapter will focus on the 'history' film, by which I mean the motion picture that attempts to depict verifiable people, events, movements and/or eras in the past. I distinguish between the 'history' film and the more common term, the 'historical', because the latter can also refer to almost any important film that has been made in the past. Sometimes a film can be both 'history' and 'historical'. Orson Welles's masterpiece, *Citizen Kane* (1941), is a history film insofar as it gives us a thinly veiled biography of powerful newspaper publisher, the Rupert Murdoch of his day, William Randolph Hearst. As a historical film, it is famous for its use of multiple perspectives on the past (long before Akira Kurosawa's celebrated film of 1950, *Rashomon*), its fragmented and contradictory way of telling a story, its special deep-focus photography, and its luscious use of black and white.

A general suspicion of the visual media has not prevented historians from becoming increasingly involved with film in recent years. Movies have invaded the history classroom, though it is difficult to specify if this is due to the 'laziness' of teachers, the post-literacy of students or the realisation that the visual media can do something that written words cannot. Hundreds of historians, at least in the United States, have become at least peripherally involved in the process of making films: some as advisers on projects, dramatic and documentary, sponsored by the National Endowment for the Humanities (which requires that filmmakers create panels of advisers, but makes no provision that the advice actually be taken); others as Talking Heads in historical documentaries. Sessions on history and film have become a routine part of history conferences and annual conventions of professional groups like the Organization of American Historians and the American Historical Association. Reviews of historical films now can be found in professional history publications.

All this activity has hardly led to a consensus on what is, or how to evaluate, the contribution, if any, of the history film to what we might call 'historical knowledge or understanding'. In 1988, the great theorist Hayden White coined an important term, *historiophoty*, which he defined as 'the representation of history and our thought about it in visual images and filmic discourse', but to date this term has been used sparingly by other scholars (White 1988: 1193). Essays and books about and reviews of film by historians usually deal with their subject in an ad hoc fashion, with little coherent or consistent theoretical underpinning.

Among those academics who do take the time to write about the history film (this includes historians and scholars in film, literary and ethnic studies), two major approaches predominate: one sees these films as less about the past than as reflections of the social tensions and political issues of the period in which they were made; the second attempts to judge history films solely by the standards that have been developed for written history over the centuries.

As an example of the first, I point to the superb work of Robert Burgoyne whose books, *Film Nation* (2010) and *The Hollywood Historical Film* (2008), are models of meticulous scholarship. His essay on *Saving Private Ryan* (dir. Steven Spielberg, 1998) is typical in the way it shows him to be less interested in the experience and events during the invasion of Normandy of June 1944 and more concerned about what the film has to say about America's current changing relationship to its own past (Burgoyne 2008: 50–73). For Burgoyne, *Saving Private Ryan* is part of a cultural project which he calls the 'reillusioning of America' after the great internal conflicts of the 1960s and the disillusionment of the Vietnam War era. The film, he argues, offers audiences a 'way home' to mythic America, 'reaffirming American national identity after the crisis of Vietnam' (Burgoyne 2008: 71–72).

Among the historians who do take the contents of history films seriously one finds Natalie Davis, an excellent scholar of early modern Europe, who served as consultant on *The Return of Martin Guerre* (dir. Daniel Vigne, 1982), wrote a micro-history by the same name (Davis 1983), and later produced *Slaves on Screen*, a study of five films about slavery (Davis 2000). Here she makes the case that such films are capable of both engaging with historical discourse and adding, through the powers of the medium, to our understanding of the past. Yet Davis is a touch uneasy that such films do not adhere to many traditional standards of history, and she suggests a variety of ways in which they might become more like books. However, one wonders, what is the point? We already have books and a sense of how to evaluate their renditions of the past. Film is a very different medium, and rather than assuming the world on film should adhere to the standards of written history, it seems more useful to see how it has created its own standards over the last century, its own techniques for turning the past into history, standards which are appropriate to possibilities and practices of the medium, as well as those of drama, the usual form in which film tells its stories, past or present.

To put this issue starkly: too many historians use written works of history to critique visual history as if that written history were itself something solid and unproblematic. They do not treat written history as what it really is: a constituted and problematic mode of thought, a process, a particular way of using the traces of the past to make that past meaningful in the present.

To talk about the failures and triumphs, strengths and weaknesses, and possibilities of the history film, it is necessary to pull back the camera from a two-shot in which we see history on film and history on the page square off against each other. We must include in our new, broader frame the larger realm of past and present in which both sorts of history are located and to which both refer – what we call the 'discourse of history', a realm that includes all the data and interpretations on a topic that have been provided over the centuries. Ultimately the question cannot be: Does the history film convey facts or make arguments as well as written history? Rather, the appropriate questions are: What sort of historical world does each film construct and how does it construct that world? How can we make judgements about that construction? How and what does that historical construction mean to us? Finally, how does the historical world on the screen relate to written history and the larger discourse on a given topic?

Varieties of historical film

We cannot talk about the history 'film' in the singular because the term covers a variety of ways of rendering the past on the screen, among them dramatic, documentary, innovative, animated and mixed genre. Written history, too, comes in different subcategories – narrative, analytic, quantitative, micro, psycho, feminist, subaltern, etc. – but we tend to see them as chapters that fit into some larger story (what theorists call 'metanarrative') about the past. Film as history may seem more fragmented because there exist no filmic overviews comparable to metanarratives of nations, eras or civilisations that could provide a broad visual historical framework for any individual recounting from the past, so the framework for thinking about film has to be that of more traditional historical discourse. While it is possible to put the history film into a number of subcategories, this chapter will focus on the one utilised in *Seediq Bale* – that is, history as drama, the genre that usually springs to mind when you think of the term 'history film'.

This form has been a staple of the screen ever since motion pictures began to tell stories in the earliest days of film, and it continues to be regularly produced all over the world. Some of the most beloved motion pictures in all national traditions have been dramatised history. Natalie Davis (2000) has suggested that history as drama can be divided into two broad categories: films based on documentable persons or events or movements (e.g. *The Last Emperor* [dir. Bernardo Bertolucci, 1987]; *Schindler's List* [dir. Steven Spielberg, 1993]; *Gandhi* [dir. Richard Attenborough, 1982]; *Selma* [dir. Ava DuVernay, 2014]), and those whose central plot and characters are fictional, but whose historical setting is intrinsic to the story and meaning of the work (e.g. *Saving Private Ryan; Dangerous Liaisons* [dir. Stephen Frears, 1988]; *The Molly Maguires* [dir. Martin Ritt, 1970]; *Black Robe* [dir. Bruce Beresford, 1991]). However, this distinction does not in fact have much explanatory power, for the categories quickly break down. Virtually all history films follow a strategy of placing fictional characters next to historical characters in settings alternately documentable and wholly invented.

How do mainstream films construct a historical world and how does *Seediq Bale* follow the pattern?

The world that the standard or mainstream historical drama constructs is so familiar that we rarely think about how it is put together. That, of course, is the point. Films want to make us think they are reality. Yet the reality we see on the screen is hardly inevitable, but rather a vision creatively constructed out of bits and pieces of images taken from the surface of a world and edited into a narrative (in a process not so different from the way a history book is constructed). Even if we know this already, we conveniently forget it in order to participate in the experience that cinema provides.

Less obvious is the fact that these bits and pieces are stuck together according to certain codes of representation, conventions of film that have been developed to create what may be called 'cinematic realism' – a realism made up of certain kinds of shots in certain kinds of sequences, seamlessly edited together and underscored by a soundtrack to give the viewer a sense that nothing (rather than everything) is being manipulated to create a world on screen in which we can all feel at home. (I leave aside here the small number of 'experimental' historical films that utilise a surrealistic or postmodern aesthetic and which I have treated elsewhere. See Rosenstone 1995b: 198–224.)

The reason to point to the codes of cinema (which have a vast literature of their own) is to emphasise the fundamental fiction that underlies the history film: the notion that we can somehow look through the window of the screen directly at a 'real' world, present or past. This 'fiction' parallels a certain convention of written history: its documentary or empirical element, which insists on the 'reality' of the world it creates and analyses, yet that reality consists of no more than words on the page.

In creating history on screen, the dramatic film regularly indulges in six common and overlapping practices:

1   Film tells history as a story, a tale with a beginning, middle and an end. A tale that leaves you with a moral message and (usually) a feeling of uplift. A tale embedded in a larger view of history that is usually progressive, if sometimes Marxist (another form of progress). If the subject matter is particularly dire – slavery, the Holocaust, the Khmer Rouge, the Rwandan genocide – the message delivered on the screen is that things are getting better, have got better, or both, for if nothing else, the very ability to tell the story can be seen as a sign of progress.

This message need not be direct. A film about the horrors of a genocide or the failure of idealistic or radical movements may seem to be a counter-example, but such works are structured to leave us feeling: Aren't we lucky we did not live in those benighted times? Isn't it nice that certain people kept the flag of hope alive? Aren't we much better off today?

Seediq Bale fits easily into this practice. It ultimately may be a work about the decimation of a tribe and the end of a way of life, but it is a glorious defeat which leads to a moral and spiritual victory. The Seediq have remained true to the values of their tradition; the men have acted in a most noble fashion (by their values if not ours) against their oppressors, and their actions allow them to cross the rainbow bridge into the glorious next world, the realm of their ancestors. Their women, too, at least in the full-length four-plus-hour version of the film, have also acted in a noble manner, killing their children and committing suicide to support the actions of their men.

2   Film insists on history as the story of individuals, either men or women (but usually men) who are already renowned, or men and women who are made to seem important because they appear before us in such a large image on the screen. Those not already famous are common people who have done heroic or admirable things, or who have suffered unusually bad exploitation and oppression. The point: dramatic features put individuals in the forefront of the historical process.

Like a typical history film, the drama in *Seediq Bale* centres around a few characters who stand in for a larger experience of Japanese colonialism and resistance. Mona Rudo, chief of one Seediq village, figures in a great deal of the main movement of the film. His actions raise questions about and reinforce tradition, and his decisions serve to move the drama. His sons and his wife, the other tribal leaders, the warriors, and children of his and other villages never achieve much individuality, though a couple of the Japanese occupiers are on screen enough for the audience to come to detest them, and two Seediq who are partially Japanised stand in for the temptation of abandoning the ancient culture for the modern.

3   Film offers us history as the story of a closed, completed and simple past. It provides no alternative possibilities to what we see happening on the screen, admits no doubts and promotes each historical assertion with the same degree of confidence. A subtle film such as *The Return of Martin Guerre* may hint at hidden historical alternatives, at data not mentioned and stories untold, but such possibilities are not openly explored on the screen.

This sort of vision of the past clearly applies to *Seediq Bale*. The audience has no way of knowing the larger problematics, if any, of the Japanese-Seediq relationships over the 20 years in which the story is told. The presence of what one might call bicultural natives with Japanese wives at least suggests some possible alternatives or accommodation at the individual level to the cycle of invasion and exploitation, but the resolution of the film forecloses any such option.

4   Film emotionalises, personalises and dramatises history. Through actors, it gives us history as triumph, anguish, joy, despair, adventure, suffering and heroism. Dramatised works use the special capabilities of the medium – the close-up of the human face, the juxtaposition of disparate images, the power of music and sound effect – to heighten and intensify the feelings of the audience about what is happening on the screen. Film thus raises the following issues. To what extent does emotion belong in historical discourse? Does it lead away from or towards knowledge and historical understanding? Does film add to our understanding of the past by making us feel immediately and deeply about particular historical people, events and situations?

Recent scholarship on this issue tends to answer in the affirmative. Alison Landsberg, the scholar who has dealt with this notion most forcefully in two books *Prosthetic Memory* (2004) and *Engaging the Past* (2015), utilises a vast array of approaches, including the latest in neuropsychological research, to argue that emotion provides its own sort of learning and can in fact be a great help in the process of cognition. From this frame of reference, the violent emotion provided by *Seediq Bale* can make for an important learning experience. Certainly it takes what (at least to a Western and, I imagine, any non-Taiwanese audience) is an extremely obscure historical incident by indulging in a highly emotional tone, involves members of the audience in the invasion, exploitation and destruction of a native people of whom many of us have never before heard.

5   Film so obviously gives us the 'look' of the past – of buildings, landscapes and artefacts – that we may not see what this does to our sense of history. So it is important to stress that more than simply the 'look' of things, film provides a sense of how common objects appeared when they were in use. In film, period clothing does not hang limply on a dummy in a glass case, as it does in a museum; rather, it confines, emphasises and expresses the moving body.

Seediq Bale shows us homes, clothing, tattoos, tools, utensils, and weapons for hunting and warfare that are not shown in a diorama or are not items on display in cases or images on the pages of books, but life-enhancing objects that the characters on screen use and misuse, objects they depend upon and cherish, objects that help to define their livelihoods, identities, lives and destinies.

6   Film shows history as process. The world on the screen brings together things that, for analytic or structural purposes, written history often has

to split apart. Economics, politics, race, class and gender all come together in the lives and moments of individuals, groups and nations. This characteristic of film throws into relief a convention of written history, the strategy that may fracture the past into distinct chapters, topics and categories; that treats gender in one section, race in another, economy in a third. Historian Daniel Walkowitz points out that written history often compartmentalises 'the study of politics, family life, or social mobility'. Film, by contrast, 'provides an integrative image. History in film becomes what it most centrally is: a process of changing social relationships where political and social questions – indeed, all aspects of the past, including the language used – are interwoven' (Walkowitz 1985: 57).

This means that a character like Mona Rudo is a son, a father, a hunter, a tribal chief, a husband, a colonial subject, a traveller who has been to Japan, a wise man who knows the world and the tribal traditions, a giver of law, a commander who finally makes the decision to attack the Japanese.

Seediq Bale and reading and judging the history film

Our sense of the past is shaped and limited by the possibilities and practices of the medium in which that past is conveyed, be it the printed page, the spoken word, the painting, the photograph or the moving image. This means that whatever historical understanding or knowledge the mainstream film can provide will be shaped and limited by the conventions outlined above: the closed story, the notion of progress, the emphasis on individuals, the single interpretation, the heightening of emotional states, the focus on surfaces.

These conventions, the demands of the medium itself, and the form in which stories are told on screen, namely drama, ensure that film will always create a past far different from the one provided by written history; indeed, they ensure that the history film will inevitably violate the norms of academic history. To obtain the full benefits of the motion picture – the dramatic story, character, look, emotional intensity, process – that is, to use film's power to the fullest, is to ensure alterations in the way we think about the past. The question then becomes: What kinds of things do we learn by approaching the past through the conventions of the dramatic film (conventions that, through the global influence of Hollywood, are understood everywhere in the world)?

These conventions have been created by filmmakers who are not trained in a discipline, and so one may wonder by what right directors speak of the past and create works of history. The answer: they speak (or film) because, much like historians, they have personal, artistic, political or monetary reasons to do so. The best certainly do research, or hire researchers to help them. In a sense they speak the way historians did before the era of professional training within standards created by a profession, by learning from other filmmakers. If this makes the production of history on film seem haphazard, it is all the more necessary that trained historians who care about public history learn how to 'read' and 'judge' such films. This means having to reconsider the standards for history in line with filmic possibilities and practice. Among the many issues in learning how to judge the history film, none is more controversial than that of invention. This most clearly sets the history film apart from written history, which in principle eschews any fictional element, save for the huge, basic and often ignored fictional move that insists people, movements and nations can be depicted in stories that are linear and ultimately have a moral meaning.

History as drama is shot through with fiction and invention from the smallest details to the largest events. Take something simple, such as the structure and its furnishings in which a historical personage such as Mona Rudo or other tribal members or the Japanese colonisers live and work. Or some process, such as the wild boar hunt at the start of *Seediq Bale*, or the reconstruction of various battles between the indigenous groups or against the Japanese. The structure and the sequences are, obviously, no more than approximate rather than literal representations. They say this is more or less the way a chief's home looked at that time; these are the sorts of artefacts that might have been in such a room. This is more or less the way boars were hunted or battles were fought on this sort of terrain. The larger point, the need of the camera to fill out the specifics of a particular historical scene, or to create a coherent (and moving) visual sequence, will always ensure large doses of invention in the history film.

The same is true of character. All films will include fictional people or invented elements of character. The very use of an actor to 'be' someone will always be a kind of fiction. If the person is 'historical', the film says what cannot truly be said: that this is how this person looked, moved and sounded. If the individual has been created to exemplify a group of historical people (a worker during a strike, a shopkeeper during a revolution, a Seediq on a hunt or in combat) a double fiction is involved: this is how this sort of person (whom we have created) looked, moved and sounded. Both can obviously be no more than approximations of particular historical individuals, approximations that carry out some sense that we already have about how such people acted, moved and behaved. The same is true of incident, where invention is inevitable for a variety of reasons – to keep the story moving, to maintain intensity of feeling, to simplify overly complex events into a plausible dramatic structure that will fit within filmic time constraints. Different kinds of fictional moves are involved here, moves we can label Compression, Condensation, Alteration and Metaphor.

One might think that the difference between fiction and history is this: both tell stories, but the latter is what we call a 'true' story. However, can this be a 'literal' truth, an exact copy of what took place in the past? Of course not. In a drama on screen it can never be. How about the printed page, is literal truth possible there? Not really. A description of a battle or a strike or a revolution is hardly a literal rendering of that series of events. Some sort of 'fiction' or 'convention' is involved here, one that allows a selection of evidence to stand for a larger historical experience, one that allows a small sampling of reports to represent the collective experience of thousands, tens of thousands, even millions who took part in or were affected by documentable events.

Film may show us the world, or the surface of part of the world, but it can never provide a literal rendition of events that took place in the past. It can never be an exact replica of what happened (as if we ever know exactly what happened). Of course historical recounting has to be based in part on evidence of what happened in the past, but the recounting itself can never be literal. Not on the screen and not, in fact, in the written word. For the word works differently from the image. The word can provide vast amounts of data in a small space. The word can generalise, can talk of great abstractions like revolution, evolution, progress and colonisation, and it can make us believe that these things exist, but of course they do not, at least not as things; they are abstractions written upon the page. To talk of such generalisations is not to talk literally, but to talk in a symbolic or metaphoric way about the past. Film, with its need for a specific image, cannot make general statements; film must summarise, synthesise, generalise, symbolise in specific images. The best we can hope for is that historical data on film will be summarised with inventions and images that are apposite to the larger meaning we impose on the past. Such generalisations on film will always come through various techniques of condensation, synthesis and symbolisation, which means that to learn to read the history film we must understand how to 'read' this filmic vocabulary.

Clearly, we must use standards different from those of academic historians, but what should they be? First we must accept that film cannot be seen as some sort of direct window onto the past. What happens on screen is never more than a distant approximation of what was said and done in the past; what happens on screen does not depict, but rather points to, the events of the past in order to make them meaningful to us in the present. This suggests it is necessary for us to learn to judge the ways in which, through various forms of invention and symbolisation, film summarises data or abstract complexities that otherwise could not be shown. We must accept that film will always include images that are at once invented and true; true in that they symbolise, condense or summarise larger amounts of data; true in that they impart an overall meaning of the past that can be verified, documented or reasonably argued.

How do we know what can be verified, documented or reasonably argued? Only from attending to the ongoing discourse of history; from the already existing body of historical texts; from their data, debates and arguments. Which is only to say that any 'history' film, like any other work of written, graphic or oral history, enters a body of pre-existing knowledge and debate. *To be considered a history film rather than simply a costume drama that uses the past as an exotic setting for romance and adventure, a work must engage, directly or obliquely, the issues, ideas, data and arguments of that ongoing discourse.* Like the book, the history film cannot exist in a state of historical innocence, should not indulge in capricious invention, or ignore the broader findings, assertions and arguments of what we already know from other sources. Like any work of history, a film must be judged in terms of the knowledge of the past that we already possess. Like any work of history, it must situate itself within a body of other works, the ongoing (multimedia) debate over the importance of events and the meaning of the past.

A new kind of history

Those attempting to determine whether *Seediq Bale* can be judged as a work of 'history' would have to evaluate how well the depiction of people and events on screen intersects with the larger discourse surrounding Japanese colonisation of Taiwan and the Wushe Incident (or 'Musha Incident' in Japanese) itself. That would have to mean taking into account any oral histories that have been carried out with participants or the descendants of those involved in the incident, along with evidence from those who remember the larger issues of the colonial period, as well as those journalists, memoirists and historians who have written about the incident or the broader social context in which it occurred. Drawing on the work of anthropologists or other historical witnesses of Seediq behaviour, values and opinions would also have to enter the mix of oral and written texts that comprise the broader discourse to which the film relates.

Any answers about the film's contribution to historical knowledge or understanding must also take account of the form in which the past is delivered. History is never simply a matter of highlighting individual facts. In the contemporary tradition, data turn into history only when they are enfolded into a narrative. In this case the narrative has visual and aural elements, most of which can be seen less as verifiable facts than as plausible inventions based upon data from the past. We may realise that the villages, settlements, battles and incidents are no more than approximations of what happened, but we must also understand that the same is true of the characters involved, who are more emblems of social roles than individuals. Mona Rudo, who dominates the film as he presumably historically dominated his tribe, seems far less an actual historical figure than an idealised portrait of a tribal leader, first as heroic youngster and then wise elder. He is always shown as stronger, more thoughtful, more steeped in tradition and more decisive than any of those around him. We can never know if the real Mona was precisely this way, but we understand that to hold his peace for so long and then lead the revolt at Wushe he must have had many of these characteristics.

The film is also a history pertaining to a larger realm here than that of the Wushe Incident. *Seediq Bale* is also a work about the costs and depredations of colonialism, in this case of the Japanese variety, and it should also be judged in that way and not only on the specifics of the Wushe Incident. The portrait it provides of militarism, exploitation, discrimination, racism and the destruction of traditional ways in the name of 'civilisation' is powerful, visceral and surely historical. It creates this effect in part by putting the spectator not only on the side of the exploited, but also in the somewhat odd position of cheering for the Seediq to slaughter their oppressors, including the non-combatant wives and children. This underlines the brutality and inherent injustice of this particular colonial project.

Of all the elements that make up a historical film, fiction or invention has to be the most problematic for historians. To accept invention is, of course, to change significantly the way we think about history. It is to alter one of written history's basic elements: its documentary or empirical aspect. To take history on film seriously is to accept the notion that the empirical is but one way of thinking about the meaning of the past. Indeed, accepting the changes in history that dramatic film proposes is not to collapse all standards of historical truth, but to accept another way of understanding our relationship to the past, another way of pursuing that conversation about where we came from, where we are going and who we are. Film neither replaces written history nor supplements it. Film stands adjacent to written history, as it does to other forms of dealing with the past such as memory and the oral tradition.

The history film may be seen as a new kind of history that, like all history, operates within certain limited boundaries. In a way it is a form close to earlier forms of history, a way of dealing with the meaning of the past that is more like oral history, or history told by bards, or history contained in classic epics. Perhaps film is a post-literate equivalent of the pre-literate way of dealing with the past, of those forms of history in which scientific, documentary accuracy was not yet a consideration, forms in which any notion of fact was of less importance than the sound of a voice, the rhythm of a line, the magic of words. One can have similar aesthetic moments in film, when objects or scenes – say the waterfall, the bridge over the gorge, the gorgeous jungle landscapes in which the *Seediq Bale* lived their days – may seem included simply for the sheer visual pleasure they impart. However, in documenting the beauties of the world in which the natives dwell, the film is also creating 'facts' of history for the onscreen world.

The major difference between the present and the pre-literate world with regard to history must be underscored: literacy has intervened. This means that however poetic or expressive it may be, history on film enters into a world where 'scientific' and documentary history have long been pursued and are still undertaken, where accuracy of event and detail has its own lengthy tradition. In a sense, this tradition raises history on film to a new level, for it provides a check on what can be invented and expressed. To be taken seriously, the historical film must not violate the overall data and meanings of what we already know of the past. All changes and inventions must engage the truths of that discourse, and judgement must emerge from the accumulated knowledge of the world of historical texts into which the film enters. If a studied analysis of *Seediq Bale* can show the film playing such a role, then it indeed can be seen as a work of history.

12 Violence and indigenous visual history

Interventional historiography in *Seediq Bale* and *Wushe, Chuanzhong Island*

Kuei-fen Chiu

Film as visual history

'Wei Te-sheng doesn't make movies; he makes history.' So remarked the editor of the film section of *Time Out Hong Kong* in a 2011 interview with Wei Te-sheng (Lee 2011). He made this statement to highlight the impressive box office success of Wei's films, particularly *Cape No.7* (2008) and *Seediq Bale* (2011), in Taiwan, but the statement can also be taken literally. History lies at the heart of Wei's filmmaking enterprise. Take a look at the two feature films he directed and *Kano* (2014) – the film with Wei as the producer and Ma Zhi-xiang (a.k.a. Umin Boya, one of the main indigenous characters in *Seediq Bale*) as the director. Each of the three aforementioned films deals with a specific historical juncture in Taiwan's colonial history, stirring up great controversies in Taiwan as the films took the island by storm. Wei is a maker of history films in the sense that his works intervene in the debates on how Taiwan's historical past should be narrated and the ideological implications of narrativity (see Rosenstone in this volume). A history film, as defined by Robert A. Rosenstone (2013: 74), is 'a mode of historical thought' that 'not only devotes itself consciously to constructing a world of the past on screen, but in doing so manages to engage the discourse of history, the body of data and debates surrounding any historical topic' (Rosenstone 2013: 71–72).

Like what happens to almost every historical representation onscreen, the question of accuracy is raised in response to the impact of the three films on the historical understanding of Taiwan's colonial past (Guo 2011). However, as Rosenstone (1995a: 7) argues, film as visual history 'must be taken on its own terms as a portrait of the past that has less to do with fact than with intensity and insight, perception and feeling, with showing how events affect individual lives, past and present'. History on film cannot be 'an exact copy of what took place in the past' (Rosenstone 1995b: 69). We must accept that 'filmic "literalism" is impossible' (Rosenstone 1995b: 70).

In addition to the question of accuracy, how the films tell stories about Taiwan's colonial past is also an important issue. In the case of *Cape No.7* and *Kano*, the portrayal of the relationship between the Taiwanese colonised and the Japanese colonisers is of special interest to film critics. *Cape No.7*, though set mainly in contemporary southern Taiwan, refers back to the beginning of the post-war era in Taiwan when many Japanese embarked on the trip home as a result of the defeat of Japan. The love story between a Taiwanese girl and a departing Japanese teacher at that historical moment is interwoven skilfully with a romance between a Taiwanese man and a Japanese actress in contemporary Taiwan, stirring up a heated debate on the ideological position of the film toward Taiwan's colonial past.

Kano resurrects the legend of a local high school baseball team in colonial Taiwan which, to everybody's surprise, made it to the national high school baseball championship in Japan. Depicting the transformation of a local baseball team in the hands of a Japanese coach, *Kano*, like *Cape No.7*, tells a story of the rapport between the Japanese colonisers and the Taiwanese colonised. Some critics argue that the film plays into the hands of colonial discourse. The question as to whether the two films imply a nostalgic romance with Japan lies at the heart of the debates (C. Wang 2009a; Y. Wang 2009b; Zhan 2010; Ma 2011: 49–58; Feng and Ling 2014; also see Liao in this volume).

Seediq Bale escapes criticism in this vein because of its focus on an indigenous uprising against Japanese colonisers in the infamous Wushe Incident. It tells the story of a rebellion under the leadership of Mona Rudo, which killed 134 Japanese but resulted in the annihilation of two-thirds of the population of the six participating Seediq groups. The incident marks a watershed in Japanese colonial governmentality, for the colonialist strategy shifted from military subjugation and economic servitude to imperial incorporation (Ching 2000: 799–803). For both the colonised Seediq and Japanese colonialists, the Wushe Incident is a catastrophe of tremendous historical significance. In spite of its deliberate focus on the perspectives of the rebellious Seediq, the film *Seediq Bale* raises a controversy because of its graphic violence. Criticised by many critics for 'blood thirst' and an astonishing number of graphic beheadings (The Economist 2011; Peng 2011; Young 2011), *Seediq Bale* is often classified as an action movie that does not help justify the indigenous resistance (also see Lee in this volume). If indigenous headhunting is often used as a trope for savagery and cruelty in colonialist discourse (Ching 2000: 806), the film's reiteration of the violence of headhunting seems to consolidate, rather than deconstruct, the dichotomy between civility and savagery.

In other words, if *Seediq Bale* is made as an intervention in the historical narration of the Wushe Incident, the film's attempt to present a visual history 'from the perspective of the [aboriginal] hunters' (Lee 2011) does not seem to serve the interests of the indigenous people. The film's visual embodiment of the violence, decapitation associated with the Seediq traditional practice of headhunting, is perceived by many critics as 'excess', too disturbing to be understood *properly*. However, if we take into account the fact that more than 100 Japanese were beheaded in the uprising and nearly 90 Tgdaya Seediq tribe people were beheaded in turn by the Japanese-recruited Toda Seediq, the violence in the movie is not excessive but realistic rendering of the historical past. It is considered 'excessive' and 'improper' because the violence of beheading is usually taken to be too uncivilised to be rendered literally onscreen. As Yomi Braester (2003: 7) remarks in his discussion of violence in twentieth-century China, 'violence accentuates and amplifies the discrepancy between history and its representation, between fact and fiction'. Violence inscribes a gap 'that makes the real inaccessible to words' (Braester 2003: 7). In other words, violence in the extreme form remains inexplicable and beyond representation.

However, it is important to recognise that the trauma of the Wushe Incident cannot be disassociated from violence. Any historical retelling of this traumatised history cannot discount its violence – the brutality of the Seediq practice of headhunting, the massacre of Japanese and that of the rebellious Seediq by Japanese-recruited Seediq. As Michael Berry (2008: 80) sums up succinctly:

> How can the spirit of the incident be endorsed when headhunting is judged as barbaric? How can the initial incident be read as a purely patriotic, anticolonial movement when it was duplicated a few months later as a cannibalistic bloodfest? And what is the fundamental difference, if any, between the original raid on the Japanese at the elementary school and the second series of raids on the detention center where the Atayal [Tgdaya Seediq] were being held for 'protection'?

How should a historical reconstruction of the Wushe Incident take on the challenge of articulating violence in visual terms as it attempts to answer these difficult questions? Rather than seeing the graphic violence of the film as the director's indulgence or inept narrativisation of a complicated historical story, this chapter proposes to analyse three visual embodiments of violence with an eye to the problematic of indigenous historiography. Crucial to this problematic are the following questions: What is the so-called Seediq's view of the violence of this traumatic history? If, as the historian Wan-yao Zhou (2011: 4) points out, the Seediq perspective has been sorely missing in all post-war historical accounts of the Wushe Incident even though the Seediq were the key historical agents and actors in that event, how would the interpretation of the violence of the Wushe Incident from a Seediq perspective impact on the historical interpretation of the Wushe Incident? How should such a perspective be rendered visually onscreen?

The first visual image chosen for analysis is a photo taken in celebration of the Japanese successful retaliation. The second is the massacre scene in *Seediq Bale*. The third is the fighting between the divided Seediq tribes during the Wushe Incident. Finally, we will juxtapose the stories suggested in these three visual embodiments with the critical responses of Seediq people from various villages to the movie in a documentary film, *Wushe, Chuanzhong Island* (*Wushe chuanzhongdao*, dir. Pilin Yapu, 2013), made by an Atayal documentary filmmaker. All visual representations discussed in this chapter – be they in the form of photo, feature film or documentary – suggest historiographic attempts marked by a specific position vis-à-vis the Wushe Incident. The fierce clash of these historiographic practices opens up an ethical space of witnessing and inheriting, where the unclaimed experience of the historical trauma of an important part of indigenous history in Taiwan returns and demands to be remembered.

A photo of layered violence

First, let's take a close look at a photo taken at the historical juncture of the Wushe Incident. As an archival document, it bears witness to the shocking violence of the historical event. This photo was apparently taken in celebration of the Japanese revenge on the rebellious Seediq, for a Japanese general in military uniform squats triumphantly in the middle, looking directly at the camera. What is so shocking about the photo is the unbearable sight of some-hundred heads cut off the rebellious Seediq. Another close examination reveals a second layer of violence superimposed on the first one: these Seediq heads are obviously trophies of a violent headhunting conducted by the Seediq surrounding the Japanese general. Thus, in addition to the conflict between the colonisers and the colonised, the photo stages the unspeakable violence of the internal division among the colonised Seediq.

Figure 12.1 Massacre of rebellious Seediq by Japanese-recruited Seediq
Permission to reproduce here by Deng Xiang-yang.

As a silent and yet powerful testimony to the brutality of the battles, this photo speaks volumes on the traumatised history of the Wushe Incident. The violence is conducted against Seediq not only by Japanese colonisers but also by Seediq themselves. Many contemporary viewers of the photo probably would see the violence of beheadings in such a great number as an unmistakable indication of the savageness of the Seediq traditional practice. Moreover, the fact that the great number of beheadings was carried out relentlessly by Seediq against Seediq seems to confirm the wide divide between civilisation and barbarianism. Such an interpretation in fact forms the backbone of Japanese colonialist ideology. This photo of Japanese colonisers' triumph over indigenous savages serves to authenticate the colonialist discourse on the so-called 'barbarianism' of the colonised indigenes. However, if this photo of excessive violence evokes a 'barbaric story' about the 1930s Taiwanese indigenes, could it be that it also throws into relief the barbarity of the Japanese themselves who cleverly played the Seediq against each other so that the great number of Seediq heads could be thus staged in a spectacular display in front of the camera? Although such a reading of the photo may deconstruct the opposition between the Japanese colonisers and the indigenous colonised, it still falls short of critiquing the so-called indigenous savagery. If headhunting is often exploited as a trope to define indigenous Seediq as savages, how would the Seediq perspective on headhunting with all its blood-shedding and violence impact on the historical narrative of the Seediq uprising in 1930? This is the task Wei took upon himself when he set out to make the movie *Seediq Bale*.

Massacre of Japanese

Central to the Wushe Incident was the massacre of Japanese at a primary school when an annual sports competition was held. Resurrecting the long-suppressed Seediq custom of headhunting, the rebellious Seediq led by the Tgdaya leader Mona Rudo killed 134 Japanese. Women and children were not spared. How should the director conduct a visual representation of the massacre that would include the Seediq hunters' perspective? How does he manage to contrive a *responsible* account of this story of massacre?

In an interview, Wei remarked that the binary opposition between the so-called good guys and bad guys does not work for history. He believed that we should be cautious in applying our present-day moral standard to the historical agents from hundreds of years ago (Zeng 2014: 369). Confronted with the daunting task of representing the massacre, he chose to highlight the Seediq's deep-rooted spiritual doctrine of *gaya*, of which headhunting is only one of the practices (Zeng 2014: 369). According to the traditional concept of *gaya*, a Seediq man with no success in headhunting would not be recognised as a 'Seediq bale' (literally a 'real man') by his tribal people. Nor would he be permitted to marry and have children of his own. A Seediq bale practises *gaya* and thereby gains the right to cross over the rainbow bridge in the afterlife to join his ancestors. This Seediq belief is reiterated throughout the film in various scenes. As Darryl Sterk (2011) puts it in a concise statement based on several scholars' explications, '[a] person who follows Gaya is a Seediq bale. Gaya is the ancestral teachings, the social norms, the ritual practices, the "law of life" [...], the "moral tradition" [...] which maintains the relationship between man and cosmos'. In a subsequent publication, Sterk (2012) further argues that 'in the film this Seediq bale belief is presented as the most significant cause of the incident' (also see Sterk in this volume).

It should be noted that when the Wushe Incident took place in 1930, the Seediq order rooted in the practices of *gaya* was breaking down as a result of the forceful implementation of Japanese colonial policies. Taiwan became Japan's colony in 1895. Ever since then, the Japanese colonial government has put in practice various policies to 'civilise the savages'. For example, traditional indigenous customs – such as headhunting and facial tattooing – were forbidden by the Japanese rulers. From the perspective of Seediq indigenes, to launch an attack on the Japanese colonisers by flaunting the suppressed headhunting practice means to resurrect the Seediq culture and reassert the manhood of the Seediq.

It is clear that Wei tries to present the Wushe Incident from the Seediq hunters' perspective so as to generate an alternative understanding of the violence of the massacre, but does this sympathetic representation of the Seediq hunters' perspective mean that Wei endorses the violence conducted by the Seediq in the massacre? In another interview, Wei speaks about the challenge of the massacre scene, which points to the complex message he tries to build into it:

> The biggest challenge was dealing with the scene of the actual Wushe Incident – the blood sacrifice. I wanted to create conflicting emotions among the audience when they are watching the scene. On [the] one hand, they want [to] cheer for the Seediq people because they feel empathetic towards their oppression. On the other hand, they may also feel antipathy, because the scene is more of a massacre instead of a man-to-man battle. Therefore, I needed to be extra careful when dealing with the aesthetics of violence in this particular scene in order to create the conflicting emotions.
>
> (Xie 2012)

We need to take a very close look at the filmic composition of the massacre scene. It is noteworthy that while the headhunting of panicking Japanese is depicted deliberately literally with a strong highlight on blood-shedding and the sheer force of the indigenous rebellious power, there appears an extra-diegetic female vocal in the Seediq language. It elevates the film viewers above the dramatic action, opening up a surreal dimension to the scene. Performing a function similar to that of the chorus in a Greek tragedy, the Seediq female vocal not only describes but also makes critical comments on the historical drama as it is being represented in the movie:

Oh, my children!
Look! The world keeps shivering.
Look! The reddened earth is silent.
Look! The bulk of Pusu Qhuni is peeling off.
Touch your blood-stained hands.
Can they still hold the sand from our hunting grounds?
Touch your angry forehead.
Can a beautiful rainbow bridge still be spread out over it?
Touch your uneasy mouth.
Can it still speak in all four seasons?

Judging from the lyrics, the singer of this song embodies the spirits of the Seediq hunters' female ancestors. The sorrowful female vocal hovering over the scene suggests a view of the massacre distinguishably different from that of the hunters in action. It conveys an ambivalent attitude toward what is going on in the diegetic world: while sympathetic to the hunters fighting against colonial oppression in defence of their pride and culture, the female ancestors' spirits also distance themselves from the Seediq hunters in their eagerness to avenge themselves through blood sacrifice. The ambiguity of the song, expressing neither complete disapproval nor a whole-hearted endorsement of the rebellious massacre, works to create the conflicting emotions that Wei mentioned in the interview quoted above.

In terms of the film as a practice of historical representation, the gap between the visual images and the soundtrack therefore enacts a curious split in the so-called 'indigenous perspective' on the historical event. Thus, rather than what Yu-lin Lee (2014b: 191) describes as 'a public enunciation of collectivity' or 'an assemblage of collective enunciations that belong to the entire

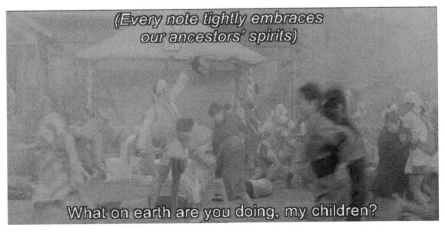

Figure 12.2 Split of 'indigenous perspective' in *Seediq Bale*
(Source: Central Motion Picture)

Seediq tribe', the Seediq utterance in this film, as dramatised in the composition of the massacre scene, designates a site of contradictions and ambiguities. It is not without reason that the vocal is gendered, suggesting a subtly different interpretation of the historical event from the perspective of Seediq women. *Seediq Bale* includes the hunters' perspective and thus acknowledges the perspective of the historical agents which has been missing in various accounts of the Wushe Incident. Interestingly, the extra-diegetic female vocal problematises this perspective without rejecting it.

The intricate interplay between different Seediq perspectives as dramatised through the audiovisual structuring of the massacre scene thus opens up an historiographical space of complex cultural negotiations. If headhunting is the most common trope for the so-called indigenous barbarity, the inclusion of the Seediq view of headhunting reinscribes the trope as one of cultural difference rather than a fundamental divide between barbarity and civilisation. The film thus performs a critique of the so-called indigenous savagery. At the same time, the intervention of the Seediq female vocal prevents a merging of the film's historical account of the massacre with that of the hunters. The complex composition of the massacre scene thus engages the traumatic indigenous history with a heightened critical consciousness, highlighting indigenous subjectivity and agency without over-simplifying the complex issues involved in the reconstruction of historical past.

Massacre of Seediq by Seediq

In a way, the film's graphic violence of the massacre implies a critical interpretation of the violence of headhunting. However, if the violence of the Wushe Incident involves at least two layers of violence – namely, the violence against Japanese in the Seediq uprising and the violence inflicted by divided Seediq groups upon each other in the wake of the Wushe Incident – how should a filmmaker of Han ethnicity portray the Toda Seediq who helped Japanese in the brutal crackdown on rebellious Tgdaya Seediq? How should he tackle the traumatic history of an internal strife that remains mostly unspeakable among the indigenes? In a working journal written during the filming process, Wei Te-sheng remarks on the hypersensitivity of Seediq people toward this issue. Before he began making the movie, he visited the Seediq villages and asked the village people to voice their opinions and suggestions:

> Everyone had his/her own worries. But they shared a common ambivalence toward the movie. They all wanted to have the story told and spread to all corners of the world, but, at the same time, they did not really want to have the movie made.
>
> I could see that they were suffering internal struggles. They needed reconciliation with one another. The Seediq is divided into three main groups – Toda, Truku, and Tgdaya. There have been conflicts among them since ancient times. Now that they were finally designated as all

belonging to the 'Seediq' tribe, they did not want the old antagonism be provoked again. They were worried that putting the past strife on screen would bring back the internal conflicts of the previous generations, or remind tribal people of the unpleasant past.

(Wei 2011: 39, my own translation)

However, avoiding the violence conducted by the Seediq against the Seediq in any serious account of the Wushe Incident would inevitably do violence to history. The photo of the massacre that we discussed at the very beginning of this chapter bears witness to the trauma of this unforgettable, though unspeakable, past. One strategy Wei uses to confront this thorny problem of historical reconstruction onscreen is to give a new interpretation of the Toda leader, Temu Walis, who played an active role in helping Japanese to crack down on the rebellious Tgdaya group. Wei makes it clear in his working journal that he wanted to create a more positive image of Temu Walis in the movie to help de-stigmatise Toda Seediq as 'pro-Japanese traitors' in official history books (Wei 2011: 248). The narration of the conflict between Tgdaya and Toda is shifted in the film from the rhetoric of 'rebellious heroes vs. pro-Japanese traitors' to the longstanding rivalry between the two Seediq groups. The violence committed by Seediq against one another in the colonial struggle is thereby implicitly justified.

The careful portrayal of the antagonism between Tgdaya and Toda, first shown in the film as a competition for the same hunting ground, culminates in the brutal fight between the groups during the Japanese counter-attacks. In addition to the violence of the battles that results in the great casualties for both Seediq groups, what is particularly noteworthy in the scene is the depiction of the death of Temu Walis in the battle. Although in historical reality Toda Seediq won the battle and Temu Walis did not die during the fight, the film departs noticeably from the historical truth by having Temu Walis beheaded by a Tgdaya during the bloody battle. This deliberate flaunting of historical accuracy generates an impression of the Toda leader as a Seediq warrior sacrificing his life in the continual rivalry between indigenous groups rather than a Seediq servile character manipulated by Japanese colonisers without his own agency.

Thus, in its head-on confrontation with the layered violence of the Wushe Incident, *Seediq Bale* enacts a filmic historiography highlighting missing indigenous perspectives in historical reconstruction. Setting multiple Seediq perspectives into play and having them speak to/against one another, the film embodies a highly self-conscious, critical historiographical practice that 'speaks with' or 'speaks alongside' indigenes, as Jay Ruby (2000: 195–219) recommends for ethnographic filmmaking. Building on a series of what Ruby calls 'ethno-dialogues', *Seediq Bale* avoids the pitfall of speaking about or speaking for indigenes in re-narrating a deeply traumatic indigenous history on the one hand, and on the other eschews romanticising a particular indigenous perspective that reduces the historical past in its full complexity to a simplified account.

Figure 12.3 Massacre of Seediq by Seediq
(Source: Central Motion Picture)

Speaking as indigenes: Pilin Yapu's documentary

With a record-breaking box office of millions of US dollars and the 'Best Feature Film Award' at the 2011 Golden Horse Film Festival (*Jin ma jiang*) held in Taipei, the overwhelming success of *Seediq Bale* as a movie blockbuster in Taiwan sparks a wave of indigenous cultural production in which indigenous writers/filmmakers voice indigenous responses to the film. *Truth, Bale* (2011) authored by Dakis Pawan of Tgdaya descent (a.k.a. Guo Ming-zheng), *Kari Toda* (2014) authored by Iwan Nawi of Toda descent, and *Wushe, Chuanzhong Island* by the Atayal documentary filmmaker Pilin Yapu are the three most prominent examples. The first book focuses on the deviation of the film from what the Tgdaya author calls 'historical truth' based on oral histories he collected from Tgdaya tribal elders. The second book is a translation of the original screenplay by Wei Te-sheng from Chinese to the Toda language, revealing the semiotic gap between the Chinese subtitles and the Seediq language spoken by the indigenous characters in the film. The authors of the two books were involved in the production of Wei's feature film. Both are of Seediq descent, though one is a Tgdaya while the other is a Toda. *Wushe, Chuanzhong Island* stresses the impact of the movie on the Seediq community and the voices of various Seediq groups in critical exchange with the historical narrative as dramatised in *Seediq Bale*.

The violent impact of the Wushe Incident on the Seediq community is registered at the very beginning of the documentary. An interviewee from the Seediq Tgdaya group remarks on the trauma: 'People of our village do not talk about the Wushe Incident. Any mention of the incident opens the old wounds. It breaks our heart.' Among Tgdaya, the traumatic history of the Wushe Incident is something unspeakable and unspoken. Interestingly, interviews with Toda reveal that not only do Tgdaya Seediq try to suppress the historical memory of the Wushe Incident, but the Toda Seediq likewise choose to leave it behind. The Wushe Incident becomes a collective trauma for the whole Seediq. 'Trauma', as defined by Cathy Caruth in her famous book, *Unclaimed Experience: Trauma, Narrative, and History*, designates an overwhelming experience of a catastrophic event that defies understanding and articulation (Caruth 1996: 5). However, the Wushe Incident leaves the Seediq traumatised in different ways. They shrink from talking about it for different reasons.

For Tgdaya Seediq, the violence of the Wushe Incident brings the survival of the Tgdaya group to a crisis. At the core of the violence is not only the encounter with death, but also the impossibility of surviving. This traumatic violence is revealed in the alienated relationship between the great granddaughter of Mona Rudo and her grandmother, a daughter of Mona Rudo. In an interview presented in the documentary film, the great granddaughter tells a story of intergenerational alienation as the descendants of Mona Rudo struggle to survive the tragedy. E. Ann Kaplan remarks that 'transgenerational trauma is a kind of unconscious vicarious trauma', as the subjects 'are haunted by tragedies, affecting their parents, grandparents, or ancestors from far back without conscious knowledge' (Kaplan 2005: 106). The subjects live with phantoms; they are haunted by ghosts that inhabit invisibly within the family space. For the Tgdaya interviewees, *Seediq Bale* is a much-welcomed resurrection of the unspoken past. The portrayal of Mona Rudo as a 'rainbow warrior' in Wei's blockbuster in defiance of Japanese colonial power onscreen provides what Kaplan called an 'ethical witness' to the historical past. Thus, the great granddaughter's story of bringing herself to a reconciliation with her grandmother who passed her life in forgetful drunkenness, becomes a story of Tgdaya coming to terms with the traumatised tragedy under the impact of the movie. For the interviewed Seediq Tgdaya, *Seediq Bale* has the healing effect of performing 'ethical witnessing' (Kaplan 2005: 122–123), for it helps shape a larger ethical framework to activate the public's recognition of the atrocities they have suffered.

It is noteworthy that the Wushe Incident remains also a taboo subject among the Seediq Toda, though for different reasons. On the one hand, any rapport with the Japanese colonisers has been viewed with strong disapproval since the Nationalists (i.e. Kuomintang or KMT) took over Taiwan after the Second World War. On the other hand, the active role of Toda in the Japanese crackdown on Tgdaya has contributed to the troubled relationship of the two Seediq groups ever since colonial times. Understandably, most Seediq Toda remain silent about the Wushe Incident, particularly the role of their ancestors in the battles. In the documentary, the suppression of the historical memory is shown by the ignorance of Away Temu – a daughter of the Toda leader Temu Walis – about her father's story. The graphic violence of the blood-shedding battle between Tgdaya and Toda warriors in *Seediq Bale* is thus most disturbing to the indigenous people, for it touches on a hypersensitive issue in Seediq communities.

In contrast to the movie which focuses mostly on the Tgdaya perspective and accentuates the role of Mona Rudo as the hero of the dramatic story, the documentary film by the indigenous filmmaker Pilin Yapu deliberately gives the Toda people more say. It calls attention to Toda people's critical responses toward the way the past is reconstructed in *Seediq Bale*. While the movie blockbuster is welcomed by many Tgdaya as ethical witnessing that helps break the silence about an unarticulated historical trauma, it is criticised by many Toda interviewees for failing to reveal the historical truth. Cutting back and forth between film clips from *Seediq Bale* and interviews with Toda, particularly the descendants of Temu Walis, the documentary presents counter-memories from Toda perspectives. Toda interviewees underscore the point that the conflict between Toda and Tgdaya in the Wushe Incident should not be interpreted in terms of the rivalry between the two groups. Toda were forced to take sides with the Japanese for their own survival. They were pawns in a game in which the indigenous groups were set to play against one another by the Japanese colonial government.

Another objection brought up by the Toda interviewees concerns the role of Mona Rudo as an anti-Japanese hero. They point out that the opposition between pro-Japanese Toda and anti-Japanese Tgdaya does not do justice to historical truth, for the so-called anti-Japanese hero Mona Rudo helped Japanese attack an Atayal village ten years before the Wushe Incident occurred. In other words, Toda interviewees in the documentary problematise the binary opposition in popular historical accounts between anti-Japanese and pro-Japanese stances in defining an indigenous hero. For them, the idea of a heroic indigenous warrior, as someone who practises *gaya* and gains the right to cross over the rainbow bridge after he dies, has nothing to do with the Japanese or Chinese nationalist sentiment. If *Seediq Bale* tells the story of an indigenous hero in an anti-Japanese uprising, the documentary voices alternative indigenous perspectives that problematise the hero-making of a movie made by a non-indigenous director. Made by an indigenous documentary filmmaker, *Wushe, Chuanzhong Island* practises an indigenous historiography highlighting the heterogeneity of indigenous voices in the interpretation of historical events.

The documentary juxtaposes interviews with Seediq with film clips from *Seediq Bale* to open up a space for an indigenous account in critical exchange with the historical narrative of the movie. Significantly, direct critical exchanges of this kind between Toda and Tgdaya seldom occur in the documentary. It is obvious that the documentary filmmaker cautiously avoids playing the opinions of the two Seediq groups against each other in their different interpretations of the Wushe Incident and the historical agents involved. Both *Seediq Bale* and *Wushe, Chuanzhong Island* try to make visual histories with a highlight on the agency of indigenes. They both involve indigenous perspectives in a complicated way to do justice to the various roles of the indigenes in the shaping of history. Rather than trying to do away with the violence of the Wushe Incident, both films underscore it as elusive memory. As ethical witnessing, these two audiovisual productions, to borrow the words of Kaplan in discussing films dealing with trauma, 'expose the structure of injustice and ... invite reviewers to take responsibility for related specific injustice' (Kaplan 2005: 135). If the representation of the headhunting Seediq as savages fails to do justice to the historical past, does the highlighting of rebellious Seediq as heroes do justice to history? This is a perplexing question raised in the indigenous documentary.

Seediq Bale and film aesthetics

If *Seediq Bale* seems to engage graphic violence in an extreme form, this chapter argues that violence lies at the very heart of the Wushe Incident. Any historical reconstruction that tried to domesticate the violence would do violence to history. Our discussion begins with an analysis of the violence embodied visually in a photo taken in the wake of the incident. It is followed by a critical examination of the historiographical practices of *Seediq Bale* to show how the film strategically tackles the issue of violence in audiovisual terms. Finally, a comparison between the framework of ethical witnessing as constructed in the feature film and that in the indigenous documentary *Wushe, Chuanzhong Island* reveals the complexity of what may be considered indigenous perspectives of history. The critical intervention of *Seediq Bale* in the debates on the storytelling of the Wushe Incident with all the historiographical issues involved makes the blockbuster a history film par excellence.

13 Archiving a historical incident

The making of *Seediq Bale* as a socio-political event

Yu-lin Lee

Introduction

Released in 2011, Wei Te-sheng's feature film *Warriors of the Rainbow: Seediq Bale* became a blockbuster and a major socio-political event. With the biggest investment in Taiwan's film history to date, the movie sought to emulate the Hollywood model, especially in terms of production value and marketing strategies, and demonstrated its ambition to enter the international film arena. Despite setbacks at major film festivals and in the international market, the film enjoyed great popularity at home. It also provoked heated debates on many issues, such as colonial historiography and identity politics, thus making a significant impact on Taiwanese society.

Many film critics, such as Leo Dai (2011) and others, have offered explanations for the film's failure in artistic composition and international reception. For example, its unbalanced narrative structure, immature cinematic techniques and absence of internationally famous stars in the movie were all blamed for its poor international reception despite world-famous director John Woo acting as producer. In addition, the dominance of Hollywood and longstanding cultural and political barriers between national borders prevented this particular film from entering the international film market successfully.

However, greater attention by critics has been given to the subject matter of the movie, which depicts an indigenous uprising organised by the Seediq tribe against Japanese colonial oppression in 1930. The uprising, known as the Wushe Incident (*Wushe shijian*), has become infamous in colonial history from the Japanese perspective. It was documented as a brutal massacre in which more than 100 Japanese officials and residents were decapitated and more than 200 were injured. This incident resulted in further Japanese military action and imposed even more rigid colonial policies in order to consolidate control over the aboriginal areas. Hundreds of Seediq indigenous people were also killed due to this incident and its backlash. Ironically, since the end of the Second World War, the incident has been portrayed as a patriotic action against Japanese colonialism in most historiographies produced by the Nationalist government (i.e. Kuomintang or KMT) in Taiwan.

The subject matter involves colonial histories, war memories, racial and cultural conflicts, and many others, and thus may not be a welcome topic for certain domestic and international audiences given the contemporary socio-political atmosphere that values racial amalgamation and multiculturalism. Indeed, the most challenging task for the director was how to interpret this contentious incident in terms of colonial historiography and how to present the indigenous people and their culture. It necessarily demanded an inter-pretative position and a justifiable attitude toward colonial history, and in this regard Wei's Han cultural background and ethnic identity only complicated an already difficult job. As a result, *Seediq Bale* is often attacked for its poor representation of history and its misunderstanding of indigenous culture. Further, its interpretation of history is accused of servicing the Han majority standpoint only and its description of the Seediq tribe as one of capitalist consumption of minority people and a minority culture. For example, in an oft-cited article, the anthropologist Kai-shi Lin criticises the film for utilising a controversial and traumatised legend simply to create a 'moral and ima-ginary space for consumption' for the majorities in Taiwanese society (Lin 2011: 39).

This chapter addresses the aesthetic values and the film's historical repre-sentation, as well as its ethical focus on the indigenous people and culture which are so central to those debates. However, instead of its historical representation, this chapter emphasises the function of the movie as a cine-matographic archive. Accordingly the discussion no longer focuses on the truthfulness of its representation and its politics, but rather on its artistic composition and the process for producing historical memories. Such an archive approach demonstrates the politics of remembering and forgetting, which is governed by the social values and aesthetic principles as defined by the director. More significantly, the archive functions as a medium by which memories concerning a historical incident can be preserved and scrutinised, in this case the Wushe Incident, by producing and distributing a new perception of colonial history to contemporary audiences.

Since its release, *Seediq Bale* has been a central topic in Taiwan's film industry for its social and political impact. In this regard, this chapter further considers its cinematic production in the context of contemporary Taiwanese socio-political conditions that are postcolonial. The term postcolonial is usually used to indicate a historical phase and set of conditions after coloni-sation. However, different ethnic groups in Taiwan perceive and use 'post-colonial' very differently, sometimes viewing it as controversial due to their different historical experiences and ideas about colonialism.[1] Despite the provocative use of this term, Taiwanese society has remained troubled by conflicting colonial historiographies, clashing cultures, racial confrontation and identity confusion. Clearly, the postcolonial historical phase and its social and political conditions are exactly the 'problem' to which the film had to respond. This chapter further argues that the cinematic production of the movie did not simply produce another version of colonial historiography on the part of oppressed people, but instead offers a philosophical inquiry into the problems of identity and subjectivity. More importantly, through its artistic expression, the film portrays a minority that is now absent and yet presents a new people still to come.

The aporia of historical representation and beyond

The tension between history film and history has long existed. Can history film be recognised as actual history? Or more precisely, how can the gap between historical facts and the fictional elements needed for the film representation of history be best reconciled? The audience must thus confront those questions when viewing the movie *Seediq Bale* as a history film, as it uses the historical Wushe Incident as its subject matter.

In Robert A. Rosenstone's chapter in this volume, '*Seediq Bale* as history', he argues that 'history film' can actually be considered an alternative form of history. For Rosenstone, as *Seediq Bale* follows the very patterns of a dramatic history film, it gives the audience an audiovisual representation of history by dramatising historical facts and fictionalising historical figures. Fiction is thus necessary when telling a historical story, and indeed, it becomes indispensible when constructing a history or historical film. Emphasising the history discourse to which a history film can contribute, Rosenstone asserts that a history film 'must engage, directly or obliquely, the issues, ideas, data and arguments' of ongoing history discourse, thereby providing a stance for its viewers to use to judge that same history. It is precisely from this perspective that Rosenstone designates a history film as 'a new kind of history' rather than a simple fictional costume drama (see Chapter 11).

Despite the fact that both written history and cinema tell stories, the readers/viewers tend to trust written texts more highly than cinematic images and will consider the former as containing and communicating more reliable historical truth than the latter. It is this tension between the perceived truth of history and the cinematic representation of that history that has provoked a variety of criticism of Wei's film, *Seediq Bale*. These criticisms address the characterisation of historical figures, the rearrangement of historical events, and its interpretation of the indigenous people and their culture, as suggested by this cinematic presentation.

Being the first mainstream movie to depict the Wushe Incident and to focus on Taiwan's aboriginals, the movie *Seediq Bale* should be praised for its tremendous effort to make the historical past visible to contemporary audiences, and more importantly, to draw attention to indigenous people and their culture. Not surprisingly, the movie's subject provoked difficult debates on several issues. It portrays Mona Rudo as an epic hero, someone who led the anti-colonialist uprising and sought a protocol for the survival of the Seediq tribe. However, this representation may have produced some confusion about, and even conflict with, certain historical facts. The so-called Seediq tribe was not actually unified, but rather consisted of at least 12 clans which all maintained a distance from the Japanese colonial administration and employed different strategies toward the uprising.

One of the controversies in the movie is its representation of the actual conflict between the Tgdaya and Toda clans. In the movie, the Tada clan is depicted as pro-Japanese, and thus it becomes the enemy of the movement led by Mona. Moreover, the relatively complicated clashes between the two clans, such as over hunting territory and trading benefits, are simplified and sometimes dramatised as only a personal rivalry between the chiefs of the two clans. As many historians and anthropologists have identified, the film's representation thus fails to portray the nuances and complicated relationship for those clans of the Seediq tribe, which could have induced further tensions between them (Guo 2011).

Apparently, the colonisers-colonised framework cannot fully explain the complexity of the colonial condition among the indigenous tribes. There has been considerable research about the historical incident, including documents, official reports, oral histories, academic studies, legends and interviews. Those discussions only reinforce the fact that the Wushe Incident is in and of itself a controversy, as is the role of Mona in the anti-Japanese uprising. Such ambiguity exists not only within various clans of the Seediq tribe, but also in neighbouring indigenous tribes. The controversy is further intensified by colonial and postcolonial historiographies produced by different governments in Taiwan during different historical periods. Unfortunately, when the movie then attempted to unveil this concealed history, it produced still more controversies.[2]

Such consequences are quite common when making films about episodes from history. The director knows well that all the scenes do not portray strict historical facts, and perhaps this is why in this instance the director freely added and subtracted from history, and modified facts to produce an epic narrative that would fulfil a heroic characterisation and create a story with a climax. For example, the film places young Mona in the Renzheguan Incident of 1902[3] to allow the epic nature of his character to develop, even though Mona did not actually participate in this episode.[4] Another instance is the characterisation of Mona's rival, Temu Walis, chief of the Toda clan. Wei expressed in an interview that he chose a handsome actor with a positive image to play this role to transform his relatively negative image in history. Clearly, the director did not maintain a neutral stance in his representation of the incident, but instead intervened in its historical truth for entertainment. As a result, Wei was caught in a contradiction, namely, a truthful representation of history and the necessary narrative structure of an epic film. Accordingly, one finds in this representation a mixture of historical facts and fiction, and an irreducible tension between actual history and the film's narrative construction.

In addition to the disagreements about cinematic representation versus historical accuracy, one also needs to address the ethical concerns and historical attitudes that are revealed in the cinematic representation of a historical incident. This is concerned with neither historical truth nor the truth of the cinema, but rather with a director's ethical, social and political stance. As mentioned earlier, Wei never hesitated to intervene in the representation of history by mixing facts and fiction, thus rearranging and altering history and historical figures. In doing so, Wei does not simply aim at creating dramatic climaxes, but rather intends to offer one explanation for the causality of historical development. As a result, episodes and scenes are carefully selected and organised to illustrate the director's perspective of historical causality.

In addition to the mixture of historical facts and fiction, cinematic designs can also serve to offer an explanation for historical causality. Violence becomes one of the dominant modes in this cinematic presentation, and in particular, the ritual of headhunting further complicates the description of Japanese colonial oppressive violence. Headhunting, which is associated with the security of the hunting fields and the survival of a clan, is regarded as a sacred ceremony and is practised faithfully according to the *gaya* doctrines on ancestral spirits.[5] However, when headhunting is depicted as a means to revenge against colonialist oppression and becomes a connotation for reconciliation with enemies and is bound with ancestors, it produces more confusion and even discomfort for a contemporary audience. Why do women and children have to be sacrificed in order to be reconciled according to the *gaya* doctrine? In addition, how can *gaya* provide an alternative rationale for the tribe to survive the causality of history by headhunting?

The description of violence is cruel and brutal, and the solution to that violence appears somehow unreliable and unrealistic.[6] Apparently, the brutality of Japanese oppression did not elucidate much of the cruelty of the massacre conducted by the indigenous people. Many clichéd images, for example falling cherry blossoms, are used to ease and even romanticise the cruelty and brutality of the battlefield. In a similar manner, Wei uses landscape shots to create a spectacle and suggest the epic mode of the film. However, these stereotypical images are created using the director's understanding of the incident, and they reveal his personal reflections on the historical causality as well as his approach toward the indigenous people and their culture.

Therefore it is not surprising that the representation of the movie invited harsh criticism, and it was accused of not only providing an erroneous interpretation of history from the Han perspective, but also viewing the indigenous other as an object of only imagination and consumption. Such criticism is not concerned with truthful historical representation, the misunderstanding of indigenous doctrines and values, or cinematic defects, but rather with an historical attitude and ethical approach toward ethnic minorities.

Further, such criticism closely relates to such questions as 'whose history?' and 'on what terms?' which are often associated with postcolonial society. Like other postcolonial societies, Taiwan is no exception and has had to confront questions that are concerned not only with postcolonial historiography, but also with the relocation of history, ethnicity and culture. If the brutality of history should not be disguised by unrealistic reconciliation, and diverse identities should not be consumed by wholesale hybridity and multiculturalism, one might wonder what benefits the fragmentary tales of this historical incident and the contesting interpretations of history and culture may bring to contemporary audiences.

Seediq Bale as a cinematographic archive

As previously discussed, the cinematic presentation of the film *Seediq Bale* seems caught in the crux of a dilemma – namely, the contradiction that rests between historical truth and the 'truth of cinema'. It underscores the cinematic realism that includes aesthetic composition. The discrepancy then between the 'truth of history' and the 'truth of cinema' seems unavoidable and often even insurmountable. To avoid this interpretative aporia, that is, to pass judgement on the extent to which a cinematic representation is truthful to actual historical facts, this chapter proposes viewing the film *Seediq Bale* as a cinematographic archive, i.e. a reproduction of the images and sounds of this particular historical incident.

Rather than questioning the truthfulness of its historical representation, the archive view emphasises the process of its construction, its function as a medium and, more importantly, its relation to the preservation of historical memories. Hence, the following discussion focuses on the question of how historical memories are reshaped through the construction of their archive, and how the very construction of that archive can forge a new concept of history regarding the historical incident.

Wei expressed in an interview that he was driven by a desire to make this movie after being inspired by the complexity of the historical incident itself and the heroic deeds of the Seediq warriors.[7] Preparation for making this film took a long time and experienced tremendous difficulties, including not only a lack of investment, but also his research into the background of the Wushe Incident. In addition to the historical record, Wei referenced a range of materials that discussed this period, including literature, TV programmes, documentary films and even comic books (also see Wang in this volume). The director was determined to create a precise historical setting so the incident could be truthfully represented. The entire Wushe village was rebuilt in the mountains on the same size and scale as the original. The indigenous costumes, tools, weapons and many other details were carefully designed to make sure they appeared faithful to history. Moreover, the director insisted on using indigenous actors for the Seediq roles and demanded that they speak onscreen in the almost extinct Seediq language.

Wei's purpose was clear: he wanted to produce a cinematographic archive to fight against official colonial historiography, or more precisely rescue and present disappearing memories from the forgotten past. This is without a doubt a massive task. Following the principle of realism, the director aimed at representing a truthful history by reproducing its images and sounds, hoping that this historical incident would be witnessed by contemporary audiences. This became Wei's initial and ultimate objective.

After all, the Wushe Incident is an actual historical event rather than an invented story. Thus, every detail on the screen had to be referenced as closely as possible to historical records, documents, legends and myths. Likewise, the philosophical principles of the indigenous rituals and values would be scrutinised by both critics and audiences. In this regard, the film not only accomplished a rewrite of colonial historiography, but also offered a visual cinematic (re)production of traumatised historical memories for contemporary audiences.

From the perspective of archive, criticism of the film should shift its focus from the politics of representation to the politics of archivisation. This chapter is concerned with the rules of archivisation instead of truthful historical representation. Just as historical truth cannot be fully represented, it is impossible to totally preserve all details of any actual historical incident. Therefore, the achievement of an archive lies in the selection and preservation of materials. This perspective can perhaps further our understanding of the director's intervention via his interpretation of history and the indigenous culture. As mentioned earlier, specific historical facts were selected, modified and reorganised in the cinematic presentation; they were apparently designed to express the director's particular views about historical causality and the indigenous civilisation. Further, his mixture of historical facts, fiction and characterisation reinforce the idea that the cinematic production followed its own aesthetic principles. Clearly, the film *Seediq Bale* as a cinematographic archive only presents what was selected and organised according to particular ideologies and aesthetic rules, all of which are controlled by the director, Wei Te-sheng.

The concept of the archive also allows us to reflect on the relationship between history and its memories. As Jacques Derrida (1996: 2) tells us: 'The concept of the archive shelters in itself ... But it also *shelters* itself from this memory which it shelters.' In other words, the archive conceals memories, while at the same time displaying them. Therefore, preserved memories should not be confused with history; they also promise no truth or accuracy of that history. Thus, the archive confronts another threat, indeed one from within. The more the archive desires to contain history, the more it loses history. This was exactly why *Seediq Bale* could not possibly have provided satisfactory explanations for history no matter how many episodes of that same history were included or how detailed the portrayal. Archivisation is the art of both remembering and forgetting. In this regard, the cinematic presentation of film renders a drama in remembering and forgetting about the historical incident, thereby demonstrating an irreducible tension between the construction and the collapse of the archive itself.

However, the function of the archive should also be emphasised. Indeed, from that perspective, *Seediq Bale* becomes a medium through which the historical incident is reviewed and scrutinised. It is particularly so when the movie is viewed on DVD or via an online resource from which the images and sound can be retrieved repeatedly. That is to say, the dead are conjured and incarnated by the actors playing them as if they were alive once again in a reinvented history made possible by the cinematic presentation. Such is the art of necromancy practised through cinema. In this sense, the film becomes a special mode of that medium that makes possible a communication between the lived and the dead, as well as between the present and the past.

The concept of the archive also sheds new light on the artistic composition of this film. The archive is itself a deliberate composition. As mentioned earlier, the director represented the Wushe Incident using a mixture of historical facts and fiction and a modification of actual historical development. Risking the criticism of untruthful representation, Wei's goal was to provide an explanation for the assumed historical causality, but from a certain viewpoint. This goal is exemplified by the frequent exchange between the subjective view presented by the characters and the objective view assumed by the camera. Often, the subjective view interrupts the objective description of the incident. As a result, the cinematic production functions as a commentary on the historical incident wherein indigenous culture and values play the major parts.

This intervention in the historical narrative and the frequent exchange of subjective and objective views underscore the archive as a specific medium. It suggests a medial quality, which is also evidenced in its cinematic composition. One of the poignant examples in the film is the massacre in the elementary school during the opening ceremony of the sports games. This plot is no doubt one of the most dramatic of the entire movie and is rendered in astounding fashion, while still disturbing. Multiple conflicts, including racial, cultural and political, reach a peak and enter an endgame where an ultimate solution must be sought. One can observe in the cinematic presentation that the camera lingers and hesitates between subjective and objective views, suggesting multiple viewpoints of the occurring massacre. Suddenly, off-screen sounds and music begin to play and join in this already confusing moment, creating an alternative world where ancestral spirits appear to be condemning the violent action occurring onscreen.

These multiple viewpoints and their worlds define the medial quality of the movie as an archive, retaining its presentation in between the past and present, facts and fiction, and the worlds on and off the screen. This episode lasts a few minutes. The movie cannot stop playing and thus sustains the occurrence of the violent massacre on the screen. In the meantime, the song of ancestral spirits suspends any episodic development, creating an interval that suggests a remote and sacred space which is fully created by the cinematic effect. The graceful and mournful rhythm from outside now mixes with the suffering cries and sorrowful weeping in the killing field, as multiple layers of time converge in the present moment while the audience reviews the agonising incident on the screen. This is a situation created by the director through his artistic composition so as to posit the essential question and also search for answers. There must be a reason for exercising such brutal violence to address the causality of history and the survival of the entire tribe. This understanding of the episode can be extended to the entire movie, which also functions as a designed medium whereby the director seeks to demonstrate his concept of the history and his understanding of the indigenous culture at the same time.

Such an understanding benefits from the view that the film functions as a cinematographic archive rather than a historical representation. In this regard, the archive becomes infinite in the sense that it can never be completed and thus never closes by shutting other resources out. Consequently the cinematic production of the film becomes a special archive that is connected to the numerous existing archives about the Wushe Incident ranging across history and popular culture. In addition, the explanation of the incident offered by the film does not define the past; on the contrary, it opens itself to the future and invites more commentary. Viewed in this light, the film as an archive not only helps preserve the past, but also manages to create a passage to the future through communication with the past. Perhaps the archive, as Jacques Derrida (1996: 36) remarks, 'is not ... a question of the past ... It is a question of the future, the question of the future itself, the question of a response, of a promise and of a responsibility for tomorrow'.

The making of *Seediq Bale* as a socio-political event

As previously argued, the concept of the archive avoids the interpretive aporia or contradiction of this film as a truthful historical representation and provides for further reflection on the intertwined relationship between history and memory. More significantly, the film as an archive functions as a medium through which historical memories are produced and preserved. This film, which features the indigenous uprising against Japanese colonialism on the part of the colonised, is accordingly seen as a postcolonial historiography. However, if the construction of the archive is seen as a 'promise' and a 'responsibility' for tomorrow, as Derrida (1996: 36) has commented, then the making of this particular film should also be considered in the contemporary Taiwanese context. In other words, the making of *Seediq Bale* should be recognised as an event, an action that responds to the contemporary Taiwanese socio-political condition and thus an attempt to bring forth a new people and a different future.

I shall argue that the contemporary Taiwanese social and political condition is postcolonial. Perhaps for Wei, filming the Wushe Incident was an endeavour to heal a historical wound by untangling the intertwined conflicts that still exist between former colonisers and the colonised and among different ethnic groups in Taiwan. From this perspective, the use of the indigenous resistance against Japanese colonialism is strategic to the contemporary condition, for it may propose a union of different ethnic groups under the code name of anti-colonialism. Behind such a wishful attempt are thoughts of racial amalgamation and multiculturalism, which are politically correct in a postcolonial atmosphere such as that in contemporary Taiwan.

Identity politics is another contentious issue of postcoloniality. In this regard, one cannot ignore in the film the two tragic indigenous characters, Hanaoka Ichirō (a.k.a. Dakis Nobing) and Hanaoka Nirō (a.k.a. Dakis Nawi). Educated by the Japanese, these two characters serve as lower Japanese officials and are the role models for the indigenous people, representing Japanese assimilation colonial policy in Taiwan. They live like their Japanese colonisers, using Japanese names, speaking Japanese, wearing kimonos, etc. Also, they represent modern civilisation and its contrasts with the indigenous tradition (also see Sterk in this volume).

However, the two characters also embody the typical identity paradigm of the colonised intellectuals. They agonise over their ethnic and cultural identities, and hesitate between obedience and resistance to their master. It is also through these two characters that the director is able to express his concern about the clashes between races and civilisations, and complicate the colonial situation of that time. In the end, the two characters are unable to overcome the insurmountable racial and social barriers that exist in the hierarchical colonial society, and find no alternative solution to the inevitable clash between modernisation and the tribal tradition. As depicted in the movie, suffering from their confused identities and colonial plight, they both commit suicide along with their wives and children.

Using such a tragic outcome as a lesson of history, the film seems to deliver a message that the same historical mistakes should now be avoided. Moreover, it suggests that mutual hatred and enmity should also be forgiven. However, this innocent proposal speaks to a more serious identity problem that still disturbs contemporary Taiwanese society. In this sense, the two agonising characters are more metaphorical than literal. Indeed, identity problems exist not only among the many indigenous tribes but also among multiple Han ethnic groups. The phrase 'I-Seediq question' is coined to summarise the identity crisis in contemporary Taiwan, which is concerned with not only identity politics, but also the subjectivity that relates to the entire territory of existence.

First of all, the I-Seediq question is one for the indigenous Seediq people and the entire tribe. Titled 'Seediq bale', which means 'a true Seediq person', this movie does not simply represent a repressed history wherein the entire tribe was suffering, but rather delves deeper into indigenous culture and history, inquiring about the very fundamental question of what being a true Seediq person means, and how to become a true Seediq person, especially when one is colliding with other races and civilisations. These questions inquire into the true meaning of violence, e.g. headhunting and massacre, in terms of the survival of the entire tribe and the sustainability of its indigenous culture. This kind of question appears both challenging and puzzling, and it is for the

Seediq people a question that concerns not just identity (who am I?) but also a focused subjectivity (how to survive?).

In this regard, the movie is not simply a painful drama of identity politics played out in colonial history. Instead, it delivers a philosophical inquiry into subjectivity, which is understood as one's *'relation to oneself'* (Deleuze 1988: 100, emphasis original).[8] The director insists on using indigenous people to play all the Seediq characters in the movie, although not all belong to the Seediq tribe. Moreover, they are required to learn and speak the Seediq language in their performances. This requirement is not simply a practice to meet the rules of realism; more significantly, in playing the roles, those indigenous actors become situated in the exact historical situation where the I-Seediq question can be addressed.

That is to say, what an actor experiences through his performance is not a request for a distinctive racial and cultural identity from the outside, but rather demonstrates how every indigenous individual is forced to confront the question of 'who am I?' from within. In that performance, the actor actually splits into two persons, one in the movie and the other in actual life. The Seediq figure is doubled and lives inside, and thus the actor finds the Other in himself. In other words, every indigenous individual understands himself/herself and considers his/her own territory of existence by becoming another person. In this regard, the name of Seediq is nothing but the Other that every indigenous individual is forced to become.

The I-Seediq question is equally important for the director. The name of Seediq, along with its people and culture, had already been an inaccessible theme for the director. The director spent tremendous effort to understand its history and civilisation by referencing the bulk of available literature and related archives. Also, the director attempts to provide an interpretation for historical development and his greater understanding of the tribal culture through a cinematic presentation. However, in the process of making this film, the Seediq appear to the director to be no longer an ethnic and cultural Other with a unique civilisation that distinguishes them from the outside world. On the contrary, the process generates a dialogue between the director and the Seediq people, and a fresh communication between the Han and Seediq civilisations. We can say that the experience of making the film was for the director a process of becoming a Seediq bale.

This process of becoming a Seediq is also true for the contemporary audiences of this film. The movie has enjoyed great popularity among domestic audiences and is one of the highest grossing local films in Taiwan's history. However, this phenomenon should not be understood simply as a sign of great sympathy for a minority group or enthusiasm for cultural nationalism. Instead, it indicates that contemporary Taiwanese audiences are willing to enter the cinema to try to understand the history and culture of a minority people, and more importantly allow their perceptions to be engrossed by and co-vibrate with the cinematic flow of sounds and images that inscribe this unforgettable historical incident on the screen in front of them. For this audience, viewing the movie is not simply an enjoyment of audiovisual exci-tement, as they actually participate in the process of becoming Seediq in their affective engagement with the film. This engagement may explain why many viewers cry out after watching the movie: 'I am a Seediq bale'.

The I-Seediq question is not just for the Seediq and other indigenous people, but also one for the director and all audiences. It is also a question that is addressed to contemporary Taiwanese society. Hence, the meaning of Seediq should not be limited to a single indigenous ethnic and cultural iden-tity, but should be recognised as an image of the Other, the anonymous identity that every Taiwanese should become.

It is from this perspective that the movie *Seediq Bale* becomes what Gilles Deleuze calls a minor cinema, or more precisely, 'modern political cinema' (Deleuze 1989: 215–224).[9] A minor cinema portrays the minority in the sense that the people are no longer representable and have been broken into frag-ments. Therefore, the people are 'missing' and thus any individual becomes first and foremost a potential component of a people. Deleuze's concept of a minor cinema is concerned with the invention of a people who do not yet exist. That is to say, the fragmentary individual can bring forth a people who can be revealed through the artistic expression of cinema.

This perspective is helpful to better understand the significance of the pro-duction of this movie in contemporary Taiwan. Seediq no longer represents any minority ethnic groups and culture; it becomes a 'minor' in every respect. Every Taiwanese encounters Seediq on the inside, allowing for a relationship to the self to emerge. However, this personal concern is then immediately political and charged with collective values. Thus, what the film has rendered is not simply a politics of recognition, but a political project concerned with the public's interest. Viewed in this light, the name Seediq no longer means a newly invented anthropological category for an indigenous identity, but instead the destiny of all Taiwanese people. As a result, the film summons from all its viewers a 'missing' people yet to come.

Conclusion

The making of this movie was driven by Wei's passion for the history of the oppressed and unknown Seediq tribe, and this passion supported his long-term research on the forgotten Wushe Incident and tribal civilisation. By referencing an immense bulk of material, the director produced an epic film with its own unique artistic composition of sound and images. It is under-standable that the movie is often regarded as a colonial historiography and accordingly invites criticism that questions whether the film is a truthful repre-sentation of the actual historical incident and offers appropriate interpretations about an indigenous culture.

This chapter considers *Seediq Bale* as a cinematographic archive, a repro-duction of images and sounds of the Wushe Incident. As a result, the material as represented and its various interpretations of the incident do not close the archive. Rather, they create an archival surface where the present meets the past and produces an intertwined history for the future. In this regard, the film is an inscription of the historical wound that implicates a reinstatement of the politics of remembering and forgetting.

More significantly, the cinematographic archive provides a medium by which one can reflect on historical violence and its causality. This reflection is not only an aesthetic-ethical vehicle, but also a socio-political concern. As suggested by its title, 'Seediq Bale', the movie inquires into the true meaning of being a Seediq person, and consequently imposes the I-Seediq question on the indigenous people, the director and contemporary audiences. This question not only requests a new identity paradigm from the perspective of an outside socio-political condition and existence, but also marks an inner process of an ethical becoming Other. In this light, what this movie achieved is the invention of a people to come rather than merely the rewriting of a colonial historiography of the past.

Notes

1 Generally speaking, Han immigrants during the seventeenth and eighteenth centuries (mostly Min/Hoklo/Hokkien and Hakka ethnic groups) tended to consider Western powers and the Japanese as the colonisers. This viewpoint becomes complicated at the point when Chiang Kai-shek's KMT government fled to Taiwan after the Second World War. Sometimes, earlier Han immigrants also recognised the KMT rule in Taiwan after the war as colonial rule. See, for example, Liao (1999). However, Western powers, the Japanese and all Han immigrants are regarded as 'invaders' in the eyes of the indigenous people, who claim that they have resided on the island for thousands of years. As a result, these different ideas about the meaning of colonialism have produced conflicting colonial historiographies and have triggered heated debate about this film.

2 After the movie's release, many materials were published and much research conducted to seek the 'ultimate' truth about the Wushe Incident. For example, Yuanliu Publishing has published a series of books on the subject. Wei's *Seediq Bale* also inspired directors to produce more documentary films, such as Tang Shiang-chu's *Pusu Qhuni* (*Yu sheng: Sai de ke ba lai*, 2014) and Pilin Yapu's *Wushe, Chuanzhong Island* (*Wushe, chuanzhongdao* (2013).

3 The Renzheguan, located at the foot of the Wushe mountains, was the doorway to the Seediq tribes. This battle occurred in 1902 and was the first military confrontation between the Seediq people and the Japanese intruders who were equipped with modern weapons. The Seediq warriors won the battle by using their traditional weapons. They successfully prevented the Japanese enemy from entering their tribal territory. See Guo (2011: 158).

4 Another episode in which Mona did not actually participate was the battle between Seediq and Amei tribes, known as the Jiemeiyen Incident in 1903. Many Seediq were killed in that battle, which represented the successful colonial policy, adopted by the Japanese administration in Taiwan, to use aborigines to fight aborigines. For the details, see Guo (2011: 161).

5 The concept of *gaya* and its contents are very complex and difficult to explain, even to the Seediq people. It can roughly be understood as a system of rules and taboos that provide a wide range of principles for everyday life of the Seediq people. See Wang (2003: 77–104).

6 For example, the reconciliation is symbolised by the scene toward the end in which the killed indigenous warriors are crossing the rainbow bridge to reach the sacred kingdom of the ancestors.

7 This interview (six minutes long), entitled 'A 12-year journey: The origin of *Seediq Bale*', is included on the DVD box set of *Seediq Bale* released by Deli company in 2012.

8 This idea of subjectivity is taken from Gilles Deleuze's reading of Michel Foucault's *The Pleasure of Sexuality* in terms of subjectivation. See Deleuze (1988: 94–123).

9 In *Cinema 2*, Deleuze (1989) makes a distinction between classic and modern political cinema and further defines the latter based on the concept of the minor literature concept that Deleuze and Félix Guattari developed in *Kafka: Towards a Minor Literature* (1986).

14 Mona Rudo's scar

Two kinds of epic identity in *Seediq Bale*

Darryl Sterk

Introduction

Ostensibly about a Seediq tribal uprising that began on 27 October 1930 against the Japanese colonial authorities in the central Taiwan town of Wushe, the historical epic film *Seediq Bale* (dir. Wei Te-sheng, 2011) has been interpreted in terms of Taiwan today.[1] *The Economist*'s review, for instance, states that the movie's 'message of a unique, empowering Taiwanese identity is unmistakable' (*The Economist* 2011). A 'Taiwanese identity' sounds like a national identity. If so, the apparent approval of the film's message is surprising, because *The Economist* has not been supportive of nationalism if it means one state per nation, one people per place; the magazine opposed the 'leave' vote both in advance of the Scottish referendum in 2014 and before British exit from the European Union, or 'Brexit', in 2016. If nationalism can encompass a modern multicultural country of which citizens feel proud, then the approval makes more sense. The problem is that a film about a ritual massacre of Japanese men, women and children and a brutal reprisal against the Seediq warriors and their families hardly seems a vote for multicultural modernity.

The Economist is not the only one to see contemporary meaning in this film. For many critics, both foreign and local, *Seediq Bale* is an allegory of Taiwan's contemporary political situation. According to American pundit Walter Russell Mead (2011), *Seediq Bale* is a work of 'romantic nationalism' that might upset the delicate cross-strait balance. To Mead, the film's inflammatory contemporary geopolitical message would be that the Taiwanese people would rather die than submit to the People's Republic of China (PRC)! There is support for a cross-strait reading of the film in the context of production. Wei Te-sheng has cited resistance to the return of Hong Kong to China as an inspiration (Kan 2011) and associated himself with cultural producers who support Taiwan independence, most notably the black metal band ChthoniC which used footage from Wei Te-sheng's 2003 fundraising short in the music video for 'Quasi Putrefaction', one of the songs on the album *Seediq Bale* (Berry 2011: 95–99). For ChthoniC, Seediq resistance to the Japanese represents Taiwanese resistance to the Chinese, whether the PRC or the Kuomintang (KMT). In the context of the 2012 presidential election, political scientist and former Democratic Progressive Party (DPP) politician Chen Ming-tong described Mona Rudo's resistance against colonial rule as representing the resolution of the Taiwan people (Chen 2012: 77), presumably against the Chinese threat or against closer ties with China, advocated by the KMT.

Commentators have remarked less upon the film's relevance to domestic politics, than upon the contemporary significance of Chief Mona Rudo's failure to unite the Tgdaya villages under his heroic leadership. Only six of the 12 Tgdaya villages around the town of Wushe joined Mona Rudo's uprising, while the Toda villages in the area ended up working for the Japanese as mercenaries during the reprisal. The film represents a population fractured along sub-ethnic lines that can at best muster a partial resolution against a foreign threat, a resolution that is shadowed by collaboration.

If Wei Te-sheng has politicised the 'Wushe Incident', as it is typically termed, in terms of contemporary national concerns, he would not be the first. As Michael Berry (2011: 57–62) has demonstrated, many retellings of Wushe in film or fiction since 1945 have read the incident in terms of Chinese or Taiwanese nationalism, taking Mona Rudo as an anti-Japanese or more generally anti-colonial hero. Nor would Wei's national politicisation of history be at all surprising. Nationalists everywhere have politicised history by reading anachronistically pre-national historical events like the Wushe Incident. Since *The Birth of a Nation* (dir. D.W. Griffith, 1915), nationalists have taken advantage of the silver screen as a vehicle for their anachronistic readings of history by shooting historical epic films. They tend to make films about traumatic historical events. Therefore, in remaking the Wushe Incident over and over, Taiwan's filmmakers (and musicians and novelists and cartoonists) seem to have been in the grips of a 'repetition compulsion'. Perhaps Wei Te-sheng hoped that this time would be different, that *Seediq Bale* could resolve the trauma once and for all and contribute to a sense of national belonging.

A sense of national belonging is what several scholars have argued the historical epic film is actually about. To one its purpose is 'to present a national or religious identity in times of change' (Elley 1984: 12). To another it is a modern myth intended to 'bind a tribe or nation together', especially 'at a time of spiritual or social crisis' (Santas 2007: 2). The way historical epic films present an identity or bind a tribe is through conflict: there has to be a 'them' to define an 'us'. In domestic conflicts, 'them' might become part of 'us', but conflict is often resolved by getting rid of 'them'. If so, the epic in question is nativist.

Outbursts of nativism at times of crisis or change worry liberals. They also worry scholars of the historical epic film like Robert Burgoyne. In a recent collection on the historical epic film around the world, Burgoyne (2011a: 1) interrogates 'the link between the epic and the imagined community of nation', not just because productions have toned down nationalist sentiment to internationalise appeal but also in order to find opposition to tyranny and tolerance for diversity in *Gladiator* (dir. Ridley Scott, 2000) and in the film's cultural impact after 9/11, which included tattooing and scarification (Burgoyne 2011b: 87).

I went to see *Seediq Bale* hoping to find the same values of opposition to tyranny and tolerance for diversity, which I would term liberal. I was initially disappointed. The film is undeniably anti-colonial, and I could agree there was a lot to be against: the Japanese employed abusive policemen, imposed an ethnic division of labour, practised corporal punishment in the schools, and failed to grant political or legal rights. In the reprisal Japan ignored international law, putting prices on Tgdaya heads (*The Rainbow Bridge* 0:56:07–0:57:12) and using mustard gas on the rebels (*The Rainbow Bridge* 1:02:41–1:03:30). However, in its opposition to a foreign tyranny *Seediq Bale* seemed to substitute the tyranny of an interpretation of tradition that rejected modernity, specifically: trade in a state-issued currency (at the Taiwanese store in Wushe), the formation of the citizenry through education (in the village schools), rule by a law that overrides communal custom (which in Seediq was called *gaya*), and the state monopoly on violence (according to which the guns in the villages around Wushe were confiscated). More than anything, Mona Rudo seems to reject multiculturalism at the personal and social levels, represented by the native policeman Dakis Nobing/Hanaoka Ichirō and by the mixed community of Paran/Musha/Bū-siā, where Seediq, Japanese and Taiwanese live together more or less in peace until the incident. Mona Rudo was not fundamentally opposed to foreigners. Before colonisation, he visited a Taiwanese tradesman to buy salt (*The Sun Flag* 0:13:56), and during the massacre spared the lives of the Han Chinese residents of Wushe, including the proprietor of the sundry goods store, with whom he shares a drink before saying goodbye (*The Rainbow Bridge* 0:14:35). He did not want to have to live with them, however. The last thing his father says to him is: keep the foreign race out of the *alang*, the tribal village (*The Sun Flag* 0:35:52). Mona Rudo took his words to heart.

The contrast between Mona Rudo in the tribal village of Mhebu on the one hand and Dakis Nobing/Hanaoka Ichirō in the colonial town of Wushe on the other has led me to read the film as a debate between two understandings of national identity – nativist versus liberal – and discuss it in terms of belonging, because we identify with groups (including nations) we (wish to) belong to. By nativist I mean a communal, ethnic, monocultural ideal of belonging of roots and passions and descent. By liberal I mean an individual, multicultural ideal of becoming of routes and principles and consent. Though I am by sensibility a liberal, I try not to take sides, because the best debates allow antagonists to find common ground.

I have been influenced in this work by two scholars in particular. For Chao-yang Liao (2013) and Yu-lin Lee (2014a, 2014b; also see Lee's chapter in this volume), *Seediq Bale* is a parable of community fragmentation and possibly re-formation respectively. Without intending to belittle Wei Te-sheng's vision of the incident in all of its historical specificity, I, too, generalise, by reading the film as a debate between liberal and nativist nationalism, with an additional contribution: a corresponding continuum of historical epic film narrative, which I develop by engaging with, of all people, Erich Auerbach.

In 'Odysseus' scar', the first chapter of *Mimesis* (1953, reprint 2003: 3–23), Auerbach cites excerpts from *The Odyssey* and 'Genesis' as two ideal-types of epic narration, externalised and internalised respectively, a contrast that guides me through the three main body sections of this chapter. The first section is a discussion of the stories implicit in visual symbols, particularly Mona Rudo's scar and the rainbows that keep appearing in the sky. The second section covers aspects of epic narration that are not medium-specific: scene arrangement and characterisation in social context. The third section attempts to 're-mediate' Auerbach by focusing on editing and perspective. It may seem fundamentally misguided to take a scholar of oral and written epic as a guide through an epic film, but I think the results I obtain are suggestive enough to justify the experiment. My results delineate two types of historical epic film: externalised epic that serves as a vehicle for nativist belonging on the one hand, and internalised epic that serves as a vehicle for liberal becoming on the other.[2] After a conclusion in which I describe *Seediq Bale* as a challenge to liberals to engage with nativists, I end with a postscript on the possibility of another, more Biblical but equally epic, treatment of the Taiwanese indigenous accommodation to the evolving project of liberal modernity.

The three arcs: on the interpretation of epic imagery

One day, Mona Rudo, Chief of Mhebu, one of the 12 Tgdaya Seediq villages in the mountains around Wushe, motions over (*The Sun Flag* 0:47:35) a village youth, Pawan Nawi, and asks him why he is not at school (Figure 14.1).

Pawan Nawi claims to be ill, but Mona Rudo sees through the lie when he spies the bruise on the youngster's cheek. Pawan Nawi is home from school

Figure 14.1 Pawan Nawi explains to Chief Mona why he is home
(Source: Central Motion Picture)

because he got smacked in the face by his Japanese teacher for beating a Japanese classmate in a race. The injustice of colonial rule is most poignant from the perspective of a boy who bears the brunt of its abusive discipline. Just then they see a rainbow (Figures 14.2–14.5).

'My grandfather says you were a hero when you were young', Pawan Nawi blurts out. 'I'm still a hero now!', Chief Mona replies. 'Hero' translates as *yingxiong*, the term in the Chinese subtitles, but the word Pawan Nawi and Mona Rudo use onscreen is *rseno bale*, a real (*bale*) man (*rseno*). A *rseno bale* is a kind of *seediq bale*, a real person. A *rseno bale* is a man who practises the traditional law of *gaya*, particularly by headhunting (Simon 2012: 165). The oldest anthropological explanation of the practice was that by bringing back an enemy's head, which contains his spiritual energy, a warrior contributed to the energy that protected the *alang* (Simon 2012: 166). According to *Seediq Bale*, the headhunter thereby turned his enemies into friends, with whom he would hunt in the afterlife on the other side of the rainbow bridge (*The Sun Flag* 2:10:56–2:11:01; *The Rainbow Bridge* 1:12:12–1:12:21). A successful headhunter had the right to receive the two facial tattoos that mark manhood. As most of the males in the film of Mona Rudo's generation have the facial tattoos, 'hero' might be too grand a translation for *rseno bale*. A *rseno bale* is simply a male adult, not necessarily a hero like Mona Rudo. Mona Rudo is no ordinary man, no ordinary *rseno bale*, but a leader of men, as his arc scar testifies.

Pawan Nawi has heard, and the audience has seen, how Mona Rudo got his scar in the first scene in the film, in which the young Mona Rudo jumped into a raging river, both to dodge bullets and to avoid losing the boar he had just stolen from his tribal enemy, a Bunun warrior, whose head was the first Mona Rudo hunted. Under water, Mona Rudo stabbed his knife into a crevice in an underwater rock to resist the current. In doing so he somehow gave himself a cut on the cheek. Thus, while there is a similarity in shape between

Figure 14.2 A rainbow appears in the sky above Mhebu
(Source: Central Motion Picture)

Figure 14.3 Pawan Nawi and Chief Mona gaze at the rainbow
(Source: Central Motion Picture)

Figure 14.4 In the same shot Pawan Nawi looks over at Chief Mona
(Source: Central Motion Picture)

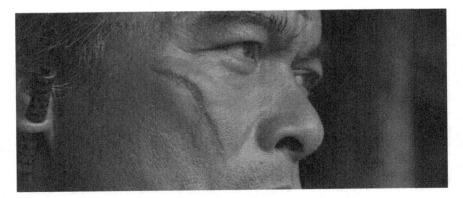

Figure 14.5 In the reverse-shot, Pawan Nawi sees the scar on Chief Mona's cheek
(Source: Central Motion Picture)

knife and scar, it is due to the fact that the knife was once contiguous with the wound that healed into Mona's scar.

The three arcs – knife, scar and rainbow – are linked by contiguity or similarity, but what do they mean? From Mona Rudo's perspective, the meaning is clear: it is partly by virtue of his scar, the mark of a hero, that he will be able to muster support for a final 'headhunt', in which the hunting knife will be the weapon of choice. Though many of the victims at Wushe will be stabbed or shot, not beheaded, their ritual killing (*The Sun Flag* 2:00:15–2:11:05) will give youngsters like Pawan Nawi the right to receive the tattoos of manhood (*The Rainbow Bridge* 0:16:14–0:16:42). After death in the Japanese reprisal, the swelled ranks of the *rseno bale* will proceed to the edge of the rainbow bridge, the *hako* (bridge) *utux* (spirit). There they will be inspected by a guardian spirit who will confirm that they really do have blood on their hands and allow them passage across the bridge into the afterlife, a happy hunting ground where the spirits (*utux*) of the ancestors (*rudan*) await.

Like many images in the film, these three arcs appear over and over again, and seem to mean the same thing each time. Anthropologist Kai-shih Lin (2011) has criticised the imagery in the film as the work of a director so juvenile he has no idea how repetitious and obvious he is (Lin 2011: 38). Lin is right about the repetition, but wrong to condemn Wei for it, because repetition is a feature of the epic form. Lin is also wrong to condemn Wei for obviousness, because according to Erich Auerbach, obviousness is a feature of a certain kind of epic. In this regard, Auerbach notes the failure of all attempts to allegorise Homer, whose significance is always right there on the surface, in contrast to the Bible, which in its minimalism practically demanded allegorisation (Auerbach 2003: 11).

Just how obvious is *Seediq Bale*? To me, Wei Te-sheng's film is somewhere between Homer and the Bible in respect to the interpretation of imagery. Homer's world seems self-contained, its meanings fixed for all time, but the world of *Seediq Bale* is more fluid, as Mhebu is opening up to modernity. In an open world, images like rainbows and scars are open to different interpretations.

What a rainbow might mean today is therefore relevant to the interpretation of what the rainbow means in *Seediq Bale*. In Wei's sleeper hit *Cape No.7* (2008), the rainbow (1:47:18–1:47:23) is a reification of romance that represents a connection between boy and girl, Taiwan and Japan, present and past. Similarly, in *Director Bale*, a director's diary about the making of *Seediq Bale*, the rainbow is a sign of connection on casting trips to central and north-eastern Taiwan, on which Wei meets with the actors who will play the young and mature Mona Rudo respectively (Wei 2011: 34–37). In his *A Little Director's Diary of Unemployment*, Wei had turned the rainbow into an ideal of Taiwan's cultural identity in which contiguity would not result in contamination:

> The concept of the national integration has compromised the integrity of the different cultural communities in Taiwan. Your hue has mixed with mine and someone else's, with the result that we have all ended up the

colour of mud. Four hundred years of hard work and Taiwan has turned into the colour of mud! If we could but separate the colours out and work to restore each one to its original hue, and then place ourselves side by side in an attitude of mutual respect, what a beautiful rainbow that would be!

(Wei 2002: 203, my translation)

Though Wei's colour metaphor seems essentialist, displaying a wariness of the mutual influence implicit in cultural connection, surely his ideal of cultural heterogeneity is preferable to homogeneity, whether Japanese or Chinese. Wei had not forgotten the rainbow of multiculturalism when he made *Seediq Bale*. He even turned it into an interpretation of his epic film. 'Why could the Seediq and Japanese not realise that there was space in the sky (symbolic perhaps of the context in which we interpret symbols) for both sun and rainbow, for both Japanese and Seediq belief?' asked the advertising blurb. With peaceful coexistence as an alternative, modern meaning of the rainbow in *Seediq Bale* in mind, let's probe further the significance of Mona Rudo's scar.

That Mona Rudo has a scar on his cheek is at first a puzzle and then an invitation to interpretation. The historical Mona Rudo did not have such a scar. Chiu Ruo-long, the cartoonist whose *Wushe Incident* (Chiu 1990) first gave Wei Te-sheng the idea for the film (Kan 2011), and who served as artistic adviser on *Seediq Bale*, did not draw Mona Rudo with a scar (Berry 2011: 83–85). There is no mention of a scar in Wei's (2000) prize-winning screen-play, nor in the novel Yan Yun-nong wrote based on the screenplay (Yan 2004). The Mona Rudo in the fundraising short Wei made in 2003 does not have a scar. Wei Te-sheng apparently added it at the last minute, right before the shoot began in 2009, on the advice of his movie make-up artists (Wei 2011: 73). How could Wei insert an ahistorical scar, especially considering that traditionally it was thought humiliating for a warrior to come home wounded (Wei 2011: 74)? Because Wei did not confine himself to history, nor is the meaning of the scar in the film limited to a traditional tribal under-standing of it. On the face of it, Wei Te-sheng added the scar for continuity. Two actors play Mona Rudo, as a 20-year-old brave and as a 50-year-old chief. The two were two centimetres apart in height (Wei 2011: 37) but did not from most angles look much alike (Wei 2011: 73). It was to make the double casting compelling that Wei Te-sheng cut continuity into his protagonist's flesh. However, once he added it, it took on a life of its own. It became Mona Rudo's most recognisable feature, both in the film and in the promotional material. On the cover of the soundtrack, for instance, the only colour is Mona Rudo's scar, in blood red. Mona Rudo's striking scar connects him with other scarred or tattooed historical epic film heroes, not just the hero of *Gladiator* mentioned above, but also the scarred and war-painted William Wallace in *Braveheart* (dir. Mel Gibson, 1995). As in *Braveheart*, the scar in *Seediq Bale* signals the protagonist's heroism: that is surely what Mona

Rudo's scar means to the young Pawan Nawi when he looks over at the chief on his day home from school. However, that is not all it means. For more indication of what else Mona Rudo's scar might mean today in Taiwan, let us delve further into 'Odysseus' scar'.

Mona Rudo's scar: two modes of epic narration

For Auerbach, Odysseus' scar becomes an emblem of various aspects of Homeric epic narration in which everything is 'externalized' (Auerbach 2003: 3). Auerbach begins with the recognition scene in *The Odyssey*, in which Odysseus's housekeeper sees the scar on his leg and realises her master has finally come home. It seems a dramatic moment, but instead of drawing out the drama Homer interrupts the scene with an account of the hunt on which Odysseus received the wound that formed his scar. The purpose of the flashback, according to Auerbach, is not to create suspense but rather simply to 'externalise' the scar by explaining its origin. In this way, Homer explicates the relation between the recognition scene and the hunt scene. Instead of consigning the hunt to the background, Homer brings it into the same depthless foreground in which every part of his narrative takes place. The Bible is the opposite. Its narrative elements are fraught with background and taut with suspense. No explanation is given for the necessity of Abraham's journey to sacrifice his son Isaac, or of the relation between the temptation of Abraham in Genesis 22 and his burial of his wife Sarah in Genesis 23. The scenes of the Bible are simply presented and juxtaposed, leaving the reader wondering why 'this' is happening and what is going to happen next.

On my viewing, *Seediq Bale* is narratively externalised. One always knows exactly what is going on. The function of the 'recognition scene' in *Seediq Bale*, for instance, is to remind the spectator that Mona Rudo is still a hero and to reveal Pawan Nawi's impressionability. As in Homer, relations between scenes are too explicit for suspense. Although Wei Te-sheng does not, like Homer, cut from his hero's scar to a flashback, the relation between the hunting expedition on which Mona wounds himself and the recognition scene is clear, as is the relation between the recognition scene and the later hunting scene. When Pawan Nawi jumps into a raging river to recover a wounded muntjac (*The Sun Flag* 0:56:27), we see how big an impression Chief Mona has made on him: Chief Mona is the kind of man he wants to become.

We can form a clearer image of what manner of man Chief Mona is by relating him to Odysseus. Odysseus and Mona Rudo seem to have a lot in common. Like Mona Rudo, Odysseus got his scar as a youth on a hunting expedition. Both hunting expeditions were led by the fathers of the future heroes, Mona Rudo's father Rudo Luhe and Odysseus's father Autolycus. For Odysseus, as for Mona Rudo, the hunt is a rite of passage (Levaniouk 2011). In the passage from youth to manhood, the two future heroes are injured in different ways: Odysseus is gored by a boar's tusk, while Mona Rudo cuts himself with his own knife. For both, though, the scar left behind is a proof of courage that distinguishes its bearer from other men. Both scars are therefore identificatory, but in different ways. Everyone knows who Mona Rudo is, while Odysseus, who has returned in disguise after 20 years away, is unrecognisable but for his scar. It is only when his housekeeper sees the scar that she recognises him. Even so, Odysseus's scar says something else about him besides the fact that he is the lord of Ithaca.

According to Auerbach, Odysseus's scar is a symbol of his superficial psychology, in which everything is externalised. As soon as he has a thought, Odysseus expresses it, and he never has any trouble expressing himself. We often talk about psychology today in terms of identity, and Odysseus's identity is skin-deep. Like a mark upon one's skin one carries for life, Odysseus's identity is also unchanging. 'Odysseus on his return is exactly the same as he was when he left Ithaca two decades earlier' (Auerbach 2003: 17). In other words, Odysseus's is a true 'identity', a word that is cognate with 'identical'. His relationship with himself never changes. His relationships with others in the small-scale feudal order in which he lived are the same, for, like all things in Homer, interpersonal relations are 'completely fixed in their spatial and temporal relations' (Auerbach 2003: 6).

Similarly, Mona Rudo seems a superficial, static character in a small-scale tribal order who says what he thinks and never has any trouble expressing himself and whose relationships – whether with himself, his wife, the other villagers, his tribal enemies, the Japanese or the ancestors, including his father – remain forever the same. Once he becomes a *rseno bale* he is always a *rseno bale*. Once he becomes a hero, a hero he will always be.

Auerbach goes on to contrast the externalised, static Homeric heroes with the internalised, dynamic patriarchs of Genesis. Characters in the Bible are internalised in several senses. They are never described in any detail, physically or psychologically. They do not have striking, easily identifiable physical or psychic features the way Odysseus does. They almost seem physical and psychological blank slates. They do not say what they are thinking; Abraham does not seem to know what to think. For the reader, it is unclear what his relationship with God or his son Isaac should be. As a result, there is a sense of fluidity (Auerbach 2003: 21) in both self and what we now call society in 'Genesis' that is entirely lacking in *The Odyssey*. For Auerbach, the contrast is between the Greek and the Hebrew ideas of the human and the social; within *Seediq Bale* there is a similar contrast between the externalised, static Mona Rudo and the internalised, dynamic Hanaoka Ichirō, who was born Dakis Nobing, and the kinds of social orders they represent.[3]

Dakis Nobing/Hanaoka Ichirō was educated along with his 'younger brother' Dakis Nawi/Hanaoka Jirō (who had the same given name but a different surname in Tgdaya) to serve as a native police officer and teacher. Unblemished with any identifying mark, whether tattoo or scar, Dakis Nobing/Hanaoka Ichirō has the freedom to present himself in different ways to different people at different times, to try on identities like sets of clothes. He has in fact at least four sets of clothes: a police officer's uniform, Japanese attire, judo *gi* and tribal garb. Each set represents one of the roles he plays. Mona Rudo, by contrast, has only one set of clothing and a unitary understanding of identity. In a scene in which Dakis Nobing/Hanaoka Ichirō asks him whether he is really going to go through with it, Mona Rudo responds by asking him to 'change clothes' (*The Sun Flag* 1:40:17), to join all the other clean-faced Seediq males and become a *rseno bale*. Chief Mona demands that he choose between Hanaoka Ichirō and Dakis Nobing, refusing him the multiple identity that allows any contemporary Taiwanese citizen to become one thing and another and something else again. The key word here is 'become'. Anyone could have predicted that a male youth of Mona Rudo's generation would aspire to become a *rseno bale*. Mona Rudo was in some sense a *rseno bale* at birth. By contrast, no one could have predicted what Dakis Nobing/Hanaoka Ichirō would become at birth, but becoming a teacher and police officer, Japanese in habit (in both senses of the word), was not Dakis Nobing/Hanaoka Ichirō's choice, nor has it brought him happiness. He is caught between two worlds, accepted in neither. He obviously resembles educated natives in colonies like India, but in his inarticulate torment also recalls the Biblical Abraham. 'I ... I am ... Seediq' (*The Sun Flag* 1:40:14), he says, tongue-tied. One cannot imagine Mona Rudo tongue-tied.

The scar of subjectivity: the presentation of perspective

Other aspects of epic narration discussed by Auerbach seem specific to written or oral epic, but can be adapted for film epic. Homer's 'syntactical culture', Auerbach (2003: 13) writes, explicated relations between clauses, relations which in Hebrew were left implicit. In film the 'syntactical' relationships would be visual, between shots. Relationships between shot and shot in *Seediq Bale* are almost always clear. The recognition scene, for instance, begins with a high-angle shot in which we see Mhebu as a whole. This shot is a master shot because it orients us in the space of the scene. A woman carrying a rattan backpack walks through the centre of the frame, covering, exposing (*The Sun Flag* 0:47:10) and therefore drawing attention to Chief Mona's slate house down below. Then, after a few connecting shots, comes the sequence I discussed above: a long shot of the rainbow, a profile shot of Pawan Nawi looking at the rainbow and turning to look at Chief Mona, and a close-up of Chief Mona's scar (Figures 14.1–14.5). The shots are spatially contiguous, so that the cinematography can be described as metonymic in Roman Jakobson's sense. An epic film grammar in which the relationships between shots (and scenes) are left somehow implicit might be a cinema of metaphor, where shots are matched not for spatial contiguity but for similarity (Jakobson 1995: 130–131). The shooting and editing of *Seediq Bale* is occasionally governed by the principle of similarity. After all, the rainbow reminds Pawan of Chief Mona's scar partly because of the similarity in shape, but one has to look very hard for cinematographically metaphorical arrangements in *Seediq Bale*. In film studies terms, *Seediq Bale* is in the tradition of continuity editing, not montage.

Another way to approach the editing would be to ask from what perspective the shots are presented. For Auerbach (2003: 7), perspective is an issue of epic narration. He contrasts the 'subjectivistic-perspectivistic' narration of the Bible with Homer, who never adopts any particular character's perspective. Homer never enters his characters' heads, while the Bible somehow seems more 'modern' in its representation of the situatedness of human subjectivity. A Homeric film would presumably be composed entirely of objective shots, as opposed to subjective shots, also known as point-of-view shots. In this respect, *Seediq Bale* seems partly Biblical in its presentation of perspective. Yu-lin Lee (2014b: 101–104) suggests that in the slaughter scene at the end of *The Sun Flag*, the seemingly objective shots, including the final bird's eye view (2:14:59–2:15:26), represent the perspectives of the ancestors, perhaps specifically of the mother figure who constitutes a kind of film epic machinery. I will instead focus on how the subjective perspectives of the characters are presented. In film studies the presentation of subjectivity is usually discussed in terms of 'suture'.

As Stephen Heath (1978) explains, 'suture' was proposed in 1966 by the Lacanian Jacques-Alain Miller and applied to cinema by Jean-Pierre Oudart in 1969. In what follows I draw on Kaja Silverman's lucid account of suture in *The Subject of Semiotics* (Silverman 1983: 194–236). A suture, literally a 'stitch', closes a wound. In Lacanian psychology it would be a wound of castration, where the phallus symbolises the pre-subjective plenitude lost when, in the mirror stage, an infant first becomes a viewing subject. At that moment, the infant supposedly realises it is limited, only able to adopt a certain perspective at a time. The realisation of limitation is a psychic castration, which the subject soon forgets. In cinema, the subject's wounding limitation is sutured over and thereby concealed by continuity editing, particularly by '[t]he shot/reverse-shot formation' as in the example with which I opened this chapter: in the shot we see Pawan Nawi looking (Figure 14.4), while in the reverse-shot we see what he sees (Figure 14.5). The shot/reverse-shot formation 'conceal[s] from the viewing subject the passivity of that subject's position … suturing over the wound of castration with narrative' (Silverman 1983: 204). Each reverse-shot offers the subject a viewing position that, depending on one's idea of how independent the subject is, either induces or invites identification. A Lacanian would probably use the word induce; I prefer invite. The reverse-shot in the recognition scene, for instance, invites identification with Pawan Nawi, who adulates Mona Rudo.

However, there are a lot of other possibilities in *Seediq Bale* for identification, many other perspectives we might choose to adopt, of characters who do not find Mona Rudo so compelling. Not all the chiefs who throw in their lot with Mona Rudo look up to him. Chief Tado Nokan, for instance, has to be arm-twisted into taking part in the rising. 'After you exchange lives (of the

Japanese people you are planning to decapitate) for the right to tattoo the faces of the young men of the village, how will you compensate for the annihilation of the tribe (in the Japanese reprisal)', he asks. 'With pride', Mona Rudo replies (*The Sun Flag* 1:53:20). Though he ends up giving in, Tado Nokan remains unpersuaded of the rightness of the rising. In this scene we switch from Mona's to Tado's perspective and back again. The viewing subject therefore has a choice. In other scenes, the shot/reverse-shot pair offers the spectator the choice of a woman's pacifist perspective, for example, when Tado Nokan's daughter Takayama Hatsuko/Obing Tado looks back at her father (*The Sun Flag* 2:13:54), or when Hakaoka Ichirō/Dakis Nobing and his wife Kawano Hanako/Obing Nawi look up to see Mona Rudo striding past right after he sees them (*The Sun Flag* 2:14:07). When a woman looks back, the cut can cut either way.

According to suture theorists, the viewing subject is particularly likely to transcend its putative passivity in moments of disconnect between the gaze and the voice. Right after Mona Rudo tells the warriors to leave him and prepare for the attack on Wushe, his wife Bakan Walis starts singing a song (*The Sun Flag* 1:43:28) in which she reminds her husband and the other warriors that they come from women and asserts that it is the women who have 'woven' together everything they have to be proud of. In this scene, Bakan Walis's implicit criticism of Chief Mona is given a voice but not a gaze. Bakan Walis appears with her daughter at 1:43:31 in a shot that is halfway between an over-the-shoulder and a profile; one cannot see what she is looking at. This shot cuts 180 degrees at 1:43:38, with the next cut at 1:43:44 to Ubus, one of Rudo Luhe's brothers in arms. This shot seems initially like it might be from Bakan's perspective, but at 1:43:49 we cut to Mona Rudo striding by, a shot that might still be from Bakan's perspective until Ubus enters the frame from the lower right. In other words, we never find out what Walis Bakan is looking at, nor does anyone acknowledge her by looking back at her. Her 'singing position' is not matched with a 'viewing position'. (In *The Rainbow Bridge* she will finally be given a viewing position, in a scene where she discovers her husband's store of gunpowder and tells her son that he and all the men are 'crazy' [0:26:26].) For a suture theorist, this moment in *The Sun Flag* is 'a moment of unpleasure in which the viewing subject perceives that it is lacking something' (Silverman 1983: 204). What we as spectators are lacking is the pacifist perspective of a woman with whom we might very much want to identify. As a result, we should pay particular attention to what she is singing.

What is Bakan Walis singing? That the men will cut asunder what the women have 'woven' together. Traditionally, a woman's qualification for passage over the rainbow bridge was calloused palms from weaving with a handloom, but Seediq women like Bakan Walis were also skilled at the use of the needle in sewing and tattooing. Mona Rudo's mother might have sewn – sutured – up the knife wound he gave himself at the same time as she gave him his tattoos (*The Sun Flag* 0:04:46–0:05:14). One might say that Seediq women were the agents of suture in a larger sense. They sutured children into language and into the tribal community. Suture can therefore be reinterpreted as a metaphor for the cohesive ties that any community needs to be more than a set of individuals. This point brings me back to the possibility I raised in the introduction of finding common ground between liberal and nativist notions of nation.

Conclusion: the role of scar nationalism in a rainbow nation

For all its explicitness, *Seediq Bale* has attracted allegorical interpretation in terms of Taiwan's contemporary domestic politics and international relations. In this chapter, I allegorised differently, interpreting the standoff between Mona and modernity in the film as a debate between a nativism that has roots in tribalism and a liberalism in which a leap of faith is made. In *Seediq Bale*, nativism is represented by Mona Rudo's metonymic understanding of belonging, metonymic because it is based on face-to-face personal connections and connections to the local landscape. The Seediq were literally 'chthonic', of the land: they believed the first humans emerged from a tree-rock or rock-tree (*The Rainbow Bridge* 2:03:37–2:04:16). It is to return to the *pusu qhuni*, the origin tree, that Hanaoka Jiro/Dakis Nawi and dozens of women and children hanged themselves from tree boughs (*The Rainbow Bridge* 0:34:16–0:37:41). To Mona Rudo, the people's connection to the origin of life was being severed under Japanese rule. Indeed, the only option for most of the young Seediq men in the film is working as loggers for slave wages, cutting down the trees that had seen their ancestors (*The Sun Flag* 0:41:46).

Liberalism in the film is represented by Dakis Nobing/Hanaoka Ichirō, who aspires to a kind of belonging based on similarity. He attempted an intellectual leap to identify with a nation of individuals, who are compatriots not just because they belong to the same territory but also because they speak the same language, share the same culture, and enjoy the same legal or political rights. Though in respect to rights they are the same, in every other respect they have the freedom to be different. Wei Te-sheng's Mona Rudo was not exactly tolerant of difference. He went headhunting to force his enemies to become friends at the cost not just of their lives, but also of their identities. He dragged them across the border of the *alang*, the boundary separating self from other. For a liberal, by contrast, the boundaries around self or society let difference in and create complicated people like Dakis Nobing/Hanaoka Ichirō, multicultural communities such as the town of Wushe, and what Wei Te-sheng himself has described as the rainbow nation of Taiwan.

As residents of a rainbow nation, we can still find Mona Rudo intensely appealing (however appalling). Mona Rudo's appeal is of someone who never doubts himself, because he has undergone a communally sanctioned rite of passage, written the successful result on his skin to display to one and all, once and for all, what he is: the potent but unquestioning upholder of an inflexible tradition. How can liberals, for whom uncertainty in the passage 'through the indeterminate and the contingent' (Auerbach 2003: 10) is a source of endless angst, possibly out-appeal Mona Rudo? At least in contemporary Taiwan, they do not have to try. What they have to try to do is articulate the benefits of an open society in which the rights of all individuals are protected, including the right to speak one's mind, to point out the tyranny and intolerance that continue to trouble Taiwan while fulfilling one's responsibility to listen. In such a society, Tado Nokan would be less likely to capitulate to a demagogue, Takayama Hatsune/Obing Tado to get caught up in a pointless uprising. In such a society, Dakis Nobing/Hanaoka Ichirō would be more likely to feel at home, and Bakan Walis to articulate a modern *gaya* that complements individual possibility with a flexible form of national belonging.

Postscript: the possibility of another kind of indigenous epic

In interpreting *Seediq Bale* as a narrative of contemporary political concerns, I seem to have left the Seediq behind. It has been argued that Wei's film leaves the Seediq behind. Lorenzo Veracini (2012: 244) describes *Seediq Bale* as 'a story of indigenous disappearance' à la *The Last of the Mohicans* (dir. Michael Mann, 1992), 'a (filmic) declaration of Taiwan's (settler) independence'. According to Veracini, the Tgdaya and Toda warriors in the film kill each other off to clear the land for the Taiwanese colonists, whose descendants would decades later identify with the aborigines in order to distinguish themselves from the Chinese and become postcolonial. The thing is that Taiwan's indigenous people have not disappeared. Actually *Seediq Bale* strongly implies the survival of the Seediq. At the end of *The Rainbow Bridge* a solitary hunter appears, on a solo expedition (*The Rainbow Bridge* 2:02:01). He hears the sound of singing and looks up to see a procession of warriors led by Mona Rudo across a rainbow (2:02:01–2:02:35), first in profile, then head on. The computer-generated imagery is atrocious, but Wei Te-sheng apparently wanted to make everything explicit, leaving nothing to the reader's imagination (also see Rawnsley 2016b). In this scene Wei implies that the Tgdaya survivors will continue to believe in the traditional rainbow bridge, but in the previous scene he shows a different procession (1:58:47–1:59:07), of Tgdaya women and children en route to the reservation of Kawanakajima, which the Tgdaya called Alang Gluban. Wei Te-sheng never gives us the reverse-shot. His purpose was not to tell the story of survivors like Dakis Nawi/Hanaoka Jirō's widow Takayama Hatsune/Obing Tado. After the war, just as Alang Gluban (a.k.a. Chuanzhong island) was renamed Qingliu, Takayama Hatsuko/ Obing Tado added a third identity, Gao Cai-yun. She ended up moving back to Mhebu, or Lushan, where she ran a hot springs hotel with her second husband, apparently managing to reconcile her personal, cultural and linguistic identities.

In *Seediq Bale*, Mona Rudo launches his rising for fear that in 20 years the Seediq people will have become Japanese (*The Sun Flag* 1:19:51), so what good is the store, the school, the post office and the police station in Wushe? Since 1930, Mona Rudo's people have crossed a different rainbow bridge, to what can idealistically be described as multicultural modernity. They no longer tattoo their faces, but their identities have not been effaced. As one indigenous critic of *Seediq Bale* put it, they each have 'the face of the inbetweener', in between Chinese and indigenous, modernity and tradition, individual and group (Pacidal 2012). That they are 'in between' attests to their survival. Eighty-five years later they are survivors of 15 years of attempts to turn them into Japanese imperial citizens, 45 years of Sinification under the KMT, and another 15 years of cultural and linguistic commodification and loss under neo-liberalism.

Viewers of Wei Te-sheng's *Cape No.7* may recall the Hakka travelling salesman of Malasang (0:18:36–54 and 1:37:06–34), a brand of millet wine, and the fired glass beads on sale at the airport store (1:31:27–38). In both cases, a ritual product of indigenous labour has become a commodity that serves as a symbol of interpersonal connection (as in the concert at the end of the film), a substitute for the social cohesion of *gaya*. Indigenous culture is obviously also commodified in *Seediq Bale* and related merchandise. Ironically, by commodifying the Seediq language – by using it to give *Seediq Bale* the aura of historical authenticity – Wei Te-sheng may have helped to slow linguistic loss, if only a little, by getting at least a few members of his audience interested. Seediq is now 'moribund', in that most native speakers are over 50 years of age. There are activists trying to revitalise the language like Guo Ming-zheng/Dakis Pawan, the translator of the Tgdaya dialogue in *Seediq Bale*, and Chiu Ruo-long's wife Iwan Nawi, a teacher and Toda native speaker, who went on to re-translate the entire screenplay into Toda (Nawi 2014). There are activists trying to reinvent the culture, often in the context of Christian belief. There are activists asserting political rights, including those who made an impression on Wei Te-sheng in 1996 by claiming that the government was occupying a traditional hunting ground in Hualian (Kan 2011). Another, more Biblical type of Taiwanese indigenous epic film should take up the suspense-filled story of the ongoing Seediq accommodation, and contribution, to the evolving project of Taiwanese modernity.[4]

Notes

1 *Seediq Bale* was released in Taiwan in September 2011 in two parts, *The Sun Flag* (*Taiyang qi*) and *The Rainbow Bridge* (*Caihong qiao*), and as a single version internationally, *Warriors of the Rainbow: Seediq Bale*. The term 'Seediq bale' means 'real person' in the Tgdaya dialect of Seediq. In the other two dialects of Seediq, Toda and Truku, the word is spelled *sediq* and *seejiq*, respectively.

2 There is a connection, however tenuous, between Homer and nativism, the Bible and liberalism, in their contrasting conceptualisations of the law: in Homer's world customary law secures the social order, while God in the Bible figures the sovereign

power that in a modern state legislates individuals, paradoxically in order to empower them.

3 Seediq bands were once nomadic, small and acephalous (Simon 2012: 171). With colonisation, they settled, grew in size and acquired chiefs (Simon 2012: 172). Clearly, Seediq society in 1930 was in flux. My claim that Mona Rudo represents a static concept of society and identity applies to *Seediq Bale*, not to history.

4 For an epistemologically humble, avant-garde narrative of the lingering trauma of Wushe in Alang Gluban, see Wu He's novel *Yusheng*, first published in 1999, due out in Michael Berry's English translation *Remains of Life* from Columbia University Press in early 2017.

Part III

Interview and supplement

15 A conversation with Taiwanese filmmaker Wei Te-sheng

Ming-yeh T. Rawnsley

Interviewers: Ming-yeh T. Rawnsley and Robert Ru-shou Chen[1]
Interviewee: Wei Te-sheng
Place: The ARS Film Production, Taipei, Taiwan
Date: 12 August 2015

Figure 15.1 Taiwanese filmmaker Wei Te-sheng
(Source: The ARS Film)

Introduction

Taiwan cinema experienced a commercial revival when Wei Te-sheng's debut feature film, *Cape No.7*, became a box office sensation in 2008 (Rawnsley 2012). Since then, there have been many commercially successful Taiwanese projects produced and directed by a variety of local filmmakers. Among the younger generation of directors, Wei Te-sheng has risen in prominence and has generated much critical interest primarily because his work focuses on the representation and rediscovery of Taiwan's recent history and identity. In other words, while Wei remains a localised talent with little exposure in the West, he is arguably one of the most representative Taiwanese filmmakers of the twenty-first century. Through the analysis of Wei's films in the second section of this volume, combined with the chapters in the first section where international film festivals and their interactions with Taiwan and Asian cinema are examined, we have demonstrated the social, political and cultural transformations in Taiwan cinema, together with the change and continuity in the international film arena. In the third section, we feature an in-depth interview with Wei Te-sheng to probe his creative vision and filmmaking practices in order to obtain further insight into how Taiwan cinema and its workforce respond and (re)adapt to a constantly evolving environment.

Q1: How did you begin making films in Taiwan?

A1: I have always wanted to make films, but I don't have a film-related background. I began working in a television production team as soon as I finished my national military service. When director Jin Ao-xun's film project, *Top Cool* (*Xiangfei: Aokong shenying*, 1993), needed a temporary floor secretary,[2] I eagerly grabbed the chance and learned on the job. Although the position lasted only two and a half weeks, it connected me to other filmmaking personnel and opportunities later on.

On reflection I also learned several valuable lessons. First, director Jin had an assistant director who then looked around 40 years old. This made me ponder on my own future. I figured at the time that I probably would never be able to direct my own films if I stayed in a studio system and waited for promotion through the ranks. I told myself that I must take a risk. I had to write my own scripts and save money to film my own works. Once I had my own creative output – even if all I could afford was short films – I would be in a better position to talk to people and to seek suitable avenues to make feature-length films.

Second, I believe that it was essential for me to develop and improve a wide range of relevant skills. For example, prior to my first short film project, *Face in the Evening* (*Xi yan*, 1995), I had never directed movies and was very nervous. I divided the script into individual frames and shot each frame one by one until the whole story was finished. I learned the procedures of shooting a film in this way. I then tasked myself to learn the entire process of filmmaking, including budget control and post-production. Thus I wrote a very short script, *Three Dialogues* (*Duihua sanbu*, 1996), in which there were only three scenes with three different shots. Once I completed my second project, I discovered that I still didn't know how to properly communicate with actors. Previously I treated actors almost as props because I shot the films frame by frame. I didn't give the cast a real opportunity to be emotionally involved in a story. Therefore in my third project, *Before Dawn* (*Liming zhi qian*, 1997), I aimed to practise communication techniques with actors. I devised the shooting script according to the stories of each scene and not simply for the sake of camera shots. I also employed a cast of more experienced professional actors and forced myself to discuss with them their performances. The result was satisfactory. In my fourth short film project, *About July* (*Qiyue tian*, 1999), I wanted to try my hands on a bigger-scale production in order to learn the art of mise-en-scène. The accumulation of these experiences finally led me to the production of *Cape No.7* in 2008.

It has been over 20 years since my first involvement in Taiwan's film industry. During this relatively short period of time, we have witnessed many dramatic changes in filmmaking, including synchronised sound recording, the disappearance of film negatives, computerisation of editing, and the digitalisation of film production and exhibition. The digital revolution has changed the boundaries of traditional processes of linear 'pre-production, production and post-production' filmmaking. This is the kind of impact we need to deal with. Some of my friends used to say that they would insist on using negatives to make films, but I find myself more flexible in this regard. I don't understand why one should insist on a certain format and thus become constrained by it. I consider content and story the more crucial elements. Format and technology are just tools to help me relay a story I want to tell. Tools may change, but you should still be able to create your imagination on screen and tell the story if you are willing to be adaptable.

Q2: Since all the feature films you have directed or produced so far are about Taiwanese history and identity, is it fair to say that the island's historiography is the core element you insist on in your films?

A2: Originally I didn't set out to make films about Taiwan's history. I stumbled into historical filmmaking by accident. My primary concern is always the story; a story moves me and so I want to make a film about it. However, following the reception of *Cape No.7, Seediq Bale* (2011) and *Kano* (2014), I must admit that the feedback from the audience has had an impact on me. Now I do feel that I need to fulfil a promise, although I have also given myself a deadline so that I won't be confined to historical subjects indefinitely. I would like to turn a 1997 novel by Mr Wang Jia-xiang, *Dao Feng Nei Hai*, [3] into a series of three films, which I call *Taiwan Trilogy* (*Taiwan sanbuqu*). One day, when I finally materialise the entire project, I know I will have said everything that I want to say on the matter and shall liberate myself from any further expectations. In other words, if I have more things to say in the future, of course I'll be happy to make more history films, but I won't see it as my responsibility any longer because I will have already delivered my promise.

The first movie of *Taiwan Trilogy* will be based on the story of *Dao Feng Nei Hai*, which is from the viewpoint of the Siraya tribes when they faced the arrival of the Dutch in Taiwan in 1624.[4] Meanwhile I would also like to tell the same story from the perspectives of the Han Chinese in Taiwan and that of the Dutch. Hence I will add two sequels to the original and make it a trilogy. I have been doing a lot of research every day and trying to integrate into my films many real experiences of the Han people and the Dutch during the period through a handful of fictionalised characters of different ethnic backgrounds. My intention is to recreate onscreen the overall structure of feeling, atmosphere and events of Taiwan 400 years ago through a number of relatable personalities.

Adapting *Dao Feng Nei Hai* into a film script is challenging. It's a wonderful novel with excellent stories and strong characters. At first I found my adaptation too literal because I allowed my creativity to be restrained by the author's words on paper. Once I identified the problem, I re-read the novel several more times to familiarise myself with it. I then put it aside completely so that I could begin developing a film script based on my own understanding and interpretation of the story in a freer manner.

If all goes well, I hope I can secure a film location and begin preparing the land in 2017, start shooting in 2018, and release the first film in 2021. In planning this, I have a bigger ambition for *Taiwan Trilogy*. I often liken Taiwan cinema to butterflies. A caterpillar takes a long time to feed on a lot of leaves to be able to turn itself into a chrysalis. It also takes ages for a chrysalis to be ready and become a fully formed butterfly. Yet on average a butterfly has an adult life span of less than two weeks. Similarly, it takes a huge amount of effort, money and time of many people to plan and produce a movie. Publicity and distribution also require much energy and attention to detail. However, many locally produced films only have a theatre life cycle in Taiwan of merely seven days. It is so short that I can't help but wonder whether or not all the work that goes into filmmaking is worthwhile. If you have done a really good job, sometimes your film will be mentioned in literature so that there may be some residual value to the film as a reference for research or as a marker for a particular year.

For this reason, I have been searching for different possibilities to lengthen the life span of a film and ways to enhance its added value. For example, we will need to reconstruct the Dutch fortress in Tainan, Fort Zeelandia (*Relanzhe cheng*, i.e. the Anping Castle today), as a location for *Taiwan Trilogy*. Once the trilogy is complete, I hope the film set will be kept and developed into an arts and cultural heritage park in which we can build a movie theatre. *Taiwan Trilogy* may be released island-wide conditionally for two to three weeks and then it will only be screened in the park for the next ten years. We don't release DVDs or cable and satellite broadcasting rights, nor do we enter any international film festivals, so the film will become a timeless production and a genuinely special feature for the park. Obviously there are still a lot of details to be negotiated and planned. Moreover, I believe there will be much room for further improvement and change. Nevertheless, this is my dream and a bold attempt to maximise the life and value of Taiwan cinema.

Q3: In addition to the innovative ways of film distribution and exhibition you mention, what are the other lessons you have learned from the previous film projects that may apply to the production of your *Taiwan Trilogy*?

A3: As far as I am concerned, the most vital lesson is about budget control. Both *Seediq Bale* and *Kano* went seriously over budget. Otherwise their market performance was similar to or above our estimate during the planning stage. *Seediq Bale* generated ticket sales worth US $24.46 million (*c.* NT $800 million) in the end, which is US $6.12 million (*c.* NT $200 million) over our original projection. When *Kano* was released, we faced an unexpected socio-political challenge (i.e. the Sunflower Movement in March 2014).[5] This means that *Kano* only had about two weeks to attract audiences to the movie theatres. By the third week when the students occupied the Legislative Yuan, ticket sales plummeted and it became impossible to turn the tide. However, within such a short space of time, *Kano* still created a box office return worth US $9.17 million (*c.* NT $300 million), similar to our initial prediction. In other words, if both films were able to stay within the production budget, they would have recouped the initial investment and made a decent profit.

Management of a film's budget is complex because many issues are interconnected, and sometimes matters are simply out of our control. For example, when we worked on *Seediq Bale* we signed a contract with one of the top special and visual effects production companies in South Korea as (1) we aspired to have the best visuals that we could afford for the film, and (2) South Korea has established a reputation, which is comparable with Hollywood and second to none in Asia, for their capacity in visual effects. Nevertheless, the Korean company went bust after we completed shooting but before post-production began, and they refused to refund the money we paid in advance. In addition, all the footage we had shot was based on their designs and we waited for them to add their digital creation to enhance individual plates. The unfortunate situation forced us to find another company half way through our project. The first alternative Korean company we talked to did not only give us a quotation beyond our reach, but also demanded a re-shoot of crucial battle scenes to fit their new special effects designs. It was impossible because many sets were already blown up or burned down in front of the cameras. I am unable to rebuild the sets and to bring back the cast for a reshoot just to satisfy different visual effects specialists. Eventually we decided to collaborate with another company in Beijing, Crystal Digital Technology. They are less experienced than the South Koreans, but they are highly motivated, and their willingness to cooperate with us made them a suitable partner in our eyes. However, these hurdles meant that the production cost of *Seediq Bale* skyrocketed.

When we made *Kano*, my role was as producer and I wanted to give the director, Umin Boya (a.k.a. Ma Zhi-xiang), as much creative freedom as possible. Originally we calculated that a production budget of around US $4.59 million (*c*. NT $150 million) should be sufficient. Nevertheless, the budget increased when shooting began. Finally, when the cost reached US $7.64 million (*c*. NT $250 million), I knew I must step in and investigate. It transpired that the production team overspent repeatedly on art designs. Once you devote most of your resources on aesthetics, much longer hours of work are required to achieve a desired outcome, which then inevitably adds significantly to staff costs. This is what I mean about the interconnection of issues for budget control.

To summarise, I think that budget control will be one of the most important lessons I need to apply to the production of *Taiwan Trilogy*. Perhaps one way to achieve this is that we should not rush into production unless we have already at least 50 per cent of the necessary funds in place. When we made the previous projects, we began shooting before the promised investment arrived, which often created its own vicious circle. For example, if you don't have enough finance to pay a particular company on time, the company may delay their work and consequently the set you need is not ready in time for shooting. Thus you have to change film schedules and shoot other scenes that don't require that specific set. Picking and shooting scenes randomly is usually much more time consuming and cost ineffective. Money and resources can be unnecessarily wasted and you'll need to find more money and resources in order to plug the holes that are left. Moreover, as I mentioned earlier, the longer the production takes, the bigger the staff costs, and a film's production budget can easily get out of hand in this way. Therefore, I would like to try and avoid falling into similar traps in the future.

Q4: It appears that visual effects are an extremely important component of your movies. Subtle and realistic digitalised imagery may help recreate and enhance a sense of historical reality in cinema. Do you have any reflection on the use of special and visual effects in your films that you can share with us?

A4: We experienced different issues in *Seediq Bale* and *Kano*. When we made *Kano*, our special effects team was based in Thailand. I remember we gave them a lot of drawings in advance in the hope that they would grasp the overall tone and ambience we wished to achieve in the film. However, when they sent us their digitalised pictures of sky and paddy fields, we felt that they looked unreal because the sky was so blue that it almost appeared purple, and it was cloudless. As landscapes of sky and rice fields are commonplace in rural Taiwan, we know the sky should be a paler blue, and there are always white clouds somewhere in the background. We went back and forth about this imagery several times and couldn't quite understand why they didn't seem to get what we meant or wanted. One day during a break in shooting some of our crew members went to Thailand for a short holiday. They were amazed at the colours of the sky and paddy fields in Thailand, which was exactly how the digitalised pictures depicted them. This tells me about the challenges of cross-cultural communication and international collaboration.

Another problem with our Thai visual effects team was that they committed a serious error in the process of file transfer by reducing the lighting range to only two settings when they finished their work and returned the digital files to us. The error was only discovered during the final stage of editing. There was no more budget or time to ask the Thai company to redo their work in order to rectify the error. In fact, it is almost impossible to demand that the entire digitalisation process be re-done because each image has layers and layers of composition. Anyway, this means that in the editing we had to sacrifice many of the better shots in order to match the lower-quality lighting in the files the Thai company gave us. This was necessary to make sure the contrast of the lighting in different scenes would not be too obvious. We are lucky that the story of *Kano* is exciting and entertaining enough to distract the audience's attention away from such technicalities. Otherwise it probably would have become an utter disaster. Nevertheless, our cameraman was heartbroken by such a careless mistake because much of his effort of creating beautiful shots and in-camera effects was needlessly wasted.

In *Seediq Bale*, I think Crystal Digital Technology did a plausible job under very difficult working conditions. By the time they took over the work, there was already a huge time pressure because the Venice International Film Festival informed us that they would like to see our film. Not only was the deadline quite tight, but also there were technically challenging effects to be made for numerous plates. Among the 2,000 plus digital pictures they created for us, perhaps fewer than ten are questionable. However, the type of visual effects we pursue in these history films is that they should appear natural and thus 'invisible'. We want the aesthetic designs and visual effects to be an integral part of the story and help construct onscreen an atmosphere of the time and place so that the audience's historical sensibility will be strengthened. For this reason, any mistakes in the moving image become particularly noticeable as they break the cinematic magic to remind viewers that nothing is real. For example, in one of the opening scenes you can see a goat drinking water. When there are little movements, the scene looks serene and realistic. However, a hunter takes a shot at the goat but misses, and the goat quickly runs away. When the goat takes off, it suddenly strikes you that the goat moves more like a rabbit instead of a real goat.

Similarly, there is a wild boar in the opening sequence. The specialists at Crystal Digital Technology had never seen a wild boar in real life before. From the many different pictures we sent them for reference, they assumed that the texture of the animal's hair is hard. Yet in reality it should be soft. Consequently, when the wild boar first appears in the movie, the still imagery looks convincing. Unfortunately, as soon as the boar runs and charges, the movement of its hair looks like a porcupine instead of a real boar. Such creative errors reduce the film's sense of quality and historical credibility. Personally I believe this may be a result of a long-term deficit in appreciation of aesthetics.

I think that perhaps both the Chinese and the Taiwanese education systems have been overly negligent in aesthetic training and sensitivity. We privilege technology and industry over arts and humanity. We don't encourage our youngsters to observe nature and the world around us. Rather, we just ask them to study textbooks so that they can obtain good grades in examinations. The digital revolution has made visual effects today an interdisciplinary craft which combines art, science and computer technology. Many visual effects technicians in Taiwan come from a background in computer science, and then they try to learn art designs and painting techniques. However, when one hasn't been immersed in aesthetics all one's life, it seems unrealistic to expect that one suddenly becomes a visual artist even if one is skilful in digital technology and various design techniques. I often wonder if perhaps this is one of the reasons why Taiwan has been weak in making special and visual effects – it is not necessarily because our knowledge and ability in digital technology falls behind our competitors, but because our aesthetic literacy seems inadequate to gain a competitive edge in the modern visual effects industry.

Q5: How may Taiwan cinema and film professionals boost aesthetic literacy?

A5: I don't think this is an exclusive issue for film professionals. The biggest challenge facing our film industry is that the number of movie-goers is decreasing each year. The most recent data show that on average, Taiwanese people watch less than one film per year while Korean people watch four.[6] I understand that the threat of foreign cinema, especially Hollywood, over home productions is an ongoing worry for many people. But if we are able to bring audiences back to cinema, even if more choose Hollywood over local features, I have no doubt that it will still give Taiwan cinema a tremendous boost. Imagine one day when our entire viewing population[7] can go and watch at least one movie per year, how it will benefit our film market! Even if nine out of ten people are attracted to foreign projects, it still means that there will be one person who will be watching Taiwan cinema. Therefore, from my perspective, the fundamental questions that we need to address are: Why don't Taiwanese people watch movies? How do we bring them to cinema? How do we create film audiences now and in the future?

This is when I envisage the influence of a much better-designed aesthetic education. In our education system, we don't place enough value on arts, humanities and experiences of immersion. In music and painting classes, students seem to simply sit in the classroom to study and practise their skills in making art. Even though the schools nowadays have developed outdoor teaching classes, the focus is still much more on teaching than experiencing.

If we are serious about improving the aesthetic sensitivity of the Taiwanese, I think we'll need to add to the curriculum – from primary schools, middle schools to colleges and universities – and provide classes which will immerse students in a wide range of activities to broaden and deepen their appreciation of the arts and humanities. For example, director Hou Hsiao-hsien's award-winning martial arts movie, *The Assassin* (*Nie yin niang*, 2015), will be an excellent choice for our hypothetical arts and cinema immersion class. Before going to see the film, students should be tasked to learn, preferably through self-study, about the Tang dynasty (618–907) – the setting of the story – and the culture, historical background and aesthetic taste of the period. After watching the movie, students should then be encouraged to discuss in the class any aspects of the film which interest them. When the arts and cinema are part of the students' living experiences and not merely a subject for study, their interest and creativity – their aesthetic sensibility – will be stimulated naturally.

Moreover, if such arts immersion classes become a reality in our schools, it will have a positive impact on our cultural and creative economy. As students must go and watch at least one movie – or a theatre production, a baseball game, an arts exhibition, etc. – per semester as part of their curriculum, the Ministry of Education and/or the Ministry of Culture should subsidise part of the entrance fees. This means that the students can enjoy the selected performances at a lower price, but the production houses/event organisers will still be able to receive the government subsidy to make up the difference in ticket sales. Imagine how many more arts and cultural audiences may be cultivated in this way, how vibrant our cinema, musical and sports venues may become, and how much economic potential may be created for our cultural and creative industries.

Interviewers: Thank you very much, Director Wei.

Notes

1 Robert Ru-shou Chen is Professor in the Department of Radio-Television at National Chengchi University. He is the co-editor (with D.W. Davis) of *Cinema Taiwan: Politics, Popularity and State of the Arts* (Routledge, 2007).
2 A floor secretary is a member of a movie production crew. The floor secretary is responsible for making a detailed record of every shot, including the camera used, the angle and length of the shot, the actors' dialogue and movements, sound effects, props, costumes, make-up, etc. The records that are maintained by the floor secretary help the director ensure continuity between shots and scenes.

3 'Dao Feng Nei Hai' is the name of an area on the south-western coast of Taiwan where the Siraya tribes lived in the 1600s. The novel is set in 1624–62, when the Dutch took over the island.

4 Roy (2003: xi–xiii) offers a chronology of major events in Taiwan from the fifteenth century to the early twenty-first century. The following provides us with useful information regarding Taiwan's early history, the setting for Wei's *Taiwan Trilogy*. Fifteenth century: first known Chinese contact with Taiwan inhabited by aborigines. 1544: Portuguese explorers discovered Taiwan and named it *Ilha Formosa*. Seventeenth century: a large number of Han Chinese migrated to Taiwan. 1624: the Dutch built Fort Zeelandia (*Relanzhe cheng*) near Tainan. 1662: Ming loyalist Cheng Cheng-kung (a.k.a. Koxinga or Zheng Chenggong) defeated the Dutch and governed Taiwan.

5 The Sunflower Movement was a student-led protest against the ruling Kuomintang administration's attempt to force through the Cross-Strait Service Trade Agreement in the legislature without subjecting it to a clause-by-clause review. It erupted into a large-scale civic movement with widespread public support, and marked the first time that Taiwan's Legislative Yuan was occupied. The occupation lasted from 18 March to 10 April 2014. For further information, see Rowen (2015).

6 The data provided by Director Wei Te-sheng have not been verified by the interviewers.

7 As of 2013, the total population in Taiwan was 23.37 million. The distribution of age groups was: 14.32 per cent (under 15 years of age), 74.15 per cent (15–64 years of age), and 11.53 per cent (65 years of age and over). If we consider the cinema viewing population as people who are 15–64 years of age, the figure is around 17.32 million. The statistics are available in *The Republic of China/Taiwan Yearbook 2014*: www.ey.gov.tw/en/cp.aspx?n=5776024635D354A6 (accessed 25 November 2015).

Appendix I

A short biography of Wei Te-sheng[1]

Compiled by Ming-yeh T. Rawnsley

Wei Te-Sheng was born in 1969 in Yongkang City, Tainan County (now part of Tainan City) in Taiwan. He joined a small production company in 1993 and learned his craft on the job. He has assistant director credits on many films, including Edward Yang's *Mahjong* (*Ma jiang*, 1996) and Chen Guo-fu's *Double Vision* (*Shuang tong*, 2002). Wei made his debut feature *About July* (*Qiyue tian*) as a modest independent production in 1999, winning praise from critics in Taiwan and a Special Mention from the Dragons & Tigers Award jury at the Vancouver Film Festival. His second feature, *Cape No.7* (2008), was also made on a relatively modest scale but became the highest-grossing Taiwanese film in the history of Taiwan cinema and picked up top prizes at the Golden Horse awards (*Jin ma jiang*), Hawaii Film Festival and Asian Marine Film Festival. The huge success of *Cape No.7* helped Wei raise the finance to make *Warriors of the Rainbow: Seediq Bale* (2011), a project he had nurtured since the mid-1990s. The film hit the movie theatres in September 2011, with the box office totalling more than NT $800 million (*c.* US $25.5 million) in Taiwan, and received several Golden Horse awards, including Best Picture and the Audience Award. In 2014, he took on the role of producer and completed two films, *Kano*, a feature film directed by Umin Boya, and *Pusu Qhuni* (*Yu sheng*), a documentary directed by Tang Shiang-chu.

Wei Te-sheng filmography

- 1995: *Face in the Evening* (*Xi yan*), video, director
- 1996: *Three Dialogues* (*Duihua sanbu*), short film, director
- 1996: *Mahjong* (*Ma jiang*, dir. Edward Yang), assistant director
- 1997: *Before Dawn* (*Liming zhi qian*), short film, director
- 1999: *About July* (*Qiyue tian*), short film, director
- 2002: *Double Vision* (*Shuang tong*, dir. Chen Guo-fu), assistant director
- 2003: *Seediq Bale* (*Sai de ke ba lai*), short film, director
- 2008: *Cape No.7* (*Haijiao qihao*), director
- 2009: *When the Rain is Over* (*Yu guo tian qing*, dir. Lin Yu-xian), producer
- 2011: *Debut* (*Deng chang*), short film, director, included in the collective short film project, *10+10*, organised by the 2011 Golden Horse awards

- 2011: *Warriors of the Rainbow: Seediq Bale* (*Sai de ke ba lai*), director
- 2014: *Kano* (*Kano*, dir. Umin Boya), producer/scriptwriter
- 2014: *Pusu Qhuni* (*Yu sheng*, dir. Tang Shiang-chu), producer
- 2017: *52 Hz I Love You* (*52 Hz wo ai ni*), director

Note

1 We thank ARS Film Production for providing us with this information.

Appendix II

Synopses of *Cape No.7, Seediq Bale* and *Kano*

Compiled by Ming-yeh T. Rawnsley

Cape No.7 (*Haijiao qihao*, dir. Wei Te-sheng, 2008)

The film is set in the present day in a small town in southern Taiwan, Hengchun (literally 'forever spring'). It is a sleepy seaside town with a beautiful beach. On the one hand, the residents of Hengchun are generally conservative with traditional values, and yet on the other hand, one can see international tourists in bikinis walking on the street during the holiday season. The town also holds an annual rock concert on the beach to attract visitors. The director and scriptwriter, Wei Te-sheng, chose Hengchun as the backdrop of this film precisely because of the interesting contrast the town offers.[1]

Another contrast in the film comes from its parallel storylines: the local residents of Hengchun decide to form a local rock band three weeks before the concert begins. As the band will perform the opening acts for the star of the concert, Japanese pop singer Kousuke Atari, the singer's company hires a Japanese lady, Tomoko, to supervise the formation of the local band in Hengchun.

The lead vocal singer of this new band, Aga, is a substitute postman. He discovers a package of undelivered love letters from the colonial period, written in Japanese. The letters are addressed to a girl whose name is also 'Tomoko', living in 'Cape No.7', an address in 1940s Taiwan which no longer exists. However, Aga finally delivers the letters just before he goes on stage to perform his music. While the Japanese writer of the love letters had to leave his Taiwanese lover Tomoko in 1945, Aga is able to persuade his Japanese girlfriend, the modern-day Tomoko, to stay with him (also see Wang in this volume).[2]

Warriors of the Rainbow: Seediq Bale (*Sai de ke ba lai*, dir. Wei Te-sheng, 2011)

As a result of the first Sino–Japanese War (*Jiawu zhanzheng*, 1894–95), the Qing dynasty acceded Taiwan to Japan in 1895. The Seediq, one of the aboriginal tribes in Taiwan, were forced to abandon many of their traditional cultural practices under the Japanese colonial rule.

The protagonist, Mona Rudo, was a Seediq chief who witnessed the Japanese repression over a period of three decades. In 1930, after a series of relatively minor incidents in tribal villages, resentment against the colonial masters accumulated. Chief Mona decided to organise armed resistance and launched attacks on the Japanese in order to regain their spiritual rights as a 'Seediq bale'. In the Seediq language and ancient belief, the term means a 'real person' who practises the traditional law of *gaya*, particularly through the rituals of headhunting and facial tattooing.

The film *Seediq Bale* depicts the historical Wushe Incident (*Wushe shijian*), which occurred in central Taiwan in 1930. Mona Rudo led 300 tribal men fighting against 3,000 Japanese troopers. While there were victories, Mona's people paid a harsh price. Many Seediq women and children committed suicide before the battles commenced so that the tribal warriors did not have to worry about them. Meanwhile, a young Seediq male, Dakis Nobing, who grew up to be a teacher and police officer under Japanese colonialism, adopted a Japanese name, Hanaoka Ichirō, married a Japanese woman and they had a baby together. When Mona forced him to choose between the identities of Dakis Nobing and Hanaoka Ichirō, he took off his police uniform and joined the bloodshed against the Japanese. However, Dakis and his young family later committed suicide as they could not bear to be caught between the two worlds but belong to neither.

Eventually the Japanese regained military control and quashed the uprising. The Seediq survivors were relocated. At the end of the film, the audiences see a young hunter on a solo expedition many years after the Wushe Incident. He hears the sound of singing and looks up to see a procession of warriors led by Mona Rudo across a rainbow bridge (also see Sterk in this volume).

Kano (*Kano*, dir. Umin Boya, 2014)

The film is set in Taiwan in the 1940s, during the colonial period. A Japanese soldier, Josha Hiromi, is on his way to the Pacific War and makes a specific detour to visit a small town on the island, Jiayi, where the Kano baseball team is based. 'Kano' is the shortened Japanese pronunciation of the Jiayi High School of Agriculture in southern Taiwan.

The story is then transported back to 1931. A Japanese coach, Hyotaro Kondo, has left for Taiwan as a high school teacher after suffering humiliation back in Japan.

At first, Kondo tries to disassociate himself from baseball in the colony. However, one day he is almost knocked down by a baseball accidentally thrown by the high school boys in the playground. Kondo's passion for baseball is rekindled and he starts to coach the boys, who are in desperate need of training and discipline. He tries to modernise the Kano team, not only using his own salary and drawing on public funds to feed the students, but also building his training programmes in response to the strengths and weaknesses of the team members, including the Japanese, Taiwanese and aborigines.

In the film, coach Kondo's training process is juxtaposed with a canal construction project engineered by Yoichi Hatta, who endeavours to build a modern irrigation system. By finishing the first canal in Taiwan and turning local farmers into the best rice growers in the empire, engineer Hatta wins adulation and support from the local communities. By reclaiming his identity as a baseball coach, Kondo successfully leads the Kano team to become domestic champions on the island and is invited to represent Taiwan in the 1931 Japanese High School Baseball Championship.

The young Josha Hiromi was a talented high school baseball player from Hokkaido at the time. When he was unexpectedly overcome by the underdogs from Taiwan, the Kano team, and in particular the Taiwanese pitcher, made a serious impression on Hiromi. Nevertheless, while the Kano team won much admiration from their rivals and audiences in Japan, they were too worn out to triumph at the last game. The film ends with views of Taiwan as the Kano team is returning on the cruise ship. Even though they did not win the game, the team and the coach show hope and confidence about the future (also see Liao in this volume).

Notes

1   Ming-yeh T. Rawnsley's interview with Wei Te-sheng, London, 20 February 2009.
2   A slightly different version of this synopsis has been published previously in Rawnsley (2012).

Chinese glossary: Selected names and terms

Aga (A Jia)　阿嘉 / 阿嘉
An, Jie-yi (An Zheyi)　安哲毅 / 安哲毅
Bai, Jing-rui (Bai Jingrui)　白景瑞 / 白景瑞
Bai, Ke (Bai Ke)　白克 / 白克
Chang, Pei-cheng (Zhang Peicheng)　張佩成 / 张佩成
Chang, Sylvia (Zhang Aijia)　張艾嘉 / 张艾嘉
Chang, Tso-chi (Zhang Zuoji)　張作驥 / 张作骥
Chen, Arvin (Chen Junlin)　陳駿霖 / 陈骏霖
Chen, Frankie (Chen Yushan)　陳玉珊 / 陈玉珊
Chen, Guo-fu (Chen Guofu)　陳國富 / 陈国富
Chen, Huai-en (Chen Huaien)　陳懷恩 / 陈怀恩
Chen, Kun-hou (Chen Kunhou)　陳坤厚 / 陈坤厚
Chen, Ying-jung (Chen Yingrong)　陳映蓉 / 陈映蓉
Chen, Yu-xun (Chen Yuxun)　陳玉勳 / 陈玉勋
Cheng, Clement (Zheng Sijie)　鄭思傑 / 郑思杰
Cheng, Fen-fen (Zheng Fenfen)　鄭芬芬 / 郑芬芬
Chiang Kai-shek (Jiang Jieshi)　蔣介石 / 蒋介石
Chiao, Peggy (Jiao Xiongping)　焦雄屏 / 焦雄屏
Chienn, Hsiang (Qian Xiang)　錢翔 / 钱翔
Chinese New Year films (*he sui pian*)　賀歲片 / 贺岁片
Chiu, Ruo-long (Qiu Ruolong)　邱若龍 / 邱若龙
Cho, Li (Zhuo Li)　卓立 / 卓立
Chou, Jay (Zhou Jielun)　周杰倫 / 周杰伦
Chuanzhong Island　川中島 / 川中岛
Fan, Van (Fan Yichen)　范逸臣 / 范逸臣
Feng, Xiaogang (Feng Xiaogang)　馮小剛 / 冯小刚
Fort Zeelandia (*Relanzhecheng*)　熱蘭遮城 / 热兰遮城
Golden Horse Film Festival (*Jin ma jiang*)　金馬獎 / 金马奖
Hakka (*Kejia*)　客家 / 客家
Han　漢 / 汉
Healthy realism (jiankang xieshi)　健康寫實 / 健康写实
Hengchun　恆春 / 恒春
Hokkien (Fujian; also see 'Hoklo' and 'Min')　福建 / 福建

Hoklo (Fulao; also see 'Min' and 'Hokkien') 福佬 / 福佬
Hou, Hsiao-hsien (Hou Xiaoxian) 侯孝賢 / 侯孝贤
Hsieh, Chinglin (Xie Qinglin) 謝慶麟 / 谢庆麟
Hsu, Li-wen (Xu Liwen) 徐麗雯 / 徐丽雯
Huang, Chao-liang (Huang Zhaoliang) 黃朝亮 / 黄朝亮
Hui, Ann (Xu Anhua) 許鞍華 / 许鞍华
Jiayi 嘉義 / 嘉义
Jin, Ao-xun (Jin Aoxun) 金鰲勳 / 金鳌勋
Kaohsiung (Gaoxiong) 高雄 / 高雄
Ke, Yi-zheng (Ke Yizheng) 柯一正 / 柯一正
Keelung (Jilong) 基隆 / 基隆
Ko, Giddens (Jiu ba dao) 九把刀 / 九把刀
Kwok, Derek (Guo Zijian) 郭子健 / 郭子健
Lam, Dante (Lin Chaoxian) 林超賢 / 林超贤
Lee, Ang (Li An) 李安 / 李安
Lee, Kang-sheng (Li Kangsheng) 李康生 / 李康生
Li, Hsing (Li Xing) 李行 / 李行
Li, Xianglan (Li Xianglan) 李香蘭 / 李香兰
Li, You-ning (Li Youning) 李祐寧 / 李佑宁
Lin, Cheng-sheng (Lin Zhengsheng) 林正盛 / 林正盛
Lin, Shu-yu (Lin Shuyu) 林書宇 / 林书宇
Liu, Jian (Liu Jian) 劉健 / 刘健
Loh, I-cheng (Lu Yizheng) 陸以正 / 陆以正
Lu, Yi-ching (Lu Yijing) 陸弈靜 / 陆弈静
mainlander (*waishengren*) 外省人 / 外省人
Mao, Zedong (Mao Zedong) 毛澤東 / 毛泽东
martial arts (*wuxia*) 武俠 / 武侠
Midi Z (Zhao Deyin) 趙德胤 / 赵德胤
Min (also see 'Hoklo' and 'Hokkien') 閩 / 闽
Mona Rudo (Mona Ludao) 莫那魯道 / 莫那鲁道
national cinema (*guopian*) 國片 / 国片
nativisation (*bentuhua*) 本土化 / 本土化
Neo, Jack (Liang Zhiqiang) 梁智強 / 梁智强
Niu, Doze (Niu Chengze) 鈕承澤 / 钮承泽
Qingliu 清流 / 清流
Renzheguan 人止關 / 人止关
sadness (*beiqing*) 悲情 / 悲情
Su, Chao-pin (Su Zhaobin) 蘇照彬 / 苏照彬
Taipei (Taibei) 台北 / 台北
Taiwan New Cinema (*Taiwan xindianying*) 台灣新電影 / 台湾新电影
Tang, Shiang-chu (Tang Xiangzhu) 湯湘竹 / 汤湘竹
Tao, De-chen (Tao Dechen) 陶德辰 / 陶德辰
Tian, Zhuangzhuang (Tian Zhuangzhuang) 田壯壯 / 田壮壮
Tsai, Ming-liang (Cai Mingliang) 蔡明亮 / 蔡明亮
Tsui, Hark (Xu Ke) 徐克 / 徐克

Umin Boya (a.k.a. Ma Zhi-xiang) 馬志翔☒马志翔
Wan, Jen (Wan Ren) 萬仁 / 万仁
Wang, Jim (Wang Chuanzong) 王傳宗 / 王传宗
Wang, Tong (Wang Tong) 王童 / 王童
Wang, Xiaoshuai (Wang Xiaoshuai) 王小帥 / 王小帅
Wei, Te-sheng (Wei Desheng) 魏德聖 / 魏德圣
Woo, John (Wu Yusen) 吳宇森 / 吴宇森
Wu, Nien-jen (Wu Nianzhen) 吳念真 / 吴念真
Wu, Zhuo-liu (Wu Zhuoliu) 吳濁流 / 吴浊流
Wushe Incident (*Wusheshijian*) 霧社事件 / 雾社事件
Yang, Edward (Yang Dechang) 楊德昌 / 杨德昌
Yang, Ya-zhe (Yang Yazhe) 楊雅喆 / 杨雅喆
Yee, Chih-yen (Yi Zhiyan) 易智言 / 易智言
Yonfan (Yang Fan) 楊凡 / 杨凡
Yu, Sunny (Yu Weishan) 于瑋珊 / 于玮珊
Zeng, Zhuang-xiang (Zeng Zhuangxiang) 曾壯祥 / 曾壮祥
Zhang, Yi (Zhang Yi) 張毅 / 张毅

Selected Chinese filmography

A Borrowed Life (*Duo sang*) 多桑 / 多桑 (dir. Wu Nien-jen, 1994)

A Brighter Summer Day (*Gulingjie shaonian sharen shijian*) 牯嶺街少年殺人事件 / 牯岭街少年杀人事 (dir. Edward Yang, 1991)

A City of Cathay (*Qingming shang he tu*) 清明上河圖 / 清明上河图 (dir. Loh I-cheng, 1960)

A City of Sadness (*Beiqing chengshi*) 悲情城市 / 悲情城市 (dir. Hou Hsiao-hsien, 1989)

A One and a Two (*Yi yi*) 一一 / 一一 (dir. Edward Yang, 2000)

A Summer at Grandpa's (*Dongdong de jiaqi*) 冬冬的假期 / 冬冬的假期 (dir. Hou Hsiao-hsien, 1984)

A Time to Live and a Time to Die (*Tongnian wangshi*) 童年往事 /童年往事 (dir. Hou Hsiao-hsien, 1985)

About July (*Qiyue tian*) 七月天 / 七月天 (dir. Wei Te-sheng, 1999)

The Assassin (*Nie yin niang*) 聶隱娘 / 聂隐娘 (dir. Hou Hsiao-hsien, 2015)

Au Revoir Taipei (*Yi ye Taipei*) 一頁台北 / 一页台北 (dir. Arvin Chen, 2010)

Banana Paradise (*Xiangjiao tiantang*) 香蕉天堂 / 香蕉天堂 (dir. Wang Tong, 1989)

Be There or Be Square (*Bu jian bu san*) 不見不散 / 不见不散 (dir. Feng Xiaogang, 1998)

Beautiful Duckling (*Yangya renjia*) 養鴨人家 / 养鸭人家 (dir. Li Hsing, 1964)

Before Dawn (*Liming zhi qian*) 黎明之前 / 黎明之前 (dir. Wei Te-sheng, 1997)

Beijing Bicycle (*Shiqisui de danche*) 十七歲的單車 / 十七岁的单车 (dir. Wang Xiaoshuai, 2001)

The Best of Times (*Meili de shiguang*) 美麗的時光 / 美丽的时光 (dir. Chang Tso-chi, 2002)

Blue Gate Crossing (*Lan se da men*) 藍色大門 / 蓝色大门 (dir. Yee Chih-yen, 2002)

Blue Kite (*Lan fengzheng*) 藍風箏 / 蓝风筝 (dir. Tian Zhuangzhuang, 1992)

The Boys of Fengkuei (*Fenggui lai de ren*) 風櫃來的人 / 风柜来的人 (dir. Hou Hsiao-hsien, 1983)

Café Lumière (*Kafei shiguang*) 咖啡時光 / 咖啡时光 (dir. Hou Hsiao-hsien, 2003)

Cape No.7 (*Haijiao qihao*) 海角七號 / 海角七号 (dir. Wei Te-sheng, 2008)

Cheerful Wind (*Feng er ti ta cai*) 風兒踢踏踩 / 风儿踢踏踩 (dir. Hou Hsiao-hsien, 1981)

Crouching Tiger, Hidden Dragon (*Wo hu cang long*) 臥虎藏龍 / 卧虎藏龙 (dir. Ang Lee, 2000)

Cute Girl (*Jiu shi liu liu de ta*) 就是溜溜的她 / 就是溜溜的她 (dir. Hou Hsiao-hsien, 1980)

Daughters of the Nile (*Niluohe nü er*) 尼羅河女兒 / 尼罗河女儿 (dir. Hou Hsiao-hsien, 1987)

Descendants of the Yellow Emperor (*Huangdi de zisun*) 黃帝的子孫 / 黄帝的子孙 (dir. Bai Ke, 1956)

Double Vision (*Shuang tong*) 雙瞳 / 双瞳 (dir. Chen Guo-fu, 2002)

The Dream Factory (*Jia fang yi fang*) 甲方乙方 / 甲方乙方 (dir. Feng Xiaogang, 1997)

Dust in the Wind (*Lianlian fengchen*) 戀戀風塵 / 恋恋风尘 (dir. Hou Hsiao-hsien, 1986)

Eat Drink Man Woman (*Yin shi nan nü*) 飲食男女 / 饮食男女 (dir. Ang Lee, 1994)

Exit (*Hui guang zou ming qu*) 迴光奏鳴曲 / 回光奏鸣曲 (dir. Chienn Hsiang, 2015)

Face in the Evening (*Xi yan*) 夕顏 / 夕颜 (dir. Wei Te-sheng, 1995)

Flowers of Shanghai (*Hai shang hua*) 海上花 / 海上花 (dir. Hou Hsiao-hsien, 1998)

Flowers of Taipei: Taiwan New Cinema (*Guangyin de gushi: Taiwan xin dianying*) 光陰的故事: 台灣新電影 / 光阴的故事:台湾新电影 (dir. Hsieh Chinglin, 2014)

Forever Love (*A ma de meng zhong qing ren*) 阿嬤的夢中情人 / 阿妈的梦中情人 (dir. Aozaru Shiao and Toyoharu Kitamura, 2013)

Gallants (*Da lei tai*) 打擂台 / 打擂台 (dir. Derek Kwok and Clement Cheng, 2010)

The Golden Era (*Huang jin shi dai*) 黃金時代 / 黄金时代 (dir. Ann Hui, 2014)

Good Men, Good Women (*Hao nan hao nu*) 好男好女 / 好男好女 (dir. Hou Hsiao-hsien, 1995)

Goodbye, Dragon Inn (*Bu san*) 不散 / 不散 (dir. Tsai Ming-liang, 2003)

Growing Up (*Xiaobi de gushi*) 小畢的故事 / 小毕的故事 (dir. Chen Kun-hou, 1983)

Hear Me (*Ting shuo*) 聽說 / 听说 (dir. Cheng Fen-fen, 2009)

Help Me, Eros (*Bang bang wo, aisheng*) 幫幫我愛神 / 帮帮我爱神 (dir. Lee Kang-sheng, 2007)

The Hole (*Dong*) 洞 / 洞 (dir. Tsai Ming-liang, 1998)

Hotel Black Cat (*Hei mao da lü she*) 黑貓大旅社 / 黑猫大旅社 (dir. Hsu Li-wen, 2010)

I Don't Want to Sleep Alone (*Hei yan quan*) 黑眼圈 / 黑眼圈 (dir. Tsai Ming-liang, 2006)

If You Are the One (*Fei cheng wu rao*) 非誠勿擾 / 非诚勿扰 (dir. Feng Xiaogang, 2008)

In Our Time (*Guangyin de gushi*) 光陰的故事 / 光阴的故事 (dir. Tao De-chen, Edward Yang, Ke Yi-zheng and Zhang Yi, 1982)

Island Etude (*Lian xi qu*) 練習曲 / 练习曲 (dir. Chen Huai-en, 2006)

Kano (*Kano*) (dir. Umin Boya, 2014)

The Kids (*Xiao hai*) 小孩 / 小孩 (dir. Sunny Yu, 2015)

Lonely Seventeen (*Jimo de shiqisui*) 寂寞的十七歲 / 寂寞的十七岁 (dir. Bai Jing-rui, 1967)

Lust, Caution (*Se jie*) 色,戒 / 色,戒 (dir. Ang Lee, 2007)

Mahjong (*Ma jiang*) 麻將 / 麻将 (dir. Edward Yang, 1996)

Millennium Mambo (*Qianxi manbo*) 千禧漫波 / 千禧曼波 (dir. Hou Hsiao-hsien, 2001)

The Missing (*Bu jian*) 不見 / 不见 (dir. Lee Kang-sheng, 2003)

Monga (*Mengjia*) 艋舺 / 艋舺 (dir. Doze Niu, 2010)

No No Sleep (*Wu wu mian*) 無無眠 / 无无眠 (dir. Tsai Ming-liang, 2015)

Orz Boyz! (*Jiong nanhai*) 囧男孩 / 囧男孩 (dir. Yang Ya-zhe, 2008)

Our Times (*Wo de shao nü shi dai*) 我的少女時代 / 我的少女时代 (dir. Frankie Chen, 2015)

Oyster Girl (*Ke nü*) 蚵女 / 蚵女 (dir. Li Hsing, 1964)

The Palace on the Sea (*Hai shang huang gong*) 海上皇宮 / 海上皇宫 (dir. Midi Z, 2014)

Piercing 1 (*Ci tong wo*) 刺痛我 / 刺痛我 (dir. Liu Jian, 2010)

Prince of Tears (*Lei wangzi*) 淚王子 / 泪王子 (dir. Yonfan, 2009)

The Puppetmaster (*Ximeng rensheng*) 戲夢人生 / 戏梦人生 (dir. Hou Hsiao-hsien, 1993)

Pushing Hands (*Tui shou*) 推手 / 推手 (dir. Ang Lee, 1992)

Pusu Qhuni (*Yu sheng: Sai de ke ba lai*) 餘生: 賽德克巴萊 / 余生: 赛德克巴莱 (dir. Tang Shiang-chu, 2014)

Red Cliff (*Chi bi*) 赤壁 / 赤壁 (dir. John Woo, 2008)

Reign of Assassins (*Jian yu*) 劍雨 / 剑雨 (dir. Su Chao-pin and John Woo, 2010)

The River (*He liu*) 河流 / 河流 (dir. Tsai Ming-liang, 1997)

Salute! Sun Yat-sen (*Xingdong daihao: Sun Zhongshan*) 行動代號孫中山 / 行动代号孙中山 (dir. Yee Chih-yen, 2014)

The Sandwich Man (*Er zi de da wan ou*) 兒子的大玩偶 / 儿子的大玩偶 (dir. Hou Hsiao-hsien, Zeng Zhuang-xiang and Wan Jen, 1983)

Second Spring of Mr. Mo (*Lao mo de di er ge chuntian*) 老莫的第二個春天 / 老莫的第二个春天 (dir. Li You-ning, 1984)

Secret (*Buneng shuo de mimi*) 不能說的秘密 / 不能说的秘密 (dir. Jay Chou, 2007)

Seven Swords (*Qi jian*) 七劍 / 七剑 (dir. Tsui Hark, 2005)

The Skywalk is Gone (*Tianqiao bujian le*) 天橋不見了 / 天桥不见了 (dir. Tsai Ming-liang, 2002)

Sorry, Baby (*Mei wan mei liao*) 沒完沒了 / 没完没了 (dir. Feng Xiaogang, 1999)

Springtime in a Small Town (*Xiaocheng zhi chun*) 小城之春 / 小城之春 (dir. Tian Zhuangzhuang, 2002)

The Stool Pigeon (*Xian ren*) 線人 / 线人 (dir. Dante Lam, 2011)
Stray Dogs (*Jiao you*) 郊遊 / 郊游 (dir. Tsai Ming-liang, 2013)
Taipei 24H (*Taipei yi xiang*) 台北異想 / 台北异想 (dir. An Jie-yi, Chen Ying-jung, Cheng Fen-fen et al., 2009)
Taipei Story (*Qingmei zhuma*) 青梅竹馬 / 青梅竹马 (dir. Edward Yang, 1985)
Teenage Fugitive (*Xiao taofan*) 小逃犯 / 小逃犯 (dir. Chang Pei-cheng, 1984)
The Terrorizers (*Kongbu fenzi*) 恐怖分子 / 恐怖分子 (dir. Edward Yang, 1986)
Thanatos, Drunk (*Zui sheng meng si*) 醉生夢死 / 醉生梦死 (dir. Chang Tso-chi, 2015)
Three Dialogues (*Duihua sanbu*) 對話三部 / 对话三部 (dir. Wei Te-sheng, 1996)
Three Times (*Zuihao de shiguang*) 最好的時光 / 最好的时光 (dir. Hou Hsiao-hsien, 2005)
Top Cool (*Xiangfei: Aokong shenying*) 想飛: 傲空神鷹 / 想飞:傲空神鹰 (dir. Jin Ao-xun, 1993)
Vive L'Amour (*Aiqing wansui*) 愛情萬歲 / 爱情万岁 (dir. Tsai Ming-liang, 1994)
Warriors of the Rainbow: Seediq Bale (*Sai de ke ba lai*) 賽德克巴萊 / 赛德克巴莱 (dir. Wei Te-sheng, 2011)
The Wayward Cloud (*Tian bian yi duo yun*) 天邊一朵雲 / 天边一朵云 (dir. Tsai Ming-liang, 2005)
We Are Family (*Wo men quan jia bu tai shou*) 我們全家不太熟 / 我们全家不太熟 (dir. Jim Wang, 2015)
The Wedding Banquet (*Xi yan*) 喜宴 / 喜宴 (dir. Ang Lee, 1993)
What Time is it There? (*Ni nei bian ji dian?*) 你那邊幾點?/你那边几点? (dir. Tsai Ming-liang, 2001)
Winds of September (*Jiu jiang feng*) 九降風 / 九降风 (dir. Lin Shu-yu, 2008)
The Wonderful Wedding (*Da xi lin men*) 大喜臨門 / 大喜临门 (dir. Huang Chao-liang, 2015)
Wushe, Chuanzhong Island (*Wushe chuanzhongdao*) 霧社: 川中島 / 雾社:川中岛 (dir. Pilin Yapu, 2013)
You Are the Apple of My Eye (*Na xie nian, wo men yi qi zhui de nü hai*) 那些年,我們一起追的女孩 / 那些年,我们一起追的女孩 (dir. Giddens Ko, 2011)
Zoom Hunting (*Lie yan*) 獵豔 / 猎艳 (dir. Cho Li, 2010)

Bibliography

Agamben, G. (2016) *The Use of Bodies*, trans. A. Kotsko, Stanford, CA: Stanford University Press.

Anderson, B. (2006) *Imagined Communities: Reflections on the Origin and Spread of Nationalism*, London and New York: Verson Books.

Anholt, S. (2002) 'Nation branding: A continuing theme', *Journal of Brand Management* 10: 59–60.

ANSA (2011) 'Venice: Aborigines for the first Taiwanese epic film' (Venezia: aborigeni per il primo colossal Taiwanese), *l'Unità*, 26 August. Available online: www.unita.it/notizie-flash/venezia-aborigeni-per-il-primo-kolossal-taiwanese-1.326309 (accessed 12 December 2015, in Italian).

Appadurai, A. (1990) 'Disjuncture and difference in the global cultural economy', *Theory, Culture & Society* 7(June): 295–310.

Appadurai, A. (1996) *Modernity at Large: Cultural Dimensions of Globalization*, Minneapolis, MN: University of Minnesota Press.

Appadurai, A. (2001) 'Grassroots globalization and the research imagination', *Public Culture* 12(1): 1–19.

Arndt, R. (2005) *The First Resort of Kings: American Cultural Diplomacy in the Twentieth Century*, Washington, DC: Potomac Books.

ASCA (2014) 'Entertainment: Rai Cinema targets Asia with the Taipei Film Commission' (Spettacolo: Rai Cinema puntasull'Asia con la Taipei Film Commission), *askanews*, 3 September. Available online: www.askanews.it/spettacolo/spettacolo-rai-cinema-punta-sull-asia-con-la-taipei-film-commission_711442253.htm (accessed 12 December 2015, in Italian).

Assmann, J. (2011) *Cultural Memory and Early Civilization: Writing, Remembrance, and Political Imagination*, New York: Cambridge University Press.

Auerbach, E. (2003 [1953]) 'Odysseus' scar', in E. Said (ed.), *Mimesis: The Representation of Reality in Western Literature*, fiftieth-anniversary edition, trans. Willard R. Trask, Princeton, NJ: Princeton University Press, pp. 3–23.

Berry, C. (2006) 'From national cinema to cinema and the national: Chinese-language cinema and Hou Hsiao Hsien's "Taiwan Trilogy"', in V. Vitali and P. Willemen (eds), *Theorising National Cinema*, London: BFI Publishing, pp. 148–157.

Berry, C. and Farquhar, M. (2006) *China on Screen: Cinema and Nation*, New York: Columbia University Press.

Berry, C. and Lu, F. (eds) (2005) *Island on the Edge: Taiwan New Cinema and After*, Hong Kong: Hong Kong University Press.

Berry, C. and Pang, L. (2008) 'Introduction, or, what's in an "s"?', *Journal of Chinese Cinemas* 2(1): 3–8.

Berry, M. (2008/2011) *A History of Pain: Trauma in Modern Chinese Literature and Film*, New York: Columbia University Press.

Bloom, D. (2012) 'Where was Taiwan in its own Golden Horse film fest?', *The Wrap: Covering Hollywood*, 30 November. Available online at: www.thewrap.com/where-was-taiwan-its-own-golden-horse-film-fest-67311/ (accessed 18 November 2015).

Bordwell, D. (2005) *Figures Traced in Light: On Cinematic Staging*, Oakland, CA: University of California Press.

Bosma, P. (2015) *Film Programming: Curating for Cinemas, Festivals, Archives*, London: Wallflower.

Box Office Mojo (2015a) 'Taiwan yearly box office 2008', *Box Office Mojo*. Available online at: www.boxofficemojo.com/intl/taiwan/yearly/?yr=2008&p=.htm (accessed 2 December 2015).

Box Office Mojo (2015b) 'Taiwan yearly box office 2011', *Box Office Mojo*. Available online at: www.boxofficemojo.com/intl/taiwan/yearly/ (accessed 2 December 2015).

Braester, Y. (2003) *Witness against History: Literature, Film, and Public Discourse in Twentieth-Century China*, Stanford, CA: Stanford University Press.

Bruno, G. (2007) *Atlas of Emotion: Journeys in Art, Architecture and Film*, New York: Verso.

Burdeau, E. (2005) 'Critique. Three Times: L'écrit le cris', *Cahiers du Cinéma* 606 (November): 24–26 (in French).

Burgoyne, R. (2008) *The Hollywood Historical Film*, Malden, MA: Blackwell Publishing.

Burgoyne, R. (2010) *Film Nation: Hollywood Looks at US History* (revised version), Minneapolis, MN: University of Minnesota Press.

Burgoyne, R. (2011a) 'Introduction', in R. Burgoyne (ed.), *The Epic Film in World Culture*, London and New York: Routledge, pp. 1–16.

Burgoyne, R. (2011b) 'Bare life and sovereignty in *Gladiator*', in R. Burgoyne (ed.), *The Epic Film in World Culture*, London and New York: Routledge, pp. 82–98.

Cahiers du Cinéma (2007) 'Un certain regard: à la pursuite du ballon rouge de Hou Hsiao-hsien', *Cahiers du Cinéma* 623(May): 34 (in French).

Cahiers du Cinéma (2011) 'Retour de Venise', *Cahiers du Cinéma* 671(October): 48–50 (in French).

Capolino, G. (2011) 'Venice 2011: Premiere review of Seediq Bale' (Venezia 2011: SaidekeBalai – La recensione in anteprima di Seediq Bale), *Cineblog – Blogo.it*, 1 September. Available online: www.cineblog.it/post/29977/venezia-2011-saideke-balai-la-recensione-in-anteprima-di-seediq-bale (accessed 12 December 2015, in Italian).

Carneiro, M.L.T. and Takeuchi, M.Y. (2011) *Imigrantes Japoneses no Brasil – Trajetória, Imaginário e Memória*, São Paulo: Edusp (in Portuguese).

Caruth, C. (1996) *Unclaimed Experience: Trauma, Narrative, and History*, Baltimore, MD: The Johns Hopkins University Press.

Chan, F. (2003) 'Crouching Tiger, Hidden Dragon: Cultural migrancy and translatability', in C. Berry (ed.), *Chinese Films in Focus: 25 New Takes*, London: British Film Institute, pp. 56–64.

Chan, F. (2011) 'The international film festival and the making of a national cinema', *Screen* 52(2): 253–260.

Chang, I.I.C. (2010) 'The colonial reminiscence, Japanophilia trend, and Taiwanese grassroots imagination in Cape No.7', *Concentric: Literary and Cultural Studies* 36(1): 79–117.

Chang, I.I.C. (2015) *Globalised Time and Space, Body, and Memory: Taiwan New Cinema and its Impact* (Quan qiu hua shi kong, shen ti, ji yi: Taiwan xin dian ying ji qi ying xiang), Hsinchu: National Chiao Tung University Press (in Chinese).

Chang, J. (2011) 'Review: Warriors of the Rainbow: Seediq Bale', *Variety* (1 September). Available online: variety.com/2011/film/markets-festivals/warriors-of-the-rainbow-seediq-bale-1117945935/ (accessed 12 December 2015).

Chang, S.S.Y. (1993) *Modernism and the Nativist Resistance: Contemporary Chinese Fiction from Taiwan*, Durham, NC: Duke University Press.

Chang, S.S.Y. (2005) 'The Terrorizer and the great divide in contemporary Taiwan's cultural development', in C. Berry and F. Lu (eds), *Island on the Edge: Taiwan New Cinema and After*, Hong Kong: Hong Kong University Press, pp. 13–26.

Chao, E.C. (2013) 'Choosing the way to die: Seediq Bale and Taiwan's new memory' (Dianyingtexie: xuanze siwang de fangshi), *Funscreen* (fangying zhoubao) 382, 5 July. Available online www.funscreen.com.tw/feature.asp?FE_NO=194 (accessed 5 June 2014, in Chinese).

Chen, I.C. (2008) 'The unrequited love between Japan and Taiwan in Cape No.7' (Haijiao qihao de tairi kulian), *China Times*, 9 October: A22 (in Chinese).

Chen, K.H. (2006) 'Taiwan New Cinema, or a global nativism', in V. Vitali and P. Willemen (eds), *Theorising National Cinema*, London: British Film Institute, pp. 138–147.

Chen, M.T. (2012) 'Taiwan in 2011: Focus on crucial presidential election', *Asian Survey* 52(1): 72–80.

Ching, L. (2000) 'Savage construction and civility making: The Musha Incident and aboriginal representation in colonial Taiwan', *Positions* 8(3): 795–818.

Chiu, K.F. (2007) 'The vision of Taiwan new documentary', in D.W. Davis and R.S.R. Chen (eds), *Cinema Taiwan*, London and New York: Routledge, pp. 17–32.

Chiu, K.F., Fell, D. and Lin, P. (eds) (2014) *Migration to and from Taiwan*, London and New York: Routledge.

Chiu, R.L. (1990) *The Wushe Incident* (Wushe shijian), Taipei: China Times (comic books, in Chinese).

Chiu, T.B. (2010) 'Localism, historical nationalism, or social transnationalism? A cultural analysis of Cape No.7' (Kongjian de zaidizhuyi lishi de guojia zhuyi haishi shehui de kuaguo zhuyi haijiao qihao de wenhua pingxi), *Film Appreciation Academic Journal* 142: 185–195 (in Chinese).

Crofts, S. (1993) 'Reconceptualising national cinema/s', *Quarterly Review of Film and Video* 14(3): 47–67.

Cull, N. (2008) 'Public diplomacy: Taxonomies and histories', *Annals of the American Academy of Political and Social Science* 616: 31–54.

Curtin, M. (2007) *Playing to the World's Biggest Audience: The Globalization of Chinese Film and TV*, Berkeley, CA: University of California Press.

Dai, L. (2011) 'What are we afraid of' (Women zai pa sheme), *Plurk Paste*. Available online: paste.plurk.com/show/722795 (accessed 31 March 2016, in Chinese).

Dalton, S. (2013) 'Taipei Factory: Cannes review', *The Hollywood Reporter*, 16 May. Available online: www.hollywoodreporter.com/review/taipei-factory-cannes-review-524072 (accessed 12 December 2015).

Davis, D.W. (2005) 'Borrowing postcolonial: Wu Nianzhen's *Dou-san* and the memory mine', in S.H. Lu and E.Y.Y. Yeh (eds), *Chinese Language Film: Historiography, Poetics, Politics*, Honolulu: Hawai'i University Press, pp. 237–266.

Davis, D.W. (2007) 'Introduction: cinema Taiwan, a civilizing mission?', in D.W. Davis and R.S.R. Chen (eds), *Cinema Taiwan: Politics, Popularity and State of the Arts*, London and New York: Routledge, pp. 1–13.

Davis, D.W. and Chen, R.S.R. (eds) (2007) *Cinema Taiwan: Politics, Popularity and State of the Arts*, London and New York: Routledge.

Davis, N.Z. (1983) *The Return of Martin Guerre*, Cambridge, MA: Harvard University Press.

Davis, N.Z. (2000) *Slaves on Screen: Film and Historical Vision*, Cambridge, MA: Harvard University Press.

De Lauretis, T. (1984) *Alice Doesn't: Feminism, Semiotics, Cinema*, Bloomington, IN: Indian University Press.

De Valck, M. (2007) *Film Festivals: From European Geopolitics to Global Cinephilia*, Amsterdam: Amsterdam University Press.

DeBoer, S. (2004) 'Sayon no Kane/Sayon's Bell, Hiroshi Shimizu, Japan, 1943', in J. Bowyer (ed.), *The Cinema of Japan and Korea*, London: Wallflower Press, pp. 23–31.

DeBoer, S. (2014) *Coproducing Asia: Locating Japanese-Chinese Regional Film and Media*, Minneapolis, MN: University of Minnesota Press.

Deleuze, G. (1988) *Foucault*, trans. S. Hand, Minneapolis, MN: University of Minnesota Press.

Deleuze, G. (1989) *Cinema 2: The Time-Image*, trans. H. Tomlinson and R. Galeta, Minneapolis, MN: University of Minnesota Press.

Deleuze, G. (2005) *Cinema 2: The Time Image*, London: Continuum.

Deleuze, G. and Guattari, F. (1986) *Kafka: Towards a Minor Literature*, Minneapolis, MN: University of Minnesota Press.

Deng, X.Y. (1998) *The Wushe Incident* (Wushe shijian), Taipei: Yushanshe Publishing (in Chinese).

Deng, X.Y. (2000) *Red Cherry Blossoms in the Wind* (Fengzhong feiying), Taipei: Yushanshe Publishing (in Chinese).

Deppman, H.C. (2009) 'Cinema of disillusionment: Chen Guofu, Cai Mingliang, and Taiwan's Second New Wave', *Positions: East Asia Cultures Critique* 17(2): 435–454.

Derrida, J. (1996) *Archive Fever*, trans. E. Prenowitz, Chicago, IL: The University of Chicago Press.

Durovicova, N. and Newman, K. (eds) (2009) *World Cinemas, Transnational Perspectives*, London and New York: Routledge.

Dyer, R. (1993) *The Matter of Images: Essays on Representations*, London and New York: Routledge.

The Economist (2011) 'A Taiwan blockbuster: Blood-stained rainbow', *The Economist*, 17 September. Available online: www.economist.com/node/21529109 (accessed 8 June 2016).

Ekman, P. (1999) *Handbook of Cognition and Emotion*, Sussex: John Wiley & Sons Ltd.

Election Study Center, National Chengchi University (2014) 'Taiwanese/Chinese identification trend distribution in Taiwan (1992/05–2015/06)', Data Archives. Available online: esc.nccu.edu.tw/course/news.php?Sn=166 (accessed 25 December 2015).

Elley, D. (1984) *The Epic Film: Myth and History*, London and New York: Routledge.

Elsaesser, T. (2005) *European Cinema: Face to Face with Hollywood*, Amsterdam: Amsterdam University Press.

Feng, Y.E. and Ling, M.X. (2014) 'Wei Te-sheng: "Do not see Kano with a bias"', *Liberty Times*, 12 March. Available online: ent.ltn.com.tw/news/paper/761278 (accessed 6 July 2015, in Chinese).

Forster, E.M. (2005 [1924]) *A Passage to India*, London: Penguin.

Frater, P. (2014) 'Taiwan Film Institute launched', *Variety*, 29 July. Available online: variety.com/2014/film/asia/taiwan-film-institute-launched-1201270814/ (accessed 5 September 2016).

Frodon, J.M. (2005a) 'Planète cinéma', *Cahiers du Cinéma* 502(June): 5 (in French).

Frodon, J.M. (2005b) 'Rencontre. Hou Hsiao-hsien: "Filmer l'histoire pour l'enlever des mains de politiciens"', *Cahiers du Cinéma* 606(November): 27 (in French).

Frodon, J.M. (2008a) 'Hou Hsiao-hsien et Juliette Binoche: c'est pas grave', *Cahiers du Cinéma* 632(February): 31–32 (in French).

Frodon, J.M. (2008b) 'Le puzzle troué de maître Hou', *Cahiers du Cinéma* 632(February): 28–30 (in French).

Fu, Y.W. (2014) 'Space and cultural memory: Te-sheng Wei's *Cape No.7* (2008)', in R. Weaver-Hightower and P. Hulme (eds), *Postcolonial Film: History, Empire, Resistance*, London and New York: Routledge, pp. 223–246.

Gao, P. (2011) 'Secret to revival', *Taiwan Review* 61(2): 4–11.

Gombeaud, A. (2005) 'DVD: HHH d'Olivier Assayas, 1 DVD, MK2. Café Lumière de Hou Hsiao-hsien, 2 DVD, Diaphana', *Positif* 537(November): 19 (in French).

Guo, M.Z. (2011) *Truth, Bale* (Zhenxiang balai), Taipei: Yuanliou (in Chinese).

Guo, Q. (2010) 'China quits Tokyo film fest', *Global Times*, 25 October. Available online at: www.globaltimes.cn/content/585192.shtml (accessed 2 November 2015).

Halbwachs, M. (1992) *On Collective Memory*, edited and translated from French by L.A. Coser, Chicago, IL: University of Chicago Press.

Hampton, H. (2006) 'Slow train coming: Who's afraid of Hou Hsiao-hsien', *Film Comment* 42(4) (July–August): 32–36.

Harrison, M. (2012) 'The impact of film and the performing arts on life in Taiwan', in S. Tsang (ed.), *The Vitality of Taiwan: Politics, Economics, Society and Culture*, New York and Basingstoke: Palgrave Macmillan, pp. 80–97.

Haslam, M. (2004) 'Vision, authority, context: Cornerstones of curation and programming', *The Moving Image* 4(1): 48–59.

Heath, S. (1978) 'Notes on suture', *Screen* 18 (Winter). Available online: www.lacan.com/symptom8_articles/heath8.html (accessed 1 July 2016).

Higbee, W. and Lim, S.H. (2010) 'Concepts of transnational cinema: Towards a critical transnationalism in film studies', *Transnational Cinemas* 1(1): 7–21.

Higson, A. (2006) 'The limiting imagination of national cinema', in E. Ezra and T. Rowden (eds), *Transnational Cinema: The Film Reader*, London and New York: Routledge, pp. 15–25.

Hjort, M. and Petrie, D. (eds) (2007) *The Cinema of Small Nations*, Bloomington, IN: Indiana University Press.

Hong, G.J. (2011) *Taiwan Cinema: A Contested Nation on Screen*, New York and Basingstoke: Palgrave Macmillan.

Hong, G.J. (2013) *Taiwan Cinema: A Contested Nation on Screen*, New York and Basingstoke: Palgrave Macmillan.

Hou, H.H., Chu, T.H., Tang, N. and Hsia, C.J. (2004) 'Tensions in Taiwan', *New Left Review* II(28) (July–August): 19–42.

Hou, H.H. and Masson, A. (2005) 'Entretien avec Hou Hsiao-hsien', *Positif* 537 (November): 16–19 (in French).

Hsiau, A.C. (2012) *Reconstructing Taiwan: The Cultural Politics of Contemporary Nationalism* (Chonggou Taiwan: Dandai minzu zhuyi de wenhua zhengzhi). Taipei: Linking Publishing (in Chinese).

Hu, B. (2012) 'Taiwan Film Showcase', The Thirteenth Annual San Diego Asian Film Festival, 1–9 November. Available online: festival.sdaff.org/2012/taiwan-film-showca se/ (accessed 26 November 2015).

Huang, R. (2008) *Japanese Cinema in Taiwan* (Riben dianying zai taiwan), Taipei: Xiu-wei (in Chinese).

Huang, R. (2014) *Long-Lasting Stars in Chinese and Foreign Cinemas II* (Zhongwai dianying yongyuan de juxing II), Taipei: Xiu-wei (in Chinese).

Huat, C.B. and Iwabuchi, K. (eds) (2008) *East Asian Pop Culture: Analyzing the Korean Wave*, Hong Kong: Hong Kong University Press.

Iordanova, D. (2010) 'Mediating diaspora: Film festivals and "imagined commu- nities"', in D. Iordanova and R. Cheung (eds), *Film Festival Yearbook 2: Film Festivals and Imagined Communities*, St Andrews: St Andrews Film Studies, pp. 12–44.

Jakobson, R. (1995) *On Language*, Cambridge, MA: Harvard University Press.

Jameson, F. (1989) 'Remapping Taipei', in *The Geopolitical Aesthetic: Cinema and Space in the World System*, Bloomington, IN: Indiana University Press, pp. 114–157.

Kan, M. (2011) 'Interview with Wei Te-sheng' (Wei desheng fangwen), *Ming Pao*, 25 Sep- tember. Available online: m.travel.sina.com.hk/news/article/147541/71/31 (accessed 16 June 2016, in Chinese).

Kaplan, E.A. (2005) *Trauma Culture: The Politics of Terror and Loss in Media and Literature*, New Brunswick, NJ: Rutgers University Press.

Kishimoto, A. (2013) *Cinema Japonês na Liberdade*, São Paulo: Estação Liberdade.

Koyama, S. (2014) 'Commentary: Manifesting the social transformations' (syakai no henbou wo tsugeru), in S. Koyama, K. Inoue, N. Makino et al. (eds), *Taiwan Cinema: Thirty Years (since Taiwan New Cinema) Manifesting the Social Trans- formations* (Taiwan eiga: syakai no henbou wo tsugeru [Taiwan new shinema kara no] sanjyuu nen), Tokyo: Koyoshobo, pp. 3–7 (in Japanese).

Kuipers, R. (2008) 'Review: Cape No.7', *Variety*, 7 November. Available online: variety. com/2008/film/reviews/cape-no-7-1200472373/945935/ (accessed 25 November 2015).

Kuo, L.H. (2009) 'After the "heat of the Cape": The vision and future of Taiwan cinema' ('Haijiao re' tuishao zhihou: Taiwan dianying de geju yu weilai), in Chinese Taipei Film Archive (ed.), *Taiwan Film Yearbook 2009* (Taiwan dianying nianjian 2009), Taipei: The Chinese Taipei Film Archive, pp. 53–57 (in Chinese).

Lai, H. and Lu Y. (eds) (2012) *China's Soft Power and International Relations*, London and New York: Routledge.

Lan, S.C.M. (2014) 'Taiwanese in China and the multiple identities, 1895–1945', in N.K. Kim (ed.), *Multicultural Challenges and Redefining Identity in East Asia*, London: Ashgate, pp. 97–122.

Landsberg, A. (2004) *Prosthetic Memory: The Transformation of American Remembrance in the Age of Mass Culture*, New York: Columbia University Press.

Landsberg, A. (2015) *Engaging the Past: Mass Culture and the Production of Historical Knowledge*, New York: Columbia University Press.

Law, K., Bren, F. and Ho, S. (2004) *Hong Kong Cinema: A Cross-Cultural View*, Lanham, MD: The Scarecrow Press, Inc.

Lee, C.C. (2013) 'Taiwanese mountain area as place/landscape presented in Seediq Bale', *NCUE Journal of Humanities* 7: 205–220.

Lee, D.M. (2012) *Historical Dictionary of Taiwan Cinema*, Lanham, MD: Scarecrow Press.

Lee, E. (2011) 'Wei Te-sheng', *Time Out Hong Kong*. Available online: www.timeout. com.hk/film/features/46851/wei-te-sheng.html (accessed 20 April 2015).

Lee, M. (2008) 'Cape No.7', *The Hollywood Reporter*, 1 October. Available online: www.hollywoodreporter.com/review/cape-no-7-125760 (accessed 12 November 2015).

Lee, Y.L. (2014a) 'The excess of affect: The technologies of history in *Seediq Bale*', in R.W. Wolny and S. Nicieja (eds), *Poisoned Cornucopia*, New York: Peter Lang, pp. 251–268.

Lee, Y.L. (2014b) 'In search of a people: Wei Te-sheng's *Seediq Bale* and Taiwan's postcolonial condition', in R. Bogue, H.P. Chiu and Y.L. Lee (eds), *Deleuze and Asia*, Newcastle: Cambridge Scholars Publishing, pp. 182–196.

Levaniouk, O. (2011) 'Odysseus and the boar', in *Eve of the Festival: Making Myth in Odyssey 19*, Center for Hellenic Studies, Harvard University. Available online: chs.harvard.edu/CHS/article/display/3759 (accessed 2 July 2016).

Li, H.R. (1992) 'Forty years of Sino-Japan film art exchanges' (zhongridianyingyishu jiaoliu sishinian), *Japan Studies* (riben yanjiu), Shenyang: Liaoning University Institute of Japan Studies, pp. 62–65 (in Chinese).

Liao, C.Y. (2013) 'Catastrophe and Oikonomia: The ethics of molecularity in Seediq Bale' (Zainan yu miyan: SaidekeBalai de fenzihua lunli), *Wenshan Review of Literature and Culture* (Wenshan pinglun: wenxue yu wenhua) 6(2): 1–33. Available online: english.nccu.edu.tw/files/archive/124_08157577.pdf (accessed 18 August 2016, in Chinese).

Liao, P.H. (1999) 'Postcolonial studies in Taiwan: Issues in critical debates', *Postcolonial Studies* 2(2): 199–211.

Liao, P.H. (2006) 'Print culture and the emergent public sphere in colonial Taiwan, 1895–1945', in P.H. Liao and D.D.W. Wang (eds), *Taiwan under Japanese Colonial Rule, 1895–1945*, New York: Columbia University Press, pp. 78–94.

Liao, P.H. and Wang, D.D.W. (eds) (2006), *Taiwan under Japanese Colonial Rule, 1895–1945*, New York: Columbia University Press.

Lim, S.H. (2006) *Celluloid Comrades: Representations of Male Homosexuality in Contemporary Chinese Cinemas*, Honolulu: University of Hawaii Press.

Lim, S.H. (2013) 'Taiwan New Cinema: Small nation with soft power', in C. Rojas and E.C.Y. Chow (eds), *The Oxford Handbook of Chinese Cinemas*, New York and Oxford: Oxford University Press, pp. 152–169.

Lin, K.S. (2011) 'A few thoughts after watching Seediq Bale' (Saideke balai guanhou gan), *Visions of Anthropology* 7: 38–40. Available online www.taiwananthro.org.tw/anthrovisions/437 (accessed 30 October 2015, in Chinese).

Lin, P.Y. (2012) 'Translating the other: On the re-circulations of the tale of *Sayon's Bell*', in J. St. André and H. Peng (eds), *China and Its Others: Knowledge Transfer through Translation, 1829–2010*, Amsterdam: Rodopi, pp. 139–164.

Lyons, M. (2013) 'Staff review: You Are the Apple of My Eye', HOME website, 11 February. Available online: homemcr.org/article/staff-review-you-are-the-apple-of-my-eye/ (accessed 12 November 2015).

Ma, K. (2015a) 'Taipei box office down in 2014', *Film Business Asia*, 13 January. Available online: www.filmbiz.asia/news/taipei-box office-down-in-2014 (accessed 2 December 2015).

Ma, S.M. (2011) *Diaspora Literature and Visual Culture: Asia in Flight*, London and New York: Routledge.

Ma, S.M. (2015b) *The Last Isle. Contemporary Film, Culture and Trauma in Global Taiwan*, Lanham, MD: Rowman & Littlefield.

Malausa, V. (2015) 'L'Asie au fil du sabre', *Cahiers du Cinéma* 712(June): 18–19 (in French).

Marks, L. (2004) 'The ethical presenter: Or how to have good arguments over dinner', *The Moving Image* 4(1): 34–47.

Masson, A. (2005) 'Three Times: un film à trois temps', *Positif* 537(November): 13–15 (in French).

Mead, W.R. (2011) 'Taiwanese film stirs Romantic nationalism', *The American Interest*, 17 September. Available online: www.the-american-interest.com/2011/09/17/ta iwanese-film-stirs-romantic-nationalism/ (accessed 17 August 2016).

Mello, C. (2013) 'Entrevista com Tsai Ming-liang', *Revista Rebeca: Revista Brasileira de Estudos de Cinema e Audiovisual* 2(3): 263–281 (in Portuguese).

Morris, A.D. (2004) 'Baseball, history, the local and the global in Taiwan', in D.K. Jordan, A.D. Morris and M.L. Moskowitz (eds), *The Minor Arts of Daily Life: Popular Culture in Taiwan*, Honolulu: University of Hawaii Press, pp. 175–203.

Motoyama, S. (2011) *Sob o Signo do Sol Levante: Uma História da Imigração Japonesa no Brasil* (Volume 1 e Volume 2), São Paulo: Instituto Brasil-Japão de Integração Cultural e Social e Associação para Comemoração do Centenário da Imigração Japonesa no Brasil (in Portuguese).

Naficy, H. (2001) *An Accented Cinema: Exilic and Diasporic Filmmaking*, Princeton, NJ: Princeton University Press.

Nagib, L. (2004) 'O Cinema Japonês em São Paulo', in *Guia da Cultura Japonesa*, São Paulo: Fundação Japão. Available at jojoscope.com/2011/06/o-cinema-japones-em -sao-paulo/ (accessed 6 June 2016, in Portuguese).

National Museum of Natural Sciences (2012) 'Press release of the Seediq Bale exhibition' (Saideke bala tezhan xinwengao), *Newsletter* (1000914). Available online www.nmns. edu.tw/public/exhibit/2011/seediq-bale/news.htm (accessed 5 June 2014, in Chinese).

Nawi, I. (2014) *Kari Toda: Seediq Bale Seediq Screenplay* (Saidekebalai saidekeyu jubenshu), Taipei: Taiwan Interminds (in Chinese and Toda Seediq).

Ng, G. (2015) 'Repeat goers make Our Times highest-grossing Taiwanese movie of all time in Singapore', *The Straits Times*, 22 November. Available online: www.straitstimes. com/lifestyle/entertainment/our-times-an-all-time-hit (accessed 22 November 2015).

Nichols, B. (1994) 'Discovering form, inferring meaning: New cinemas and the film festival circuit', *Film Quarterly* 47(3): 16–30.

NYAFF (New York Asian Film Festival) (2012) 'Warriors and romantics: The new cinema from Taiwan', New York Asian Film Festival programme booklet, New York: NYAFF, pp. 49.

Nye, J.S. (1990) 'Soft power', *Foreign Policy* 80: 153–171.

Nye, J.S. (2011) *The Future of Power*, New York: Public Affairs.

Nye, J.S. (2012) 'China's soft power deficit', *The Wall Street Journal*, 8 May. Available online: www.wsj.com/articles/SB10001424052702304451104577389923098678842 (accessed 28 November 2015).

Pacidal, N.E. (2012) 'The face of the inbetweener: The image of the historical researcher in Seediq Bale' (Zhongjianzhe zhi lian: SaidekeBalai de yuanzhumin lishi yanjiuzhe yingxiang), *Humanitas Taiwanica* (Taidawenshizhe xuebao) 77 (November): 167–197. Available online: homepage.ntu.edu.tw/~bcla/index_ebook.htm (accessed 16 June 2016, in Chinese).

Peng, P. (2011) 'Fighting the good fight: The bloody battleground of Seediq Bale', trans. G. Aberhart, *Taiwan Panorama* (September). Available online: www.taiwan-panorama. com/en/show_issue.php?id=201190009046E.TXT&distype=text (accessed 10 July 2015).

Peranson, M. (2009) 'First you get the power, then you get the money: Two models of film festivals', in R. Porton (ed.), *Dekalog 3: On Film Festivals*, London: Wallflower Press, pp. 23–37.

Phillips, A. and Stringer, J. (eds) (2007) *Japanese Cinema: Texts and Contexts*, London and New York: Routledge.

Pollacchi, E. (2014) 'The rules of the game: How film festivals and sales agents have shaped the consumption of Chinese (independent) films', in M. Abbiati and F. Greselin (eds), *The Lute and the Books* (Il liuto e ilibri), Venezia: Edizioni Ca' Foscari, pp. 713–724 (in Italian).

Pontiggia, F. (2011) 'Seediq Bale', *Cinematografo*, 1 September. Available online: www.cinematografo.it/recensioni/seediq-bale/ (accessed 12 December 2015, in Italian).

Radhakrishnan, R. (2009) 'Why compare?', *New Literary History* 40(3): 453–471.

Rastegar, R. (2012) 'Difference, aesthetics and the curatorial crisis of film festivals', *Screen* 53(3): 310–317.

Rawnsley, G.D. (2000) *Taiwan's Informal Diplomacy and Propaganda*, London: Macmillan.

Rawnsley, G.D. (2003) 'Selling democracy: Diplomacy, propaganda and democratisation in Taiwan', *China Perspectives* 47(May–June). Available online: chinapersp ectives.revues.org/361 (accessed 2 November 2015).

Rawnsley, G.D. (2015) 'To know us is to love us: Public diplomacy and international broadcasting in contemporary Russia and China', *Politics* 35(3–4): 273–286.

Rawnsley, M.Y.T. (2009a) 'Cape No.7 film notes', HOME website, 1 May. Available online: homemcr.org/media/cape-no-7-film-notes/ (accessed 4 May 2016).

Rawnsley, M.Y.T. (2009b), 'Taiwan New Cinema', in C. Neri and K. Gormley (eds), *Taiwan Cinema*, Lyon: Asiexpo, pp. 78–96.

Rawnsley, M.Y.T. (2011) 'Cinema, historiography and identities in Taiwan: Hou Hsiao-hsien's A City of Sadness', *Asian Cinema* 22(2): 196–213.

Rawnsley, M.Y.T. (2012) '*Hai jiao qi hao/Cape No.7*', in G. Bettinson (ed.), *Directory of World Cinema: China*, London: Intellect, pp. 139–140.

Rawnsley, M.Y.T. (2013) 'The distribution and exhibition of Chinese and Asian cinema in the UK: A Chinese Film Forum UK symposium, Cornerhouse, Manchester, 28–29 March 2012', *Screen* 54(4): 534–539.

Rawnsley, M.Y.T. (2016a) 'Cultural democratisation and Taiwan cinema', in G. Shubert (ed.), *Routledge Handbook of Contemporary Taiwan*, London and New York: Routledge, pp. 373–388.

Rawnsley, M.Y.T. (2016b) 'An interview with director Wei Te-sheng' (Wei desheng daoyan zhuanfang), *Chung Wai Literary Quarterly* 45(3): 211–221 (in Chinese).

ROC Diplomatic Missions (2013) 'Japan-Taiwan cultural and art performance events' (Nittai bunka geino dekigoto), *Portal of Republic of China (Taiwan) Diplomatic Missions*. Available online: www.taiwanembassy.org/public/Data/110519543571.pdf (accessed 20 November 2015, in Japanese).

Rosenstone, R.A. (1995a) 'Introduction', in R.A. Rosenstone (ed.), *Revisioning History: Film and the Construction of a New Past*, Princeton, NJ: Princeton University Press, pp. 3–13.

Rosenstone, R.A. (1995b) *Visions of the Past: The Challenges of Film to Our Idea of History*, Cambridge, MA: Harvard University Press.

Rosenstone, R.A. (2013) 'The history film as a mode of historical thought', in R.A. Rosenstone and C. Parvulescu (eds), *A Companion to the Historical Film*, Sussex: Wiley-Blackwell, pp. 71–87.

Rowen, I. (2015) 'Inside Taiwan's Sunflower Movement: Twenty-four days in a student-occupied parliament, and the future of the region', *The Journal of Asian Studies* 74: 5–21.

Roy, D. (2003) *Taiwan: A Political History*, Ithaca, NY: Cornell University Press.

Ruby, J. (2000) *Picturing Culture: Explorations of Film and Anthropology*, Chicago, IL: The University of Chicago Press.

Ryans, T. (2005) 'Coffee, time, light: Hou Hsiao-hsien's Café Lumière', *Cinemascope* 21(Winter): 10–12.

Ryans, T. (2006) 'Hou Hsiao-hsien: Song for swinging lovers', *Sight and Sound* 16(8) (August): 14–19.

Santas, C. (2007) *The Epic in Film: From Myth to Blockbuster*, Lanham, MD: Rowman & Littlefield.

Sato, H. (2002 [1936]) 'Musha' (in Japanese), ed. and trans. by J.S. Chiu, *Travels in the Colony* (Zhimindi zhi lü), Taipei: Caogen (in Chinese).

Sato, T. (1997) 'Taiwan cinema and Japan' (Taiwan eiga to nihon), in A. Morimune, T. Sato, H. Sato and H. Fukushima (eds), *Taiwanese Film Festival – Documents Taiwan Cinema's Yesterday, Today and Tomorrow* (Taiwan eigasai – shiryoushuu taiwaneiga no sakujitsu konnichi to myōnichi), Tokyo: Genndaienngekikyoukai, 10–19 (in Japanese).

ScreenCraft (2016) 'Hollywood and Chinese cinema: The future of movies', *The Huffington Post*, 5 July. Available online: www.huffingtonpost.com/screencraft/holly wood-and-chinese-cin_b_10819380.html (accessed 5 September 2016).

Shiau, H.C. (2009) 'Spectatorships, pleasures, and social uses of cinema: A tentative study of the reception of Cape No.7', *Asian Cinema* 20(1): 189–202.

Shih, H.C. (2011) 'Minister says "no bottom line" over film name debate', *Taipei Times*, 18 November. Available online: www.taipeitimes.com/News/front/archives/ 2011/08/18/2003511010 (accessed 12 December 2015).

Shih, S. and Liao, P. (2014) 'Introduction: Why Taiwan? Why comparatize?', in S. Shih and P. Liao (eds), *Comparatizing Taiwan*, London and New York: Routledge, pp. 1–10.

Shohat, E. and Stam, R. (1994) *Unthinking Eurocentrism: Multiculturalism and the Media*, London and New York: Routledge.

Sight and Sound (2009) 'The New Wave at 50: Riding the wave', *Sight and Sound* 19(5) (May): 26.

Silverman, K. (1983) *The Subject of Semiotics*, Oxford: Oxford University Press.

Simon, S. (2012) 'Politics and headhunting among the Formosan Sejiq: Ethnohistorical perspectives', *Oceania* 82: 164–185.

Sing, S.Y. (2010) 'The telepathy in downgrading history: On the fluid imaging of Taiwan's "post-New Cinema"' (Qing lishi de xinling ganying: Lun Taiwan hou-xin dianying de liuti yingxiang), *Film Appreciation Academic Journal* 142: 137–156 (in Chinese).

Spivak, G. (1988) 'Can the subaltern speak?', in C. Nelson and L. Grossberg (eds), *Marxism and the Interpretation of Culture*, Champaign, IL: University of Illinois Press, pp. 271–313.

Sterk, D. (2011) 'Nativization and foreignization in the translation of "Seediq Bale"', *Savage Minds: Notes and Queries in Anthropology*, 31 December. Available online: savageminds.org/2011/12/31/the-translation-of-seediq-bale/ (accessed 20 April 2015).

Sterk, D. (2012) 'Mona Rudao's scars: Epic identity in "Seediq Bale"', *Savage Minds: Notes and Queries in Anthropology*, 1 January. Available online: savageminds.org/ 2012/01/01/mona-rudaos-scars/ (accessed 20 April 2015).

Su, C. (2009) 'Beyond south of the border: A textual analysis of the Taiwanese blockbuster Cape No.7', *Asian Cinema* 20(1): 176–189.

Taipei Film Commission (2013) 'Taipei Factory debuts in Cannes', *Marketwired*, 17 May. Available online: www.marketwired.com/press-release/taipei-factory-debuts-in-ca nnes-1792294.htm (accessed 7 September 2016).

Taiwan Education Society (2008) *Happy Farmers: Colonial Japanese Documentaries on Taiwan* (Xingfu de nongmin), Tainan: National Museum of Taiwan History (in Chinese).

Taiwan.gov.tw (2013) 'Economy and finance: National competitiveness', The Official Website of the ROC. Available online at: www.taiwan.gov.tw/ct.asp?xItem=126570& CtNode=3766&mp=1 (accessed 25 December 2015).

Taubin, A. (2005) 'Distributor wanted: Café Lumière. Light fantastic', *Film Comment* 41(2) (March–April): 6.

Teruoka, S. (ed.) (2005) *Winds of Asia 2005: 18th Tokyo International Film Festival*, Tokyo: Kinemajunposha (in Japanese).

Tezuka, Y. (2012) *Japanese Cinema Goes Global: Filmmaker's Journeys*, Hong Kong: Hong Kong University Press.

Tharoor, I. (2014) 'Could this map of China start a war?', *Washington Post*, 27 June. Available online at: www.washingtonpost.com/news/worldviews/wp/2014/06/27/ could-this-map-of-china-start-a-war/ (accessed 25 December 2015).

Thornber, K. (2009) *Empire of Texts in Motion: Chinese, Korean, and Taiwanese Transculturations of Japanese Literature*, Cambridge, MA: Harvard University Press.

Tomkins, S.S. (1962) *Affect Imagery Consciousness Volume I: The Positive Affects*, New York: Springer Publishing Company.

Torgovnick, M. (2013) *Primitive Passions: Men, Women, and the Quest for Ecstasy*, New York: Alfred A. Knopf.

Tourism Bureau, M.O.T.C., Republic of China (Taiwan) (2015) 'Yearly statistics', *Executive Information System*. Available online at: admin.taiwan.net.tw/statistics/ year_en.aspx?no=15 (accessed 25 December 2015).

Tsai, M.C. (2001) 'Dependency, the state, and class in neoliberal transition of Taiwan', *Third World Quarterly* 22: 359–379.

Tweedie, J. (2013) *The Age of New Waves Art Cinema and the Staging of Globalization*, Oxford: Oxford University Press.

Udden, J. (2009) *No Man an Island: The Cinema of Hou Hsiao-hsien*, Hong Kong: Hong Kong University Press.

Veracini, L. (2012) 'Review of Warriors of the Rainbow: Seediq Bale, directed by Wei Te-sheng', *Transnational Cinemas* 3(2): 233–244.

Villanueva, C. (2007) *Representing Cultural Diplomacy, Soft Power, Cosmopolitan Constructivism and Nation Branding in Sweden and Mexico*, Växjo: Växjo University Press.

Vitali, V. (2008) 'Hou Hsiao-hsien reviewed', *Inter-Asia Cultural Studies* 9(2): 280–289.

Voci, P. and Hui, V. (eds) (2017) *Screening Soft Power in China*, London and New York: Routledge.

Walkowitz, D.J. (1985) 'Visual history: The craft of the historian-filmmaker', *Public Historian* 7(1): 52–64.

Wang, C.S. (2009a) 'Cape No.7 and Taiwan's national consciousness', *Asian Cinema* 20(2): 244–259.

Wang, C.S. (2012a) 'Memories of the future: Remaking Taiwaneseness in Cape No.7', *Journal of Chinese Cinemas* 6(2): 135–151.

Wang, D.D.W. and Rojas, C. (eds) (2007) *Writing Taiwan: A New Literary History*, Durham, NC: Duke University Press.

Wang, G. (2012b) 'No sign of slowing down: The renaissance of Taiwanese cinema', in Los Angeles Asian Pacific Film Festival 2012 program booklet, Los Angeles: Visual Communications, pp. 24–29.

Wang, G. (2015) *Film in Our Time: Taiwan New Cinema on the Road* (Guangyin zhi lü: Taiwan xindianying zai lushang), Taipei: Department of Cultural Affairs, Taipei City Government (in Chinese).

Wang, J.X. (1997) *Dao Feng Nei Hai*, Taipei: Yushanshe publishing (in Chinese).

Wang, M.H. (2003) 'Exploring the social characteristics of the Dayan multiple meanings of gaga' (Cong gaga de duoyixing kan taiyazu de shehui xingzhi), *Taiwan Journal of Anthropology* (Taiwan renlei xuekan) 1(1): 77–104 (in Chinese).

Wang, Y.B. (2009b) 'Love letters from the colonizer: The cultural identity issue in Cape No.7', *Asian Cinema* 20(2): 260–271.

Wei, T.S. (2000) *Seediq Bale* (Saidekebalai), Taipei: Government Information Office (screenplay, in Chinese).

Wei, T.S. (2002) *A Little Director's Diary of Unemployment* (Xiao daoyan shiye riji), Taipei: China Times (in Chinese).

Wei, T.S. (2011) *Director Bale* (Daoyan balai), Taipei: Yuanliou (in Chinese).

White, H. (1988) 'Historiography and historiophoty', *American Historical Review* 93(5): 1193–1199.

Willemen, P. (1994) *Looks and Frictions: Essays in Cultural Studies and Film Theory*, London: British Film Institute.

Willemen, P. (2006) 'The national revisited', in V. Vitali and P. Willemen (eds), *Theorising National Cinema*, London: British Film Institute, pp. 29–43.

Williams, R. and Orrom, M. (1954) *Preface to Film*, London: Film Drama Limited.

Willis, A. (2010) 'Cinema curation as practice and research: The Visible Secrets project as a model for collaboration between art cinemas and academics', *Screen* 51(2): 161–167.

Winfrey, G. (2016) 'Fortissimo Films goes bankrupt: 3 reasons the respected arthouse distributor lost its groove', *IndieWire*, 23 August. Available online: www.indiewire.com/2016/08/3-lessons-fortissimo-films-bankruptcy-metrodome-1201719375/ (accessed 7 September 2016).

Wong, C.H.Y. (2011) *Film Festivals: Culture, People and Power on the Global Screen*, New Brunswick, NJ: Rutgers University Press.

Wu, C. (2007) 'Festivals, criticism and international reputation of Taiwan New Cinema', in D.W. Davis and R.S.R. Chen (eds), *Cinema Taiwan: Politics, Popularity and State of the Arts*, London: Routledge, pp. 75–91.

Wu, C.R. (2014) 'Re-examining extreme violence: Historical reconstruction and extreme violence in Warriors of the Rainbow: Seediq Bale', *ASIA Network Exchange* 21(2): 24–32.

Wu, H. (2011) *Remains of Life* (Yusheng), Taipei: Ryefield (in Chinese).

Wu, M. (2005) 'Postsadness Taiwan New Cinema: Eat, drink, everyman, everywoman', in S.H. Lu and E.Y.Y. Yeh, *Chinese-Language Film: Historiography, Poetics, Politics*, Honolulu: University of Hawai'i Press, pp. 76–95.

Wu, Z.L. (1959) *Orphan of Asia* (Yaxiya de guer), translated from Japanese by Z.Q. Yang, Kaohsiung: Huanghe Publishing (in Chinese).

Wu, Z.L. (2006) *Orphan of Asia*, translated from Chinese by I. Mentzas, New York: Columbia University Press.

Xie, C. (2012) 'Blood sacrifice: Interview with Seediq Bale director Wei Te-sheng', *Asia Pacific Arts*, 30 May. Available online: asiapacificarts.usc.edu/article@apa?blood_sa crifice_interview_with_seediq_bale_director_wei_te-sheng_18169.aspx (accessed 10 August 2015).

Xu, G.G. (2007) *Sinascape: Contemporary Chinese Cinema*, New York: Rowman & Littlefield Publishers.

Yamashita, M., Matsukura, R. and Yamashita, H. (2014) 'The chronicle of Taiwan cinema 1980–2010' (Taiwan eigashi nennhyo 1980–2010), in S. Koyama, K. Inoue and N. Makino (eds), *Taiwan Cinema: Thirty Years (since Taiwan New Cinema) Manifesting the Social Transformations* (Taiwan eiga: syakai no henbou wo tsugeru [Taiwan new shinema kara no] sanjyuu nen), Tokyo: Koyoshobo, pp. 85–148 (in Japanese).

Yan, C.M. (2012) 'The postcolonial paradox in the (self-)Orientalization of Taiwanese history in Wei Te-sheng's action saga', *Theory and Practice in Language Studies* 2(6): 1114–1119.

Yan, Y.N. (2004) *Seediq Bale* (Saidekebalai), Taipei: Pingzhuangben (in Chinese).

Yang, E. (2001) 'Taiwan stories', *New Left Review* II(11) (September–October): 129–136.

Yau, E.C.M. (2015) 'Watchful partners, hidden currents: Hong Kong cinema moving into the mainland of China', in E.M.K. Cheung, G. Marchetti and E.C.M. Yau (eds), *A Companion to Hong Kong Cinema*, Maiden, MA: John Wiley & Sons, 15–50.

Yeh, E.Y.Y. (1999) 'Taiwan New Cinema: Localism's other' (Taiwan xindianying bentu zhuyi de tazhe), *Chung Wai Literary Quarterly* 27(8): 43–67 (in Chinese).

Yeh, E.Y.Y. and Davis, D.W. (2005) *Taiwan Film Directors: A Treasure Island*, New York: Columbia University Press.

Yen, C.Y. (2006) 'Colonial Taiwan and the construction of landscape painting', in P.H. Liao and D.D.W. Wang (eds), *Taiwan under Japanese Colonial Rule, 1895–1945*, New York: Columbia University Press, pp. 248–261.

Yip, J. (2004) *Envisioning Taiwan: Fiction, Cinema and the Nation in the Cultural Imaginary*, Durham, NC: Duke University Press.

YoungD. (2011) 'Warriors of the Rainbow: Seediq Bale. Venice film review', *The Hollywood Reporter*, 1 September. Available online: www.hollywoodreporter.com/review/warriors-rainbow-seediq-bale-venice-230239 (accessed 12 December 2015).

Yu, S.L. (2009) 'Cape No.7 gets green light in mainland China', *Screen Daily*, 15 January. Available online: www.screendaily.com/cape-no7-gets-green-light-in-mainla nd-china/4042692.article (accessed 12 November 2015).

Zarrow, P. (2009) 'In case you missed it: Cape No.7', *The China Beat: Blogging How the East is Read*, 16 January. Available online: thechinabeat.blogspot.co.uk/2009/01/in-case-you-missed-it-cape-no-7.html (accessed 12 November 2015).

Zeng, Z.Y. (2014) 'Achieving mission impossible with rebellion: Interview with Wei Te-sheng the director of *Seediq Bale*' (Yong panni wancheng bukeneng de renwu: Saidekebalai daoyan wei tesheng), in Y.Y. Wang (ed.), *Paper Projection: Interviews with Taiwan Film Directors* (Zhishang fangying: Tankan taiwan daoyan benshi), Taipei: Bookman, pp. 364–373 (in Chinese).

Zhan, M.X. (2010) 'The shaping of Taiwanese grassroots imagination in Cape No.7' (Cong haijiao qihao tan caogen Taiwan xiangxiang de xingsu), *Film Appreciation Academic Journal* 142: 170–184 (in Chinese).

Zhang, Y. (2002) *Screening China: Critical Interventions, Cinematic Reconfigurations, and the Transnational Imaginary in Contemporary Chinese Cinema*, Ann Arbor, MI: Center for Chinese Studies Publications.

Zhang, Y. (2004) *Chinese National Cinema*, London and New York: Routledge.

Zhou, W.Y. (2010) 'Discussing the interpretations of the Wushe Incident in post-war Taiwan' (Shilun zhanhou taiwan guanyu wushe shijian de quanshi), *Taiwan Folkways* 60(3): 11–57 (in Chinese).

Zhou, W.Y. (2011) 'Preface: Hero, hero-worship, and their antitheses' (Xu: Yingxiong, yingxiong chongbai ji qi fanmingti), in M.Z. Guo, *Truth* (*Bale*), Taipei: Yuanliou, pp. 2–8 (in Chinese).

Zhu, Y. and Robinson, B. (2010) 'The cinematic Transition of the Fifth Generation auteurs', in Y. Zhu and S. Rosen (eds), *Art, Politics, and Commerce in Chinese Cinema*, Hong Kong: Hong Kong University Press, pp. 145–162.

Index